PLATE by PLATE

PLATE by PLATE
플레이트 바이 플레이트

초판 1쇄 인쇄 2025년 07월 1일
초판 1쇄 발행 2025년 07월 15일

지은이 김도윤, 송홍윤, 김미령, 박성배, 방기수, 옥동식, 최지형, 신계숙, 임태훈, 조광효,
황진선, 김승민, 심성오, 이진곤, 장호준, 김낙영, 김민석, 김세경, 남정석, 데이비드 리,
류태환, 박준우, 박지영, 박찬일, 성시우, 이대건, 장지수, 조우람, 이은희, 조은주
영문 번역 김유진, Kim Eunice | **펴낸이** 박윤선 | **발행처** (주)더테이블

기획 책임편집 박윤선 | **디자인** 김보라 | **사진** 신동민
영업·마케팅 김남권, 조용훈, 문성빈 | **경영지원** 김효선, 이정민

주소 경기도 부천시 조마루로385번길 122 삼보테크노타워 2002호
홈페이지 www.icoxpublish.com | **쇼핑몰** www.baek2.kr (백두도서쇼핑몰) | **인스타그램** @thetable_book
이메일 thetable_book@naver.com | **전화** 032) 674-5685 | **팩스** 032) 676-5685
등록 2022년 8월 4일 제 386-2022-000050 호 | **ISBN** 979-11-92855-20-2 (13590)

- (주)더테이블은 '새로움' 속에 '가치'를 담는 요리 전문 출판 브랜드입니다.
- 이 책은 저작권법에 따라 보호받는 저작물이므로 무단 전재 및 복제를 금하며,
  이 책 내용의 전부 또는 일부를 이용하려면 반드시 저작권자와 (주)더테이블의 서면 동의를 받아야 합니다.
- 도서에 관한 문의는 이메일(thetable_book@naver.com)로 연락주시기 바랍니다.
- 잘못된 책은 구입하신 서점에서 바꾸어드립니다.
- 책값은 뒤표지에 있습니다.

❖ 이 책의 저자 인세 전액과 출판사 수익금 일부는 '세이브더칠드런'을 통해 아이들에게 기부됩니다.

30

서른 명의 셰프가 쌓은 인생의 맛,
당신의 식탁에 놓일 온기 한 접시

PLATE by PLATE

30 Culinary Journeys, Bringing Warmth to Your Table

더 테이블
THE TABLE

PROLOGUE

'요리'라는 행위는 때론 말보다 더 많은 것을 전합니다. 정성스레 손질한 재료들, 불 앞에서 쌓인 시간, 조심스레 담아낸 한 접시의 음식에는 말로는 다 표현하지 못할 셰프의 삶의 태도와 마음이 깃들어 있습니다. 이 책은 그렇게 '요리'를 통해 자신의 이야기를 전한 서른 명의 셰프들과 함께 만든, 조금은 특별한 책입니다.

이번 프로젝트는 셰프들에게도, 에디터로 참여한 저에게도 새로운 도전이었습니다. 작년 11월부터 서른 명이 훌쩍 넘는 셰프들을 만나 이 프로젝트를 소개하고, 최종적으로 섭외된 서른 명의 셰프들에게 책에서 선보일 두 가지 요리의 주제에 대해 설명했습니다. 한식, 일식, 중식, 양식, 비건 요리 등 이 책에 참여하는 셰프들의 전공은 다르지만, 모두에게 동일한 주제를 제안했습니다. 하나는 셰프의 경험과 추억, 철학이 담긴 '이야기가 있는 요리', 나머지 하나는 독자들이 집에서 어렵지 않게 따라할 수 있는 '가정식 레시피'입니다. 셰프들은 이 주제에 맞춰 자신들이 소개할 두 가지 요리를 꽤 긴 시간 고민하였고, 글과 사진, 인터뷰로 자신들의 요리에 담긴 이야기와 레시피를 자세하게 풀어냈습니다.

촬영이 끝난 후, 참여한 모든 셰프들에게 똑같은 질문을 던졌습니다. "요리할 때 가장 중요하게 생각하는 것이 무엇인가요?" 놀랍게도 모든 셰프들의 대답은 같았습니다. "제철에 나는 좋은 식재료를 사용하고, 내 가족이 먹는다는 마음으로 정성껏 조리하는 것이죠." 수십 년을 주방에서 살아온 이들의 입에서 최신 기술이나 트렌드보다 먼저 나온 이 한결같은 대답은 요리가 무엇이어야 하는지를 새삼 일깨워 주었습니다. 이 책은 그런 요리 철학이 고스란히 담긴 기록입니다.

셰프들은 단순히 두 가지 요리를 책에 소개하는 것을 넘어 그들의 기억과 감정, 요리사로서 살아온 삶의 이야기를 들려주었습니다. 어린 시절 먹던 밥상에 대한 기억, 스승에게 혼나며 배운 기술, 식당을 운영하며 마주한 삶의 기쁨과 슬픔, '나'라는 존재를 대중에게 알린 시그니처 레시피까지. 그 모든 이야기가 글이 되고 요리가 되어 책 속에 담겼고, 그 결과 이 책은 단순한 레시피 북을 넘어 '요리라는 언어로 이어진 60가지의 인생 이야기'로 완성되었습니다. 독자 여러분은 이 책을 통해 누군가의 주방을, 누군가의 인생을 훔쳐보듯 요리를 둘러싼 삶의 여러 장면들을 만나게 될 것입니다.

이 책의 저자 인세 전액과 출판사 수익금 일부는 '세이브더칠드런'을 통해 아이들에게 기부됩니다. 누군가의 밥상이 따뜻해지는 데 작게나마 보탬이 되기를 바라는 마음을 담았습니다. 이 책을 펼치는 모든 독자 여러분들에게, 이 의미 있는 나눔이 또 하나의 따뜻한 울림으로 전해지기를 바랍니다.

이 책에 참여해준 서른 명의 셰프들에게 감사의 인사를 전합니다. 눈코 뜰 새 없이 바쁜 일정 속에서도 원고 집필과 촬영, 인터뷰에 진지하게 임해주셨고, 무엇보다 본인들의 인세 전액을 기부하는 것에 흔쾌히, 기쁜 마음으로 참여해 주셨습니다. 고맙습니다. 그리고 감사합니다.

끝으로, 이 모든 연결의 시작을 만들어준 박준우 셰프에게 진심 어린 감사를 전합니다. 셰프들과 출판을 잇는 다리 역할을 자처하며 기꺼이 발 벗고 나서준 그의 따뜻한 마음이 없었다면, 이 책은 지금의 모습을 갖추지 못했을 것입니다. 감사합니다.

이 책에 담긴 한 접시의 음식이, 하나의 문장이, 하나의 이야기가 누군가의 마음속에 오래도록 머물 수 있기를. 그 바람을 담아 이 책을 독자 여러분께 전합니다.

2025년 6월의 어느 날

발행인 **박윤선**

PROLOGUE

The act of 'cooking' sometimes speaks louder than words. The carefully mise en place ingredients, the time spent in front of the heat, and the sincere presentation of a plate of food convey more about a chef's heart and attitude towards life than words can. This book is something special, a collaboration with thirty chefs who share their stories through the art of cooking.

This project was a new challenge for the chefs and for me as the editor. Starting last November, I met with over thirty chefs to propose the project and explain the theme of the two dishes that would be featured in the book to the thirty chefs who would ultimately join us. The chefs participating in the book come from diverse cuisines – Korean, Japanese, Chinese, Western, and vegan – but I suggested the same theme to all of them. One would be a 'dish with a story,' which includes the chef's experiences, memories, and philosophy, and the other is a 'home-style recipe,' which is easy for the readers to recreate at home. The chefs devoted a significant amount of time selecting the two dishes they wanted to feature under these themes; through writing, photography, and interviews, they elaborated on the stories and recipes behind their dishes.

After the photoshoot, I asked every chef who participated the same question: "What is the most important element to you when you cook?" To my surprise, the answers were the same: "Using good ingredients that are in season and cooking with care, as if to serve my own family." Coming from those who have spent decades in the kitchen and before the latest techniques or trends, this consistent answer was a reminder of what cooking should be about. This book is a record of such culinary philosophy.

The chefs didn't just share two dishes in the book; they shared memories, feelings, and stories of their lives as chefs: memories of childhood meals, techniques they learned while being scolded by their mentors, the joys and sorrows of running a restaurant, and the signature recipes that made them known to the public as who "I" am. All of these stories were written, cooked, and captured in a book, and the result is more than just a recipe book- it's 60 life stories told through the language of cooking. Throughout the book, you'll be taken on a journey into someone's kitchen, a peek into someone's life, and a glimpse into the lives that surround cooking.

All of the author's royalties from the book and a portion of the publisher's proceeds will be donated to children through Save the Children Federation, Inc. We hope that this small contribution will make a difference in warming up someone's meal and that this meaningful sharing will resonate with every reader who opens this book.

I want to thank the thirty chefs who participated in this book. They took time out of their busy schedules to write, shoot, and conduct interviews sincerely, and most importantly, they were willing and happy to donate full royalties. Thank you. And most of all, grateful.

Last but not least, a heartfelt thank you to Chef Park Joonwoo for making the connection that started it all. Without his willingness to step out of his comfort zone and act as a bridge between chefs and publishing, this book would not be what it is today – my deepest gratitude to you.

I hope that a plate of food, a sentence, or a story in this book will linger in someone's heart for a long time. It is with such hope that I present this book to you.

A day in June 2025

Publisher **Bak Yunseon**

CONTENTS

KIM DOYUN 018
김도윤

간장게장 • Ganjang-gejang (Soy Sauce Marinated Crab)

무 만두 • Korean Radish Mandu (Korean Radish Dumplings)

020   026

SONG HONGYUN
송홍윤

반건조 생선과 석박지 무침 •
Half-Dried Fish and Seokbakji Salad
(Half-Dried Fish and Radish Kimchi Salad)

멸치 강된장 • Anchovy Gangdoenjang
(Seasoned Soybean Paste with Korean Dried Anchovies)

034   040

KIM MIRYEONG 046
김미령

돼지 수육과 겉절이 • Dwaeji Suyuk and Geotjeori
(Korean Boiled Pork and Fresh Kimchi)

밑반찬 4종과 김구이, 그리고 비빔밥 •
Four Kinds of Banchan, Roasted Seaweed, and Bibimbap

048   054

PARK SUNGBAE 062
박 성 배

백자 두부 • Baekja Bean Curd

대구구이와 홍합 톳밥 •
Pan-fried Cod with Mussel and Brown Seaweed Rice

064   070

BANG KISOO 076
방 기 수

콩즙 냉채 • Soybean Purée Naengchae
(Chilled Vegetables in Soybean Purée)

활전복 한우 갈비찜 • Hanwoo Galbijjim and Abalone
(Braised Korean Beef Short Ribs and Abalone)

078   086

OK DONGSIK 094
옥 동 식

구엄닭곰탕 • Gueom Dakgomtang (Gueom Chicken Soup)

양지곰탕 • Yangji-gomtang (Beef Brisket Soup)

096   102

CHOI JIHYUNG 108
최 지 형

양배추 디시 • Cabbage Dish

녹두전 • Nokdujeon (Mung Bean Pancake)

110   116

SHIN KYESOOK *122*
신 계 숙

탕수갈비 • Tangsu Galbi (Sweet and Sour Ribs)
난자완스 • Nanja Wans (Stir-fried Chinese Meatballs)

124   *130*

LIM TAEHOON *136*
임 태 훈

팔보완자 • Eight Treasures Meatball
비파두부 • Pipa Tofu

138   *146*

CHO KWANGHYO *152*
조 광 효

비룡 떡볶이 & 볶음밥 •
Biryong Tteokbokki (Biryong Stir-Fried Rice Cake)
마파두부 • Mapo Tofu

154   *160*

HWANG JINSEON *166*
황 진 선

작춘권 • Egg-Wrapped Spring Rolls
홍쇼대구 • Hong Shao Cod (Soy-Braised Cod)

168   *176*

KIM SEUNGMIN *184*
김승민

고등어 완자 • Mackerel Balls

두반장 가라아게 • Doubanjiang Karaage (Doubanjiang Fried Chicken)

SIM SUNGOH *200*
심성오

등푸른 생선 사시미와 로메스코 소스 • Blue-Backed Fish Sashimi with Romesco

도미 턱살을 이용한 일본식 간장 조림 • Soy-Braised Tai Kama (Japanese Soy-Braised Snapper Collar)

LEE JINGON
이진곤

사시미 케이크 • Sashimi Cake

미소 치킨 • Miso Chicken

JANG HOJOON *228*
장호준

쿠로 다마네기 • Kuro Damanegi (Black Onion)

소고기 대파 우동 • Beef and Green Onion Udon

KIM NAKYOUNG
김 낙 영

라자냐 알라 볼로네제 • Lasagne alla Bolognese

탈리아텔레 콘 라구 알라 볼로네제 •
Tagliatelle con ragù alla bolognese

KIM MINSEOK
김 민 석

성게알을 올린 카초 에 페페 소스의 피치 •
Cacio e Pepe Pici with Sea Urchin Roe

가정식 카초 에 페페 • Homemade Cacio e pepe

KIM SEAKYEONG
김 세 경

대게살과 레몬 바이트 • Snow Crab Meat and Lemon Bite

미니 양배추와 체리 콜라 게스트릭 •
Brussels sprouts with Cherry Cola Gastrique

NAM JEONGSEOK
남 정 석

구운 채소를 곁들인 백태콩 후무스 •
Yellow Soybean Hummus with Roasted Vegetables

로메스코를 곁들인 양배추 슈니첼 •
Cabbage Schnitzel with Romesco

DAVID LEE *308*
데이비드 리

갈비 부르기뇽 A.K.A 가르비뇽 •
Galbi Bourguignon A.K.A. Garlbignon

된장 할라페뇨 맥적 •
Doenjang Jalapeño Maekjeok (Doenjang Jalapeño Marinated Pork)

310 *318*

RYU TAEHWAN *324*
류태환

충무공 이순신을 위한 보양식 •
Boyangsik for Chungmugong Yi Sunsin
(Energy-Boosting Dish for Admiral Yi Sunsin)

반건조 청어 오픈 샌드위치 •
Open-Faced Sandwich with Half-Dried Herring

326 *332*

PARK JOONWOO *338*
박준우

통밀 리소토와 샴페인 소스를 곁들인 아귀 메다이용 •
Monkfish Médaillon with Whole Wheat Risotto and Champagne Sauce

표고버섯 사블레와 표고버섯 리에트를 곁들인 표고버섯 크림 •
Shiitake Mushroom Trilogy: Cream, Rillettes and Sablé

340 *350*

PARK JIYOUNG *358*
박지영

허브 김 버터 전복 구이 • Abalone in Herb and Seaweed Butter

백골뱅이 알 아히오 • White Whelk al Ajillo

360 *368*

PARK CHANIL *374*
박찬일

대파와 칼국수 짜장면 •
Kalguksu with Jjajang Sauce and Green Onion
(Korean Knife-Cut Noodles with Black Bean Sauce and Green Onion)

토마토 내장찜 • Tomato-Braised Trippa

SUNG SIWOO *388*
성시우

참깨 소스를 발라 구운 가지찜 꼬치 •
Steamed Eggplant Skewer with Sesame Sauce

참두릅 커틀릿 • Cham-Dureup Cutlets (Angelica Tree Shoot Cutlets)

LEE DAEGEON *402*
이대건

훈연한 관자와 콜리플라워 에멀전 •
Smoked Scallops and Cauliflower Emulsion

애호박 로얄, 새우 파르메산 소스 •
Zucchini Royale with Shrimp Parmesan Sauce

JANG JISOO *418*
장지수

동해안 대구 스테이크와 매시드 포테이토 & 초리소 소시지 •
East Sea Cod Steak with Mashed Potatoes & Chorizo Sausage

참문어 플레이트 • Octopus Plate

JO WOORAM *436*
조 우 람

파테 오 피멍 데스플레트 (바스크 스타일 파테) •
Pâté au Piment d'Espelette (Basque-Style Pâté)

소 부채살 콩피 • Beef Top Blade Confit

438

444

LEE EUNHEE
이 은 희

키슈 로렌 • Quiche Lorraine

초리소 사블레 • Chorizo Sablé

450

456

CHO EUNJU *462*
조 은 주

트러플 풍미의 돌문어 랍스터 전채 •
Truffle-Flavored Octopus and Lobster Appetizer

굴 크림과 매생이 아로마 오일을 곁들인 전복 요리 •
Abalone with Oyster Cream and Seaweed Fulvescens Aroma Oil

464

472

ABOUT THE BOOK
이 책에 대해

이 책은 한식, 일식, 중식, 양식, 비건 등 다양한 분야에서 활약 중인 서른 명의 셰프가 함께 만든 요리책입니다. 전공과 스타일은 제각각 이지만, 모든 셰프에게 두 가지 공통된 주제를 제안했습니다. 하나는 셰프의 경험과 추억, 요리에 대한 철학이 담긴 '이야기가 있는 요리', 다른 하나는 독자들이 집에서도 어렵지 않게 따라 할 수 있는 '가정식 레시피'입니다. (각 레시피 페이지에는 '이야기', '가정식'으로 표기해 쉽게 구분할 수 있도록 했습니다.)

It is a cookbook created by thirty chefs from a variety of cuisines, including Korean, Japanese, Chinese, Western, and vegan. Despite their different specialties and styles, we suggested two common themes for all the chefs: "a dish with a story," which includes the chef's experiences, memories, and philosophies about cooking, and "a home-style recipe," which is easy for the readers to replicate at home. (Each recipe page is labeled 'story' and 'home-style' to make it easy to distinguish between them.)

서른 명의 셰프가 전하는 60가지 요리에는 각자의 맛과 이야기, 요리에 대한 철학과 기술이 고스란히 담겨 있습니다. 같은 재료를 사용하더라도 셰프마다 전혀 다른 방식으로 풀어내는 조리법과 테크닉의 차이를 느껴보는 것도 이 책의 또 다른 즐거움이 될 것입니다.
셰프들의 손끝에서 시작된 요리가, 독자 여러분의 주방에서 새로운 이야기로 이어지길 바랍니다.

Each of these 60 recipes, contributed by thirty chefs, brings their flavors, stories, culinary philosophies, and techniques to the table. It's a joy to see how different chefs can use the same ingredients but approach them in entirely different ways.
We hope that what began at the fingertips of these chefs will lead to new stories in your kitchen.

ABOUT THE UNITS OF MEASUREMENT USED IN THE BOOK

이 책에서 사용된 계량 단위에 대해

이 책에서 사용된 계량 단위는 다음과 같습니다. 서른 명의 셰프가 가지고 있는 각자의 레시피를 소개한 책인 만큼 같은 재료라도 g, ml, cup으로 단위가 다를 수 있습니다. 아래의 계량 단위를 참고하되, 되도록 레시피에 적힌 단위로 계량하시는 것을 추천합니다.
예를 들어 물의 경우 1g = 1ml로 분량이 동일하나, 물을 제외한 다른 액체류나 고체류는 완전히 동일하지 않습니다.

The following units of measure are used in this book. Because this book is a collection of recipes from thirty different chefs, the same ingredient may be measured differently in grams, milliliters, or cups. Use the units of measure below as a guide; however, we recommend measuring in the units listed in the recipe.
For example, for water, 1 g equals 1 ml, but other liquids or solids are not quite the same (1 g ≠ 1 ml or 1 g ≠ 1 cup).

단위 Unit	약어 Abbreviation	설명 Note
그램	g	무게 단위 Weight
밀리리터	ml	부피 단위 Volume
리터	L	부피 단위 volume
컵	cup	부피 단위 (약 240ml 기준) Volume (about 240 ml)
테이블스푼	tbsp	큰술, 약 15ml Tablespoon, about 15 ml
티스푼	tsp	작은술, 약 5ml Teaspoon, about 5 ml

KIM DOYUN
김도윤

SONG HONGYUN
송홍윤

김도윤, 송홍윤 셰프가 이끄는 윤서울은 2019년 미쉐린 1스타를 획득한 이후 지금까지 별을 지켜내며, 한국의 미감과 정서를 담은 식탁을 선보이고 있다.

윤서울은 하루하루 주어진 재료에 따라 메뉴를 구성하며, 제철 식재료를 그대로 다루거나 발효, 건조, 숙성시키는 과정을 거쳐 그날 가장 좋은 생선이나 고기를 곁들여 요리를 완성한다. 계절마다 코스를 교체하기보다는, 매일 주방에 들어온 식재료를 중심으로 유연하게 구성하는 이 방식은 윤서울의 가장 큰 특징이자 철학이다.

윤서울의 요리에서 '발효, 건조, 숙성'은 빼놓을 수 없는 핵심이다. 실제로 이곳에서는 김치만 해도 13가지에 이를 정도로 발효 음식에 대한 애정과 깊이가 남다르며, 이밖에도 반건조 생선, 말린 해산물, 건조시킨 채소, 숙성시킨 장아찌 등의 재료들이 단순한 곁들임을 넘어, 음식의 맛과 구조를 이끄는 중심 요소로 자리한다.

두 셰프는 앞으로 지금보다 더 여유 있는 공간에서 직접 발효, 건조, 숙성한 재료를 보다 자유롭게 다루며, 더욱 다양한 음식 실험을 이어가고자 한다. 긴 시간과 손길이 필요한 일이지만, 그만큼 긴 호흡으로 요리를 이어가겠다는 다짐이기도 하다.

겉보기엔 조용한 윤서울의 주방에서는, 매일 새로운 재료와 시간이 겹쳐지며 맛의 깊이가 차곡차곡 쌓여간다. 두 셰프는 그 흐름 속에서 서울이라는 도시의 맛을 자신들만의 방식으로 담담히 써 내려가고 있다.

윤서울
@ yunseoul.restaurant

면서울
@ myeonseoul

@ projectsyun
@ hongyoon_song

Led by chefs Kim Doyun and Song Hongyun, the restaurant Yun Seoul has has maintained its first Michelin star since earning it in 2019, continuing to serve dishes with Korean aesthetics and flavors.

Each day, Yun Seoul creates a menu based on the ingredients at hand, either working with the seasonal ingredients as they are or fermenting, drying, and aging them and then pairing them with the best fish or meat of the day. Rather than rotating courses from season to season, Yun Seoul's philosophy of flexibility is centered around what comes into the kitchen each day.

Fermenting, drying, and aging are key to Yun Seoul's cuisine. In fact, there are 13 kinds of *kimchi* alone, and the love for fermented foods is so deep that other ingredients, such as semi-dried fish, dried seafood, dried vegetables, and aged pickles, are more than just accompaniments; they are central to the flavor and structure of the food.

In the future, the two chefs hope to have more space, greater freedom to work with their own fermented, dried, and aged ingredients, and more opportunities for food experimentation. It's a long and labor-intensive process, but it's also a commitment to continue cooking with a sustained effort.

In Yun Seoul's seemingly quiet kitchen, new ingredients and time are layered on top of each other every day, building up the depth of flavor. In the midst of all this, the two chefs are writing the flavors of Seoul with equanimity in their own way.

김도윤
KIM DOYUN

Ganjang-gejang
(Soy Sauce Marinated Crab)

이야기
STORY

간장게장

간장게장은 흔히 '밥도둑'이라는 별명을 가질 정도로 짜고 강렬한 맛의 요리로 떠올리는 분들이 많을 것입니다. 이 책에서 소개하는 윤서울의 간장게장은 자극적이지 않고 심심한 간장 양념으로 게의 감칠맛이 자연스럽게 배어날 수 있도록 만들었습니다.

이 요리는 알과 살이 꽉 찬 제철 암꽃게만을 사용하는 것, 간장 양념의 농도와 게를 숙성하는 시간이 포인트입니다. 짜지 않지만 깊은 풍미가 느껴지고, 강하지 않지만 오래 기억에 남는 맛으로 완성한 레시피입니다.

Often dubbed a "rice thief," *Ganjang-gejang* typically conjures up a salty, intensely flavored dish. But this version, crafted at Yun Seoul, lets the crab's *gamchilmat** gently infuse through a delicately balanced ganjang-based marinade.

The essence of this dish lies in the use of seasonal female crabs brimming with roe and meat, a meticulously balanced marinade, and an aging period timed to perfection. The recipe achieves a flavor that runs deep but not overly salty—unforgettable, yet never overpowering.

* ***Gamchilmat*** (감칠맛): One of the five basic taste sensations in Korean cuisine, also known as *umami* (うま味) in Japanese. It is often described as the meaty, savory richness that deepens flavor.

Ingredients

꽃게 4마리 분량

For 4 crabs

암꽃게	1kg (약 4마리)
진간장	2400ml
정수물	3000ml
맛술	900ml
청주	900ml
물엿	800ml
매실청	50ml
통후추	5알
생강	50g
통마늘	100g

1 kg	female crabs (about 4 crabs)
2400 ml	jin-ganjang (Korean dark soy sauce)
3000 ml	filtered water
900 ml	matsul (Korean cooking wine)
900 ml	cheongju (Korean refined rice wine)
800 ml	mulyeot (Korean corn syrup)
50 ml	maesil-cheong (Korean plum extract)
5	black peppercorns
50 g	ginger
100 g	garlic cloves

How to make

1. 꽃게는 흐르는 물에서 브러시를 이용해 깨끗이 세척해 준비합니다.
- 여기에서는 암꽃게(활꽃게)를 사용했습니다.
2. 세척한 꽃게를 통에 담고 꽃게가 잠길 정도의 진간장을 부은 후 1시간 정도 둡니다.
- 꽃게 1kg(약 4마리) 기준 1시간~1시간 30분 정도 담가두면 적당합니다.
3. 꽃게를 담갔던 진간장 전량을 냄비로 옮깁니다.

1. Clean the crabs thoroughly with a brush under running water.
- This dish uses live female crabs.
2. Place the cleaned crabs in a container and add enough jin-ganjang to cover. Let them steep for 1 hour.
- Steep for 1 to 1.5 hours for 1 kg (approximately 4 crabs).
3. Transfer the entire jin-ganjang marinade into a pot.

4. 나머지 재료를 모두 냄비에 넣고 가열합니다.
5. 국물이 팔팔 끓어오르고 마늘이 노랗게 변하면 불을 끄고 얼음물에 받쳐 완전히 식힙니다.

4. Add the remaining ingredients to a pot and bring to a boil.
5. Once the marinade reaches a rolling boil and the garlic turns yellow, turn off the heat and place the pot in an ice bath until fully cooled.

6. 꽃게가 담긴 통에 **5**를 붓습니다.
7. 냉장고에 보관한 후 2~3일 후에 먹습니다.

6. Pour (**5**) into the container with the marinated crabs.
7. Store in the refrigerator for 2 to 3 days before serving.

김도윤
KIM DOYUN

Korean Radish Mandu

(Korean Radish Dumplings)

무 만두

가정식
HOME COOKING

이 메뉴는 무의 고유한 맛을 살리는 데 초점을 맞춰 만든 요리입니다.

만두의 속이 되는 무는 쌀뜨물에 살짝 삶은 후 간장 베이스의 양념에 졸여 짜지 않고 은은하게 간장의 향이 배도록 만들었고, 만두피는 중력분과 강력분을 섞어 반죽의 식감과 탄력을 조절함과 동시에 콩가루와 녹두가루로 고소함을 더했습니다.

찜기에 쪄 완성한 무 만두는 한입 베어물면 간장 양념이 스며든 촉촉한 무와 쫄깃하고 고소한 만두피가 어우러져 입안 가득 은은하고 부드러운 맛을 선사합니다. 자꾸 생각나는 질리지 않는 담백한 맛이 특징입니다.

This dish is designed to showcase the natural flavor of Korean radish.

For the filling, the radish is gently simmered in boiling rice water, then reduced in a ganjang-based seasoning to allow subtle savoriness to infuse without making it overly salty. The wrappers are made from a blend of all-purpose and bread flours for the ideal texture and elasticity, while soybean and mung bean powders offer a delicate nuttiness to the dough.

This steamed *mandu* presents a harmonious balance between the moist radish filling and chewy, nutty wrappers, delivering a mouthful of delicate, mellow flavors. With its clean, understated taste, it is the kind of dish that keeps drawing you back for more.

Ingredients

25인 분량
Serves 25

속재료

무	500g
쌀뜨물	1000ml
물	1200ml
진간장	55g
페페론치노	1개
청주	100ml
맛술	30ml
소금	2g

만두피

강력분	300g
중력분	210g
로스팅한 콩가루 ◆	5g
로스팅한 녹두 가루 ◆	5g
정수물	200ml

◆ 특유의 풋내가 날 수 있으므로 콩가루와 녹두 가루는 160℃에서 약 30분간 구운 후 식혀 사용합니다. 구우면 고소함도 배가 됩니다.

FILLING

500 g	Korean radish
1000 ml	rice water
1200 ml	water
55 g	jin-ganjang (Korean dark soy sauce)
1	peperoncino
100 ml	cheongju (Korean refined rice wine)
30 ml	matsul (Korean cooking wine)
2 g	salt

MANDU WRAPPERS

300 g	bread flour
210 g	all-purpose flour
5 g	roasted soybean powder ◆
5 g	roasted mung bean powder ◆
200 ml	filtered water

◆ To avoid any unpleasant beany flavor, roast the soybean and mung bean powders at 320°F (160°C) for about 30 minutes. This roasting process enriches their nutty flavor.

How to make

속재료

1. 무는 껍질을 벗긴 후 약 5cm 두께로 자릅니다.
2. 지름 3~4cm 원형 틀로 무를 찍어냅니다.
- 무 안쪽의 부드러운 부분만 사용합니다.
3. 냄비에 쌀뜨물과 자른 무를 넣고 1시간 정도 가열합니다.

FILLING

1. Peel the Korean radish and cut it into 5 cm thick slices.
2. Use a 3 to 4 cm ring cutter to cut rounds from each slice.
- Use only the tender inner part.
3. Place the radish and rice water in a pot, then simmer for about 1 hour.

4. 쌀뜨물을 버리고 무를 가볍게 씻습니다.
5. 냄비에 씻은 무와 나머지 재료를 모두 넣고 1~2시간 정도 가열합니다.
6. 무에 국물의 양념이 충분히 배어들면 키친타월에 올리고 잠시 두어 겉면의 물기를 제거합니다.

4. Discard the rice water and gently rinse the radish.
5. Return the radish to the pot, add the remaining ingredients, then simmer for about 1 to 2 hours.
6. Once the radish has absorbed the liquid, place it on a kitchen towel to drain any surface moisture.

만두피

1. 믹싱볼에 강력분, 중력분, 로스팅한 콩가루와 녹두 가루를 넣고 저속으로 정수물을 조금씩 흘려가며 믹싱합니다.
- 강력분과 중력분을 섞어 사용해 반죽에 찰기를 더했습니다.
- 반죽기가 없는 경우 손으로 치대어 작업해도 좋습니다.
2. 정수물이 다 들어가면 중속으로 약 5분 정도 믹싱합니다.
3. 날가루가 보이지 않고 정수물이 충분히 흡수되면 믹싱을 마무리합니다.

MANDU WRAPPERS

1. In a mixing bowl, combine the bread flour, all-purpose flour, and roasted soybean and mung bean powders. Gradually mix in the filtered water at low speed.
- The combination of bread flour and all-purpose flour gives the dough elasticity.
- If a stand mixer is unavailable, knead by hand.
2. Once all the water has been added, increase the speed to medium and mix for about 5 minutes.
3. Continue mixing until no dry flour is visible and the dough has absorbed enough water.

4. 반죽을 한 덩어리로 만들고 밀대나 기계를 이용해 적당한 두께로 밀어 펍니다.
5. 원형 틀을 사용해 만두피를 자릅니다.
● 원형 틀 없이 밀대로만 밀어 펴도 되지만, 원형 틀을 이용하면 작업도 편리하고 모양도 더 동그랗게 만들 수 있습니다.
6. 밀대를 이용해 지름 약 12cm로 밀어 펍니다.

4. Bring the mixture together into a single dough, then roll it out to a moderate thickness using a rolling pin or pasta machine.
5. Cut the dough into rounds using a round cutter.
● While a rolling pin works for shaping the dough, a round cutter makes the process easier and ensures a rounder shape.
6. Roll out each round to 12 cm in diameter using a rolling pin.

  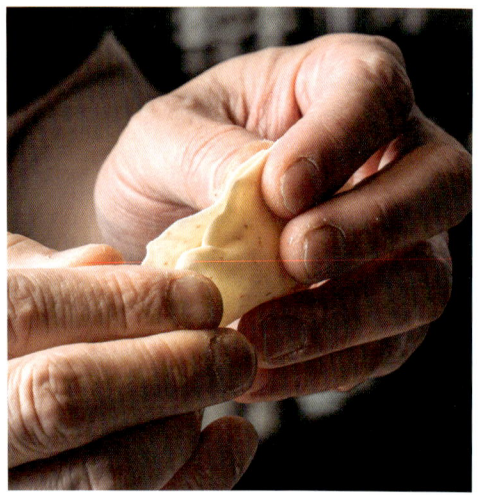

마무리

1. 만두피에 무를 올린 후, 반죽 가장자리를 겹쳐 접고 양끝을 고정시켜 만두 모양으로 빚어줍니다.

FINISH

1. Place the radish filling onto each wrapper, fold in half, and pinch the edges to seal into a *mandu* shape.

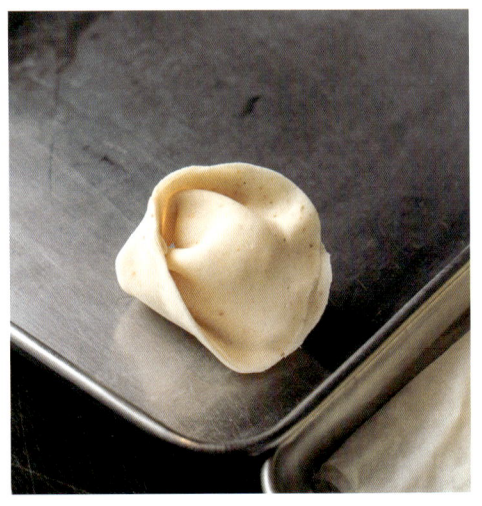 

2. 찜기에서 약 7분간 쪄 완성합니다.

2. Steam for about 7 minutes.

송홍윤
SONG HONGYUN

이야기
STORY

Half-Dried Fish and Seokbakji Salad

(Half-Dried Fish and Radish Kimchi Salad)

반건조 생선과 석박지 무침

한국의 반건조 생선은 저장과 유통을 위해 발전해온 방식이지만, 그 속에는 특별한 감칠맛과 식감이 담겨 있습니다. 하지만 오늘날의 소비자들은 잘 말려진 생선의 맛과 향보다 신선한 생선을 더 선호하는 경향이 있습니다. 그래서 저는 이 요리를 통해 반건조 생선이 지닌 고유한 매력을 다시금 소개하고자 합니다.

반건조 생선의 대표적인 예로 '굴비'를 들 수 있습니다. 선조들은 조기의 비린 향을 없애기 위해 녹차를 우린 물에 씻고, 소금에 절인 뒤 해풍에 말리는 과정을 거쳤습니다. 저는 이 전통을 현대적으로 재해석해, 녹차를 우린 물에 염지한 후 통째로 말려 겉은 바삭하고 속은 촉촉하게 조리했습니다. 또한, 생선의 가마살과 뼈를 우려내어 만든 진한 소스를 더해 생선 본연의 풍미를 더욱 깊게 표현했습니다. 여기에 한식에서 빠질 수 없는 김치를 곁들였는데요. 묵은 석박지의 양념을 걷어내고, 석박지 특유의 은은한 산미와 발효된 향을 생선과 함께 어우러지도록 구성했습니다.

한식이 가진 핵심 요소들인 숙성, 건조, 발효를 모두 담은 한 접시입니다.

While half-drying fish in Korea was a traditional way to preserve it for longer periods and ease distribution, it also brings out a unique *gamchilmat* and texture. Today, however, consumers tend to favor the flavor and aroma of fresh fish over dried. Through this dish, I hope to shed light on the distinct appeal of half-dried fish.

One classic example is gulbi (dried yellow croaker). Our ancestors would rinse the fish in green tea to remove any unpleasant fishy odor, then salt and dry it in the sea breeze. Taking a modern approach to this tradition, I brined the fish in salted green tea and dried it whole to achieve a texture that is crispy on the outside and moist within. This dish is further enriched with a deeply flavored sauce made from the fish collars and bones, and is served with kimchi—a staple never absent from Korean cuisine. With the kimchi paste scraped off, aged *seokbakji* offers a subtle tang and fermented notes that gently complement the fish.

This single plate brings together three essential elements of Korean cuisine: aging, drying, and fermentation.

Ingredients

6인 분량
Serve 6

반건조 생선

신선한 생선◆	1마리 (700~800g)
녹찻잎	2g
물	2000g
소금	80g

◆ 여기에서는 두줄촉수를 사용했습니다.

소스

구운 생선 뼈와 아가미	약 10조각
무	250g
알배추	200g
후춧가루	0.5g
대파	100g
물	4000g
생크림	200g
버터	15g

석박지 무침

묵은 석박지	60g
알배추	66g
참나물	1.5g
들기름	12g

HALF-DRIED FISH

1	fresh fish (700 to 800 g) ◆
2 g	loose leaf green tea
2000 g	water
80 g	salt

◆ This recipe uses black-spot goatfish.

SAUCE

about 10	roasted fish bones and gills
250 g	Korean radish
200 g	baby napa cabbage
0.5 g	ground black pepper
100 g	green onion
4000 g	water
200 g	fresh cream
15 g	butter

SEOKBAKJI SALAD

60 g	aged *seokbakji*
66 g	baby napa cabbage
1.5 g	chamnamul
12 g	perilla oil

How to make

반건조 생선

1. 생선의 비늘과 내장을 제거한 후, 녹찻잎을 우려낸 소금물(물+소금)에 넣어 1~2일 염지합니다.
2. 염지한 생선을 꺼내 4~8일 정도 드라이에이징 전용 냉장고(5~6℃)에 걸어 말려줍니다.
• 생선의 껍질을 만졌을 때 잘 건조된 느낌이 들 때까지 말려줍니다. 단시간에 말리기보다는 천천히 숙성시키며 건조해야 생선 살의 감칠맛이 올라갑니다.

HALF-DRIED FISH

1. Remove the scales and innards of the fish, then brine it in green tea-infused salt water (water + salt) for 1 to 2 days.
2. Hang the brined fish upside down in the dry-aging fridge at 41 to 43°F (5 to 6°C) and dry for about 4 to 8 days.
• Dry until the skin feels dry to the touch. Rather than drying the fish quickly over a short period, dry it slowly to allow aging, which helps deepen the *gamchilmat*.

3. 건조한 생선은 뼈와 살로 분리한 후 적당한 크기로 잘라줍니다. 생선을 손질하고 남은 뼈와 아가미는 다시 한번 2~3달 정도 드라이에이징 전용 냉장고에서 건조시켜줍니다.
4. 건조시킨 생선 뼈와 아가미는 지느러미를 제거하고, 145℃로 예열된 오븐에서 황금빛이 돌도록 천천히 구워줍니다.

3. Separate the fillets from the bones of the dried fish, then cut them into moderately sized slices. Place the fish bones and gills left after filleting in the dry-aging fridge, then dry for another 2 to 3 months.
4. Slowly roast the dried bones and gills, excluding the fins, in an oven preheated to 293°F (145°C) until golden brown.

소스

1. 냄비에 구운 생선 뼈와 아가미, 적당한 크기로 썬 무, 알배추, 후춧가루, 대파, 물을 넣고 48시간 이상 뭉근하게 끓여줍니다. 생선 뼈 육수를 체에 거른 후 다시 냄비로 옮겨 아주 진한 베이스가 될 때까지 천천히 졸여줍니다.

- 천천히 끓여가며 졸아든 물의 양만큼 중간중간 물을 추가하며 끓여줍니다.

2. 졸인 베이스에 생크림을 넣고 최종 소스 농도로 졸인 후 버터를 넣고 섞어줍니다.

SAUCE

1. In a pot, combine the roasted fish bones and gills with bite-sized pieces of Korean radish, baby napa cabbage, black pepper, green onion, and water. Simmer gently for at least 48 hours. Strain the fish bone stock, return it to the pot, and continue simmering slowly until it reduces into a rich sauce base.

- Replenish water as needed to make up for the amount lost during simmering.

2. Stir in the fresh cream and simmer until the base thickens to a sauce consistency. Add the butter and stir until incorporated.

석박지 무침

1. 석박지는 칼로 긁어내 겉에 묻은 양념을 벗겨낸 후, 찜기에 5분간 찌고 식혀줍니다.
2. 1과 알배추, 참나물을 아주 얇게 채 썰고 들기름과 함께 버무립니다.
3. 식용유를 두른 팬에 손질한 생선을 올리고 껍질이 바삭해질 때까지 구워줍니다. 이때 생선 살이 오그라들지 않도록 평평하게 누르고, 식용유를 끼얹어가며 위쪽 살까지 익힙니다.

SEOKBAKJI SALAD

1. Scrape off the kimchi paste from the seokbakji with a knife, steam for 5 minutes, and let it cool.
2. Finely slice the baby napa cabbage, chamnamul, and (**1**), then toss with perilla oil.
3. Pan-fry the fillet in cooking oil until the skin turns crispy. Press down evenly to prevent curling, and baste the top continuously with the pan liquid until cooked through.

플레이팅

1. 접시에 생선과 석박지 무침을 올려줍니다.
2. 소스를 부어 마무리합니다.

PLATING

1. Arrange the fish and *seokbakji* salad on a plate.
2. Gently pour the sauce.

송홍윤
SONG HONGYUN

가정식
HOME COOKING

Anchovy Gangdoenjang

(Seasoned Soybean Paste with Korean Dried Anchovies)

멸치 강된장

어릴 적, 어머니가 자주 해주시던 강된장의 기억 속 맛과 향을 되살려 만들어본 음식입니다. 자작하게 끓인 강된장을 쌉싸름한 나물과 함께 비벼 먹기도 하고, 찐 호박잎에 싸서 한입 가득 넣으면 잃었던 입맛도 돌아오곤 했습니다.

손이 많이 가기는 하지만, 멸치의 뼈와 머리를 정성껏 제거하면 더 깔끔하고 깊은 맛을 낼 수 있습니다. 또한 청양고추를 더하면 마지막에 치고 올라오는 매운맛으로 입맛을 돋울 수 있습니다. 짭짤한 강된장과 단맛이 도는 채소를 곁들이면 짠맛과 단맛의 조화를 이룰 수 있으니 꼭 한번 만들어보시길 바랍니다.

This dish is created to revive the nostalgic flavor and aroma of the seasoned soybean paste my mother often made when I was a child. I would mix it with pleasantly bitter *namul* (wild greens), or wrap it in a steamed pumpkin leaf. Each mouthful was so satisfying that it could bring back even a lost appetite.

While removing the bones and heads of anchovies by hand takes time and care, the effort yields a deeper, more refined flavor. A touch of cheongyang green chili peppers adds a gentle heat that kicks in at the end, subtly awakening the palate. The savory *gangdoenjang* pairs beautifully with vegetables that carry a delicate sweetness, creating a perfect balance of salty and sweet—truly worth trying.

Ingredients

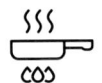

약 800g 분량
Yields about 800 g

건멸치	150g
다시마	20g
물	1500g
대파	200g
양파	140g
무	180g
집된장	약 120g
청양고추	70g

150 g	Korean dried anchovies
20 g	dried kelp
1500 g	water
200 g	green onion
140 g	onion
180 g	Korean radish
about 120 g	jip-doenjang (homemade soybean paste)
70 g	cheongyang green chili peppers

How to make

1. 기름을 두르지 않은 팬에 건멸치를 넣고 천천히 잘 볶아 비린 맛을 날려줍니다.
2. 멸치를 한번 털어 가루를 없애고 머리, 내장, 뼈, 지느러미를 제거합니다.
- 멸치의 뼈는 따로 모아두었다가 육수를 끓일 때 사용합니다.
3. 냄비에 멸치 뼈, 다시마, 물을 넣고 80°C 온도를 유지하며 30분 정도 천천히 가열합니다.
- 다시마는 마른 천으로 닦아서 사용하고, 가능하면 전날 물에 미리 담궈 천천히 우린 후 우린 물과 함께 사용하면 더 좋습니다.

1. Slowly stir-fry the dried anchovies in a dry pan to remove any unpleasant fishy odor.
2. Shake off any surface powder from the anchovies, then remove the heads, innards, bones, and fins.
- Reserve the anchovy bones for stock.
3. In a pot, combine the anchovy bones, dried kelp, and water. Gently simmer at 176°F (80°C) for about 30 minutes.
- Wipe the dried kelp with a dry cloth. If possible, soak it in water a day in advance and use both the kelp and its soaking water.

4. 완성된 육수를 체에 걸러줍니다.
5. 다시 냄비로 옮긴 후 **2**를 넣고 15분 정도 끓여줍니다.

4. Strain the stock through a sieve.
5. Return the stock to the pot, add (**2**), and simmer for about 15 minutes.

6. 사방 1cm 정도로 썬 대파, 양파, 무를 넣고 푹 익을 때까지 뭉근하게 끓여줍니다.

7. 어느 정도 자작하게 졸아들면 된장을 넣고 더 졸여줍니다.

- 여기에서는 윤서울의 두 가지 된장을 섞어 사용했습니다. 집된장이 없다면 시판 재래식 된장을 사용해도 좋습니다. 다만 된장마다 염도가 조금씩 다르므로 80% 정도의 양만 넣고 간을 보며 조금씩 추가해주는 것이 좋습니다. 혹시나 묵은 된장이 있다면 1작은술 정도 섞어 사용해 풍미와 향을 더해도 좋습니다.

8. 원하는 정도의 농도로 졸아들면 청양고추를 넣고 한 번 더 끓여 마무리합니다.

- 마지막에 넣은 청양고추로 매운맛을 더하고 아삭한 식감을 만들어줍니다.
- 조금 덜 짜게 완성하려면, 덜 졸여진 상태에서 전분 푼 물을 넣어 농도를 잡아줍니다.

6. Add the green onion, onion, and Korean radish, each cut into about 1 cm squares, then simmer until cooked through.

7. Once slightly reduced, add the doenjang and continue simmering to reduce further.

- This recipe uses two types of doenjang crafted at Yun Seoul. If jip-doenjang is unavailable, substitute with store-bought traditional doenjang. Meanwhile, since saltiness may vary depending on the doenjang, start with 80% of the amount and adjust gradually to taste. If available, add 1 teaspoon of aged doenjang to enhance flavor and aroma.

8. Once reduced to the desired consistency, add the cheongyang green chili peppers and bring to a boil.

- A final touch of cheongyang green chili peppers adds heat and a crunchy texture.
- For a less salty flavor, add a starchy slurry before fully reducing to achieve the desired consistency.

KIM MIRYEONG

김미령

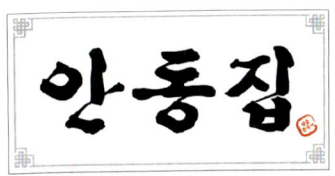

안동국시
Andongjip Sonkalguksi

즐거운 술상
Cheerful Drinking Table

auntieomakase_no.1

처음 요리는 생계를 위한 선택이었다. 중학교 2학년, 아버지의 사업 부도와 건강 악화로 가세가 기울자 어머니는 경동시장에서 국수를 팔기 시작했다. 어린 시절엔 그 국수가 가난의 상징처럼 느껴졌지만, 시간이 흐를수록 한 그릇에 담긴 정성과 따뜻함을 알게 되었다.

20대에 어머니의 가게를 물려받으며 본격적으로 요리의 길에 들어섰다. 발레리나의 꿈을 내려놓고 선택한 길이었지만, 한식의 깊이에 매료되면서 어느새 요리는 삶이 되었다. 전통을 지키면서도 그녀만의 감각을 더한 '이모카세' 스타일은 그렇게 탄생했다.

넷플릭스 <흑백요리사: 요리 계급 전쟁>에서 '캐비어보다 맛있다'는 극찬을 받은 김 요리로 주목을 받았고, 창동의 '즐거운 술상'은 하루 1000통이 넘는 예약 전화로 화제가 되었다.

김미령 셰프는 말한다. 음식은 결국 '정성과 반복의 결과'라고. 화려하진 않아도 오래도록 기억되는 맛. 그 맛을 담아 손님들에게 편안한 식사 경험을 제공하는 것이 그녀의 철칙이다.

Initially, cooking was a means of survival. During the second year of middle school, Chef Kim's mother began selling noodles at Gyeongdong Market due to the bankruptcy of her father's business and deteriorating health. As a child, the noodles seemed like a symbol of poverty, but as she grew older, she came to appreciate the sincerity and warmth that went into each bowl of noodles.

She started cooking in her 20s as she took over her mother's restaurant. Although she had to give up her dreams of becoming a ballerina, cooking became her life as she was fascinated by the depth of Korean cuisine. Thus, the "*Imokase* (Auntie Omakase)" style was born, a style that honors tradition while adding her own flair.

Netflix's *Culinary Class Wars* drew attention to her seaweed dish, which was highly praised as being "tastier than caviar," and Chang-dong's "Cheerful Drinking Table" went viral for receiving more than 1,000 calls for reservations per day.

Chef Kim Miryeong says that food is ultimately the result of sincerity and repetition. It may not be fancy, but taste is one that is remembered for a long time. Her philosophy is to provide a comfortable dining experience for her guests with such taste.

Dwaeji Suyuk and Geotjeori

(Korean Boiled Pork and Fresh Kimchi)

이야기 / STORY

돼지 수육과 겉절이

잔치나 기념일, 좋은 날 빠질 수 없는 음식이 바로 수육이 아닐까 싶습니다. 한국 사람이라면 누구나 좋아하는 음식이죠. 부드럽고 구수한 맛 덕분에 어린아이들부터 어르신들까지 함께 즐기기에도 참 좋은 메뉴입니다.

수육을 만들 때 보통 삼겹살을 사용하지만, 저는 앞다리 살을 권하고 싶습니다. 삶았을 때 쫄깃하면서도 부드러운 식감으로 완성되기 때문이죠. 기름기가 적당히 빠진 담백한 맛도 앞다리 살만의 매력입니다.

그리고 수육 하면 빠질 수 없는 것이 바로 겉절이입니다. 저는 통배추 대신 쌈배추, 그중에서도 알배추를 사용했습니다. 절이는 시간이 짧고, 샐러드처럼 가볍고 상큼하게 즐길 수 있어 수육과도 훨씬 잘 어울리기 때문이죠. 양념도 과하지 않게, 필요한 재료만으로 담백하게 만들었습니다.

Whenever there is a party, anniversary, or any special occasion, *Dwaeji suyuk* (Korean boiled pork) is a must on our table. With its tender and savory flavor, it is beloved by Koreans of all ages—from children to the elderly.

While it is typically made with pork belly, I recommend using picnic shoulder for its clean flavor, lower fat content, and a texture that is chewy yet tender when cooked.

And no *suyuk* is complete without *Geotjeori* (fresh kimchi). Instead of using whole napa cabbage, I use baby napa cabbage, which salts more quickly and is light and refreshing—like a salad—and pairs even better with *suyuk*. Made only with essential ingredients, the seasoning is also kept simple and clean, not overpowering.

Ingredients

돼지 수육 – 고기 한 덩어리 분량
겉절이 - 알배추 한 통 분량

Dwaeji Suyuk –
For 1 picnic shoulder cut

Geotjeori – For 1 baby napa cabbage

돼지 수육

돼지고기 앞다리 살 (생고기)	한 덩어리
찬물	적당량
된장	약 1큰술

겉절이

알배추	1통
물	1L
굵은 소금	25g
대파	65g
다진 마늘	38g
고춧가루	27g
액젓 ◆	22g
물엿	20g
참깨	11g
미원	3g

◆ 액젓은 멸치, 까나리 모두 사용 가능합니다.

DWAEJI SUYUK (Korean boiled pork)

1	picnic shoulder
Q.S.	cold water
1 tbsp	doenjang (Korean soybean paste)

GEOTJEORI (Fresh kimchi)

1	baby napa cabbage
1 L	water
25 g	coarse salt
65 g	green onion
38 g	minced garlic
27 g	Korean chili powder
22 g	aekjeot (Korean fish sauce) ◆
20 g	mulyeot (Korean corn syrup)
11 g	whole sesame seeds
3 g	Miwon (MSG)

◆ Either myeolchi (Korean anchovy) aekjeot or kkanari (sand lance) aekjeot can be used.

How to make

돼지 수육

1. 냄비에 돼지고기 앞다리 살, 고기가 덮일 정도의 찬물, 된장 한 스푼을 넣고 고기가 익을 때까지 삶아줍니다.

- 고기가 신선하다면 삶을 때 많은 재료를 넣을 필요가 없습니다. 냉동한 고기나 냉동 후 해동한 고기 대신 신선한 생고기를 사용해주세요.
- 앞다리 살을 사용하는 이유는 살코기와 지방의 비율이 가장 이상적이기 때문입니다.

2. 고기가 익으면 적당한 크기로 썰어줍니다.

- 젓가락으로 고기 중심부를 찔렀을 때 부드럽게 들어가는 정도가 되면 익은 것입니다.

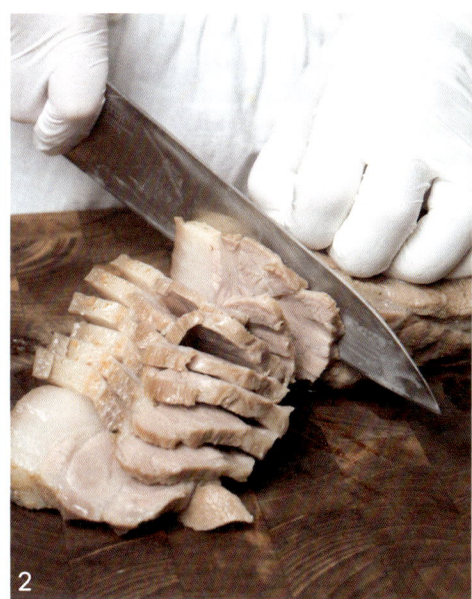

DWAEJI SUYUK

1. Place the picnic shoulder in a pot, and add enough cold water to cover. Stir in 1 tablespoon of doenjang, then cook until the meat is done.

- When using fresh meat, there is no need to add many ingredients while boiling. It is best to use fresh meat rather than frozen or thawed.
- This recipe uses picnic shoulder for its ideal balance of lean and fat.

2. Once the meat is cooked, cut it into moderately sized pieces.

- The pork is done when a chopstick easily pierces through the center.

겉절이

1. 알배추를 4등분으로 먹기 좋게 잘라줍니다.

- 자르는 크기에 정답은 없지만, 저의 경우 잎을 좋아하는 사람과 줄기를 좋아하는 사람 등 먹는 이를 배려해 잎과 줄기로 구분해 자릅니다.

GEOTJEORI

1. Cut the baby napa cabbage leaves into four pieces each for easier eating.

- There is no strict rule about size, but I usually separate the leafy parts and the white stems to satisfy both leaf lovers and stem lovers.

2. 넉넉한 볼에 알배추와 물, 굵은소금을 넣고 5~10분 정도 절여줍니다. 이때 중간중간 알배추를 뒤집어줍니다.

3. 배춧잎을 구부렸을 때 유연하게 휘어지면 잘 절여진 것입니다. 단, 너무 오래 절여지지는 않게 주의합니다.

- 알배추를 사용한 이유는 일반 배추보다 부드럽기 때문입니다. 일반 배추를 사용할 경우 절이는 시간을 더 늘려주세요.

- 알배추에 따라 절이는 시간은 달라질 수 있습니다. 중요한 것은 바로 무쳐 샐러드처럼 먹는 김치이므로 숙성하는 김치처럼 오래 절이면 안 된다는 점입니다. 숨이 살짝 죽을 정도로만 가볍게 절여주세요. 어차피 양념을 버무리는 과정에서도 숨이 죽습니다. 좀 더 빨리 절이고 싶으면 소금의 양을 늘려주세요.

2. Toss all the pieces of baby napa cabbage with the coarse salt and water in a large mixing bowl. Let sit for about 5 to 10 minutes, turning occasionally.

3. The cabbage leaves are well salted when they bend easily. However, be careful not to oversalt by leaving them in the salt too long.

- This recipe uses baby napa cabbage for a more tender texture than regular napa cabbage. When using regular napa cabbage, allow more time for salting.

- Salting time may vary depending on the baby napa cabbage. *Geotjeori* is meant to be eaten fresh, like a freshly tossed salad. Make sure not to salt it for too long, unlike other types of kimchi that are aged before eating. Salt just enough to slightly wilt the cabbage, as it will continue to wilt when tossed with the kimchi paste. Add more salt to speed up the salting process, if desired.

4. 절인 알배추를 흐르는 물에 가볍게 씻고 체에 받쳐 물기를 제거한 후, 볼에 모든 재료를 담고 골고루 버무려줍니다.

- 기호에 따라 참기름을 추가해도 좋습니다. 이 경우 먹기 직전 참기름을 겉절이에 한 바퀴 둘러주세요.

4. Gently rinse the salted baby napa cabbage under running water, then drain over a sieve. Place all the ingredients in a large mixing bowl and toss thoroughly.

- Add sesame oil, if desired. If using it, finish with a swirl over the *geotjeori* right before serving.

Four Kinds of Banchan, Roasted Seaweed, and Bibimbap

가정식
HOME COOKING

밑반찬 4종과 김구이, 그리고 비빔밥

한국 사람이라면 누구나 좋아하고, 밥상에 빠지지 않는 반찬 중 하나가 바로 콩나물무침입니다. 콩나물은 저렴하면서도 누구나 맛있게 즐길 수 있는 재료라, 매일 먹어도 질리지 않죠. 겨울에 특히 맛이 좋은 무는 그 자체로도 단맛이 뛰어나 많은 양념이 필요 없습니다. 간단한 손질만으로도 시원하고 칼칼한 무생채가 완성되지요. 들기름을 살짝 두르고 볶아낸 애호박은 볶는 동안 퍼지는 향만으로도 입맛을 돋워줍니다. 여기에, 잔칫상이나 차례상에서 빠지지 않는 고사리도 더해보았습니다. 고사리는 부드러우면서도 쫄깃한 식감이 매력적이고, 다른 나물들과 조화롭게 어우러집니다.

이 네 가지 반찬을 고른 이유는 함께 상에 올렸을 때 맛과 색감이 조화를 이루고, 비빔밥 재료로도 더할 나위 없이 잘 어울리기 때문입니다. 각각 따로 먹어도 좋고, 고추장과 참기름을 곁들여 밥에 비벼 먹으면 한 그릇 뚝딱할 만큼 맛있습니다.

마지막으로 소개할 메뉴는 바로 김구이입니다. 요즘은 조미김이 흔하지만, 예전 어머니가 불 위에서 기름을 바르고 정성껏 구워주시던 그 김의 맛이 그리워 직접 구워보았습니다.

네 가지 반찬과 김구이, 그리고 정갈한 비빔밥은 모두 '즐거운 술상'의 인기 메뉴입니다. 익숙하지만 정성스러운 맛으로, 따뜻한 식탁을 만들어보시길 바랍니다.

One of Korea's most beloved *banchan* (side dishes), never absent from the table, is none other than seasoned bean sprouts. Affordable and flavorful, this humble dish is something anyone can enjoy every day without ever growing tired of it. Korean radish, at its winter peak, needs little seasoning, as its natural sweetness speaks for itself. With just a simple preparation, it becomes a salad with clean, peppery heat. Zucchini is gently stir-fried with perilla oil, and its aroma alone is enough to awaken the appetite as it cooks. Fernbrake, traditionally served at parties or ancestral rites, offers a tender yet springy texture that blends harmoniously with other greens.

These four kinds of *banchan* are chosen for their balance of flavor and color when served together, and they come together just as well in *bibimbap* (mixed rice with vegetables). They can be enjoyed separately or mixed with rice, gochujang (Korean red chili paste), and sesame oil—so delicious that the bowl will be empty in no time.

The last is roasted seaweed. While seasoned seaweed is easy to find these days, I made my own, longing for the kind that my mother used to prepare—gently brushing each sheet with oil and carefully roasting it over the flame.

These four kinds of *banchan*, along with the roasted seaweed, are beloved fare at Jeulgeoun Sulsang. Though familiar in taste, these dishes are prepared with sincerity. I hope they bring a touch of comfort and warmth to your table.

Ingredients

밑반찬 4종 - 1접시 분량

Four kinds of *banchan* - Makes 1 plate each

콩나물무침

데친 콩나물	200g
대파	16g
다진 마늘	11g
소금	4g
참깨	4g
미원	1g

호박 볶음

호박	1개
식용유	적당량
다진 마늘	19g
대파	15g
들기름	9g
참깨	5g
미원	3g

고사리 볶음

고사리	210g
식용유	적당량
대파	22g
다진 마늘	18g
양조간장	9g
들기름	6g
참기름	6g
소금	3g
미원	2g

무 생채

채 썬 무	315g
대파	36g
다진 마늘	25g
고춧가루	17g
물엿	17g
소금	8g
참깨	5g
미원	4g

김구이

들기름과 참기름	1:1 비율
재래김	적당량
맛소금	적당량

SEASONED BEAN SPROUTS

200 g	blanched bean sprouts
16 g	green onion
11 g	minced garlic
4 g	salt
4 g	sesame seeds
1 g	Miwon (MSG)

STIR-FRIED ZUCCHINI

1	zucchini
Q.S.	cooking oil
19 g	minced garlic
15 g	green onion
9 g	perilla oil
5 g	sesame seeds
3 g	Miwon

STIR-FRIED FERNBRAKE

210 g	fernbrake
Q.S.	cooking oil
22 g	green onion
18 g	minced garlic
9 g	yangjo-ganjang (naturally brewed soy sauce)
6 g	perilla oil
6 g	sesame oil
3 g	salt
2 g	Miwon

RADISH FRESH SALAD

315 g	julienned radish
36 g	green onion
25 g	minced garlic
17 g	Korean chili powder
17 g	mulyeot (Korean corn syrup)
8 g	salt
5 g	sesame seeds
4 g	Miwon

ROASTED SEAWEED

1:1 ratio perilla oil and sesame oil

Q.S.	Korean dried seaweed
Q.S.	seasoning salt

How to make

콩나물무침

1. 냄비에 콩나물과 콩나물이 덮일 정도의 찬물을 넣은 후 뚜껑을 닫고 가열합니다.
2. 물이 끓어오르면 콩나물을 건져내 식혀줍니다.
3. 볼에 모든 재료를 넣고 골고루 버무립니다.
- 기호에 따라 참기름 6g을 함께 버무려도 좋습니다.

SEASONED BEAN SPROUTS

1. Place the bean sprouts in a pot and add enough cold water to cover. Bring to a boil with the lid on.
2. Once it comes to a boil, remove the bean sprouts and let them cool in a strainer.
3. Combine all the ingredients in a mixing bowl and toss thoroughly.
- If desired, add 6 g of sesame oil before tossing.

호박 볶음

1. 호박을 반달 모양으로 썰어줍니다.
2. 식용유를 두른 팬에 호박을 넣고 볶아줍니다.
3. 호박의 숨이 살짝 죽으면 남은 양념 재료를 모두 넣고 볶아줍니다.
- 새우젓을 좋아한다면 소금 대신 넣어도 좋습니다.

STIR-FRIED ZUCCHINI

1. Cut the zucchini into half-moon slices.
2. Stir-fry the zucchini in a pan with cooking oil.
3. When the zucchini is slightly wilted, add the remaining seasoning ingredients and continue stir-frying.
- If desired, add saeu-jeot (salted shrimp) instead of salt.

고사리 볶음

1. 식용유를 두른 팬에 고사리를 넣고 가볍게 볶아줍니다.
- 고사리는 흐르는 물에 가볍게 씻은 후 적당한 크기로 잘라 사용합니다.
- 시중에 판매되는 고사리는 대부분 한 번 삶아져 나온 고사리이므로, 오래 볶지 않아도 됩니다.
2. 남은 양념 재료를 모두 넣고 볶아줍니다.
3. 대파가 너무 익지 않을 정도로 살짝 볶아 마무리합니다.

STIR-FRIED FERNBRAKE

1. Gently stir-fry the fernbrake in a pan with cooking oil.
- Rinse the fernbrake under running water and cut it into moderately sized pieces before cooking.
- Since most fernbrake sold in markets is already blanched, it does not need to be stir-fried too long.
2. Add the remaining seasoning ingredients and continue stir-frying.
3. Finish cooking before the green onion becomes overcooked.

무 생채

1. 무는 먹기 좋은 크기로 채 썰어줍니다.

RADISH FRESH SALAD

1. Julienne the radish into bite-sized pieces.

2. 볼에 모든 재료를 넣고 버무려줍니다.

- 기호에 따라 고춧가루의 양을 가감합니다. 매운 걸 좋아하는 분이라면 고춧가루의 양을 늘리고, 아이와 함께 먹는다면 주황빛이 돌 정도로만 고춧가루를 사용합니다.
- 참기름의 사용 여부에 따라 전혀 다른 맛으로 완성할 수 있습니다. 참기름을 사용하면 고소한 맛이 추가되고, 사용하지 않으면 깔끔한 맛으로 완성됩니다. 참기름을 사용할 경우 6g 정도가 적당합니다.

2. Combine all the ingredients in a bowl and toss thoroughly.

- Adjust the amount of Korean chili pepper as desired. If you prefer it spicy, add more; if you're eating with kids, use just enough to give the radish a light orange tint.
- The flavor of the dish can change significantly depending on whether sesame oil is used. If added, it brings a nutty flavor; if omitted, the dish has a clean finish. If using sesame oil, about 6 grams is ideal.

김구이

1. 들기름과 참기름을 1:1 비율로 섞어 준비합니다.
- 참기름만 사용하면 맛이 너무 가볍고, 들기름만 사용하면 맛이 무겁고 산패도 빠르게 진행됩니다. 저는 1:1로 섞어 사용하지만 기호에 따라 비율을 조절해도 좋습니다.
2. 재래김에 **1**을 고르게 펴 발라줍니다.
3. 맛소금을 뿌려줍니다.
- 맛소금의 사용량은 기호에 따라 달라집니다. 저의 경우 엄지와 검지에 잡히는 소금(약 한 꼬집)을 재래김 한 장에 사용하지만 기호에 따라 가감해도 좋습니다.

ROASTED SEAWEED

1. Make the oil blend by mixing perilla oil and sesame oil in a 1:1 ratio.
- Sesame oil alone makes the seaweed too mild, whereas perilla oil alone makes it too heavy in flavor and causes it to turn rancid quickly. The recipe uses a 1:1 ratio, but feel free to adjust it to taste.
2. Evenly brush (**1**) onto a sheet of dried seaweed.
3. Sprinkle with seasoning salt.
- The amount of seasoning salt can be adjusted to taste. The recipe uses about a pinch per sheet, but feel free to adjust it to taste.

4. 재래김을 계속 올려가며 동일하게 반복합니다.
- 아래에 있는 재래김에 기름과 소금이 뿌려져 있으므로 윗면만 작업하면 됩니다. 이 상태로 소분해 냉동 보관하면서 필요할 때마다 꺼내서 구워 먹으면 매일매일 바삭하고 맛있는 김을 먹을 수 있습니다.
5. 뜨겁게 달군 팬에 재래김을 올려 굽습니다. 이때 주걱으로 김 사방을 눌러 고르게 구워지도록 합니다.

4. Stack the seaweed sheets, repeating the oiling and seasoning process for each layer.
- Since the underside is already coated, apply oil and salt only to the top side of each subsequent sheet. Divide the stack into single-serving portions and store in the freezer. Roast directly from frozen as needed to enjoy crispy, flavorful seaweed anytime.
5. Roast the seaweed in a well-preheated pan. Use a spatula to press down on all sides to ensure even roasting.

6. 김의 색이 살짝 파래지고, 처음보다 비치는 상태가 되면 적당하게 구워진 것입니다.
7. 구운 재래김을 먹기 좋은 크기로 잘라줍니다.

6. The seaweed is properly roasted when it turns slightly green and becomes more translucent.
7. Cut the roasted seaweed into moderately sized pieces.

PARK SUNGBAE

박 성 배

ONJIUM

어린 시절부터 음식은 그에게 단순한 끼니가 아닌, 정성과 깊이가 깃든 예술이었다. 대학 시절, 본격적으로 요리의 길을 걷기로 결심한 그는 한식이 지닌 고유한 맛과 조리법에 매료되었고, 특히 조선 시대 반가 음식의 정신과 구조에 깊이 빠져들었다.

그가 10년 넘게 수석 셰프로 활동하고 있는 온지음은 2019년 미쉐린 1스타를 획득한 후 현재까지 유지하고 있으며, 전통 한식을 현대적으로 계승하는 데 집중해왔다. 특히 발효와 채소 조리법을 중심으로, 자극적인 맛이 아닌 재료 본연의 깊고 담백한 맛을 담은 요리들을 선보이고 있다. 과학적 조리법과 현대적 감각을 더한 그의 요리는 한식의 본질을 잃지 않으면서도 세계적인 미식 트렌드 속에서 조화를 이루는 방향으로 발전하고 있다.

한국의 식문화는 그에게 단지 과거의 유산이 아니다. 그는 한식을 '살아 있는 문화'로 바라보며, 한국인의 미감과 정서를 담은 식탁을 세계에 전하고자 한다. 음식은 결국 본질을 잃지 않고 시간과 손길을 머금었을 때 비로소 완성된다는 것. 박성배 셰프는 그 진리를 매일의 식탁 위에서 증명하고 있다.

Since childhood, food has been more than just a meal to Chef Park; it was an art imbued with sincerity and depth. During his college years, he decided to pursue his culinary career in earnest. He was fascinated by the unique flavors and recipes of Korean cuisine, especially the spirit and structure of Joseon Dynasty Banga cuisine.

Onjium, where he has been the executive chef for over a decade, was awarded one Michelin star in 2019, a distinction he has maintained to this day, and he has focused on modernizing traditional Korean cuisine. With a particular focus on fermentation and vegetable-based recipes, his dishes are not excessive but rather intensely flavorful and light in nature. With scientific preparations and modern touches, his cuisine is evolving in a way that harmonizes with global gastronomic trends while retaining the essence of Korean cuisine.

Korean food culture is not just a heritage of the past for him; he sees it as a "living culture" and wants to convey to the world the aesthetics and emotions of the Korean people. In the end, food is only perfect when it is made with time and care without losing its essence. Chef Park proves this verity every day at the table.

온지음
@ onjium_restaurant

@ sung252825

Baekja Bean Curd

백자 두부

이야기
STORY

어렸을 적, 강원도 양구 산골 마을에서 지내시던 할머니가 자주 만들어 주던 음식이 바로 이 백자 두부입니다. 해가 잘 드는 마당 끝 부엌에서 두부를 만들던 할머니의 모습은 아직도 제 머릿속에 선명합니다. 시간이 흐르고 요리사가 되어 전국의 다양한 두부를 맛보았지만, 아직까지도 저에게 가장 깊이 남은 맛은 여전히 그 시골집에서 갓 만든, 따뜻하고 담백한 할머니표 두부입니다.

이 책에서 소개하는 백자 두부는 강원도 특산물인 잣을 백태콩과 함께 곱게 갈아 넣어 은근한 고소함을 살리는 것이 가장 큰 특징입니다. 현재 제가 몸담고 있는 온지음에서도 이 두부를 활용한 메뉴를 자주 선보이고 있습니다. 단순한 한 그릇의 음식이지만, 그 속에는 추억과 손맛 그리고 지금도 이어지는 저만의 요리 이야기가 담겨 있습니다.

When I was a child, my grandmother, who lived in a mountain village in Yanggu County, Gangwon Province, used to make this *baekja** bean curd. I can still vividly recall her preparing it in the kitchen across the sunlit yard. Over the years, I became a chef and have tasted countless varieties of bean curd from across the country, but the warm, clean one she crafted fresh by hand in that countryside home remains the most deeply rooted in my memory.

The distinctive quality of this *baekja* bean curd is its gentle nuttiness, achieved by grinding pine nuts—a specialty of Gangwon Province—together with yellow soybeans. At Onjium, where I currently work, we often showcase dishes that incorporate this bean curd. Though it may seem simple, this dish holds layers of cherished memories, personal touches, and ongoing stories behind my journey.

* *Baekja* literally means "white porcelain," and this bean curd is named for its porcelain-whiteness.

Ingredients

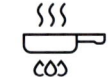

두부 약 2모 분량

For 2 bean curds

백태콩	3컵 (약 480g)
물	3L
로스팅한 잣◆	1컵
참기름	적당량
얼음	700g
간수 (시판)	적당량

◆ 잣은 프라이팬이나 오븐에서 노릇해질 때까지 구워 사용합니다.

3 cups	yellow soybeans (about 480 g)
3 L	water
1 cup	roasted pine nuts ◆
Q.S.	sesame oil
700 g	ice
Q.S.	bittern (store-bought)

◆ Roast the pine nuts in a pan or oven until golden brown before use.

How to make

1. 백태콩은 물(분량 외)에 담가 하루 정도 충분히 불린 후, 손바닥으로 비벼 껍질을 벗겨 준비합니다.
2. 믹서에 껍질 벗긴 백태콩과 물 3L를 넣고 갈아줍니다. 절반 정도 갈렸을 때 로스팅한 잣 1/2컵을 넣고 곱게 갈아줍니다.
- 휴롬과 같은 즙용 믹서를 사용하면 좋습니다.

1. Soak the yellow soybeans in water for about a day, then rub them between your hands to remove their skins.
2. Combine the peeled yellow soybe ans with 3 liters of water in a blender, and blend until roughly ground. Once halfway ground, add 1/2 cup of roasted pine nuts, and continue blending until smooth.
- A juicer and blender in one, like a Hurom, is recommended.

3. 냄비에 옮겨 한소끔 가열합니다.
- 이때 약간의 참기름을 넣으면 끓는 동안 넘치지 않습니다.
4. 불을 끈 후 얼음을 넣고 식혀줍니다.
- 두부를 수차례 만들다 보니 터득하게 된 방법입니다. 얼음을 사용해 온도를 낮춰주면 면포에 거르고 짜내는 과정이 더 수월합니다.

3. Pour the mixture into a pot and bring it to a boil.
- A dash of sesame oil can help prevent the mixture from boiling over.
4. Turn off the heat and add the ice to cool it down.
- This is a pro tip from many trials in making bean curd. Cooling with ice makes the mixture easier to strain and squeeze through muslin (cheesecloth).

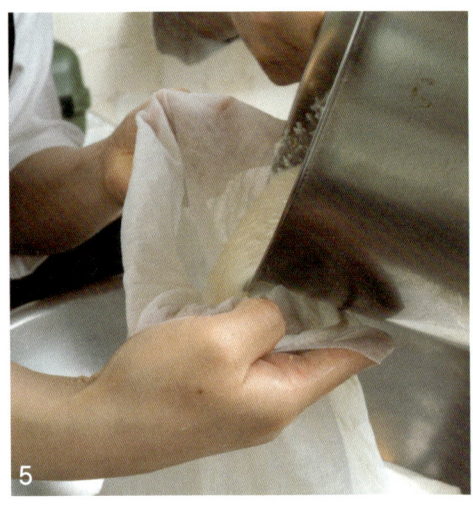

5. 식힌 백태콩을 면포에 담고 짜줍니다.
6. 걸러진 콩물을 다시 냄비로 옮겨 가열합니다.

5. Pour the cooled mixture over a piece of muslin and squeeze out the liquid.
6. Return the liquid to the pot and bring to a boil again.

7. 한번 끓어오르면(약 85℃), 불을 끄고 남은 로스팅한 잣과 간수를 넣고 섞어줍니다.
8. 몽글몽글한 질감이 될 때까지 잠시 기다립니다.

7. Once it reaches a boil (approximately 185°F / 85°C), turn off the heat. Add another 1/2 cup of roasted pine nuts and bittern, then stir gently.
8. Let the mixture sit for a while until it begins to curdle and forms soft lumps.

9. 면포를 깐 네모난 틀에 붓고 면포 밖으로 나온 수분은 버립니다.

9. Pour it into a muslin-lined rectangular mold, then discard any liquid that seeps out.

10. 잠시 두고 굳혀 완성합니다.

10. Let the bean curd sit for a while until fully set.

068 - 069

Pan-fried Cod with Mussel and Brown Seaweed Rice

가정식
HOME COOKING

대구구이와 홍합 톳밥

대구 특유의 시원한 감칠맛과 쫀득한 식감을 최대한 살린 대구구이, 그리고 함께 곁들이기에 좋은 홍합 톳밥을 만들어 보았습니다.

집간장을 넣어 만든 양념을 대구에 정성스럽게 발라 구워 입안에서 착 감길 만큼 풍미 깊은 대구구이는 밥반찬으로도, 손님상에도 잘 어울리는 메뉴입니다.

홍합 톳밥은 최근에 액젓이 들어간 톳밥을 무척 맛있게 먹은 경험에서 착안해 만들게 되었는데요. 톳의 식감에 감칠맛을 더하기 위해 양념장에 액젓을 살짝 넣고, 여기에 탱글탱글한 홍합살을 더해 맛과 영양, 두 마리 토끼를 모두 잡았습니다. 톳의 향긋함과 홍합의 바다 향이 어우러져 대구구이와도 훌륭하게 어울립니다.

두 가지 요리 모두 복잡한 과정 없이 가정에서도 충분히 따라 만들 수 있는 레시피입니다. 특히 대구와 홍합이 제철인 겨울철에는 재료 본연의 맛이 한층 살아나니, 따뜻한 집밥이 생각나는 계절에 꼭 한 번 만들어 보시길 추천합니다.

Prepared to highlight its mild *gamchilmat* and springy texture, pan-fried cod is served with mussel and brown seaweed rice that pairs beautifully with it.

Brushed with a homemade ganjang-based seasoning before pan-frying, the cod takes on a savory flavor with gentle depth on the palate, making it perfect for an everyday meal or a special offering when entertaining guests.

I recently had a memorable mussel and brown seaweed rice with aekjeot (Korean fish sauce), which inspired me to create this dish. The addition of aekjeot brings out the *gamchilmat* in the seaweed's delicate texture, while the mussels add a pleasantly bouncy bite, making the dish both flavorful and nourishing. The gentle aroma of brown seaweed mingles with the fresh ocean scent of mussels, which makes a wonderful complement to pan-fried cod. The natural flavors of cod and mussels are at their peak in winter—the perfect season to enjoy them, when we often crave warm, comforting homemade food.

Ingredients

4인 분량

Serves 4

대구 구이

손질한 대구	600g
식용유	10g

대구 양념

국간장	40g
맛술	40g
다진 파	30g
다진 마늘	15g
식용유	35g
생강즙	5g
고춧가루	적당량
참깨	적당량
후춧가루	적당량

홍합 톳밥

홍합 살	200g
참기름	적당량
쌀	1컵
물	1컵
생톳	100g

양념장

다진 미나리	1큰술
깨소금	1큰술
들기름	1큰술
액젓 ◆	1큰술
다진 마늘	1큰술
다진 파	1큰술
소금	약간

◆ 맛이 좋은 액젓이라면 종류는 상관 없습니다.

PAN-FRIED COD

600 g	cleaned cod
10 g	cooking oil

COD SEASONING

40 g	guk-ganjang (Korean soup soy sauce)
40 g	matsul (Korean cooking wine)
30 g	chopped green onion
30 g	minced garlic
35 g	cooking oil
5 g	ginger juice
Q.S.	Korean chili powder
Q.S.	sesame seeds
Q.S.	ground black pepper

MUSSEL AND BROWN SEAWEED RICE

200 g	mussel meat
Q.S.	sesame oil
1 cup	rice
1 cup	water
100 g	fresh brown seaweed

SAUCE

1 tbsp	chopped water parsley
1 tbsp	roasted sesame seeds
1 tbsp	perilla oil
1 tbsp	aekjeot (Korean fish sauce) ◆
1 tbsp	minced garlic
1 tbsp	chopped green onion
Q.S.	salt

◆ Any variety of aekjeot works, as long as it is flavorful.

How to make

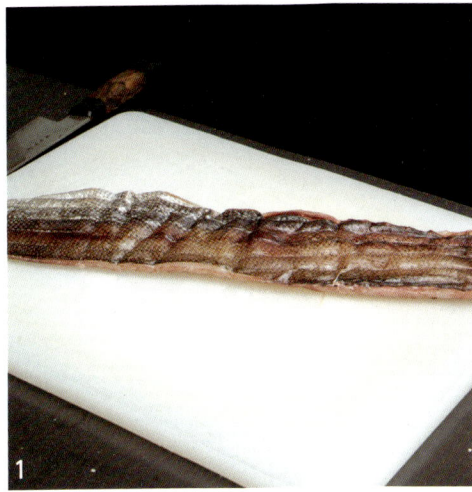
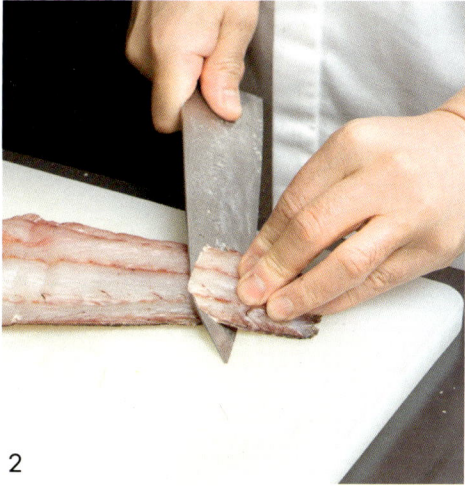

대구 구이

1. 대구는 손질하여 하루 정도 건조시킵니다.
- 대구 손질이 어렵다면 손질된 것을 구매해 사용합니다. 냉동된 대구를 사용할 경우 냉장고에서 해동한 후 소금을 뿌려두었다가 씻어내 살짝 건조시킨 후 사용하면 살이 쫀쫀해집니다.
2. 건조시킨 대구는 껍질을 살려 도톰하게 썬 후 잠시 두어 수분을 날립니다.

PAN-FRIED COD

1. Clean the cod and let it dry for about a day.
- If cleaning the cod is not feasible, use pre-cleaned cod instead. If using frozen cod, thaw it in the refrigerator, sprinkle with salt, then rinse. Let air-dry gently before use to achieve a springy texture.
2. Cut the dried cod into moderately thick fillets, leaving the skin on. Let them air-dry for a while to release any remaining moisture.

3. 볼에 양념 재료를 모두 넣고 골고루 섞어줍니다.
4. 손질한 대구에 양념을 골고루 묻힙니다.
- 대구 살 600g 기준 40g의 양념을 사용합니다.
5. 식용유를 두른 팬에서 중불로 익히다가, 색이 나면 뒤집고 약불로 줄여 완전히 익혀줍니다.

3. In a mixing bowl, combine all the cod seasoning ingredients and mix well.
4. Add the dried cod fillets and toss until evenly coated.
- Use 40 g of seasoning for every 600 g of cod fillet.
5. Pan-fry the cod fillets in cooking oil over medium heat. Once golden brown, reduce the heat to low and cook through.

홍합 톳밥

1. 홍합 살은 소금물에 씻어 준비합니다.
2. 참기름을 두른 팬에 홍합 살을 넣고 익힙니다. 익힌 홍합 살은 익힐 때 나온 국물과 함께 통에 담아둡니다.

MUSSEL AND BROWN SEAWEED RICE

1. Wash the mussel meat in salted water.
2. Pan-fry the mussel meat in sesame oil. Reserve the mussel meat and the pan liquid together in a bowl.

3. 솥에 쌀, 물, **2**에서 나온 홍합 국물을 넣고 밥을 짓습니다.
- 홍합을 익힐 때 나온 국물을 물과 함께 사용하면 홍합의 풍미와 감칠맛이 더 깊어집니다.
4. 뜸을 들이는 시점에 익힌 홍합 살, 생톳, 참기름 1큰술을 넣고 뚜껑을 덮어 뜸을 들입니다.
- 생톳은 깨끗이 씻어 물기를 제거한 후 잘게 썰어 사용합니다.

3. In a cast iron pot, combine the rice, water, and reserved pan liquid from (**2**), then set over heat.
- The pan liquid enhances the mussel's flavor and deepens the *gamchilmat*.
4. When it is time to let it rest, add the mussel meat, fresh brown seaweed, and 1 tablespoon of sesame oil. Cover with a lid, and allow it to finish cooking in residual heat.
- Wash the brown seaweed thoroughly, drain, and finely chop before use.

양념장

1. 소금을 제외한 양념장 재료를 모두 섞어줍니다. 소금은 가장 마지막에 조금씩 넣어가며 간을 맞춰 완성합니다.
2. 완성된 양념장은 홍합 톳밥과 곁들여 먹습니다.

SAUCE

1. Mix all the sauce ingredients, except salt. Add salt as needed at the end to adjust the seasoning.
2. Serve the sauce alongside the mussel and brown seaweed rice.

BANG KISOO

방기수

강원도 양구에서 태어난 방기수 셰프는 자연과 함께한 유년기를 통해 재료 본연의 맛에 대한 감각을 키웠다. 대학을 졸업한 뒤, 국내 최초 미쉐린 3스타 한식당 '가온'에 입사하며 본격적으로 요리사의 길을 걷기 시작했다. 전통 한식의 정수와 깊이를 익힌 그는, 2008년 베이징올림픽 기간 동안 수석 셰프로 활약하고, 브라질 상파울루에서의 한식 교류를 통해 세계 무대에서의 경험도 쌓았다.

2012년에는 '비채나'의 오픈 멤버로 참여해 총괄 셰프로서 미쉐린 1스타를 획득하는 데 큰 기여를 했으며, 2017년에는 시그니엘 호텔의 한식당 입점을 총괄하며 고급 한식의 방향성을 제시했다.

2018년에는 자신의 요리 철학을 담은 한식당 '깃든'을 열고, 한식의 전통을 존중하면서도 현대적인 감각을 더한 요리를 선보이고 있다. 그는 재료가 가진 이야기와 계절의 흐름을 한 접시에 고스란히 담아내며, 깃든에서의 한 끼가 단순한 식사가 아닌 마음에 오래 남는 따뜻한 기억으로 남길 바라고 있다.

Chef Bang Gi-su was born in Yanggu County, Gangwon Province, where a childhood immersed in nature nurtured his appreciation for the natural flavors of ingredients. After graduating, he began his culinary career at Gaon, Korea's first three-Michelin-starred restaurant, where he learned the excellence and depth of the traditional Korean cuisine. He broadened his global perspective by serving as head chef during the 2008 Beijing Olympics and participating in Korean culinary exchange in Sao Paulo, Brazil.

In 2012, he became part of the opening team at Bicena, where he contributed significantly to the restaurant's Michelin star achievement as executive chef. In 2017, he led to the launch of a Korean restaurant at the Signiel Hotel, presenting a new vision for high-end Korean cuisine.

The following year, he opened 'Gitdeun,' a Korean restaurant that embodies his culinary philosophy, showcasing a modern take on Korean cuisine with respect for tradition. He captures the story of each ingredient and the passage of the seasons on the plate, hoping that a meal at Gitdeun will linger not just as a meal, but as a heartfelt memory.

깃든
@ gitdeun_bang

Soybean Purée Naengchae

이야기
STORY

(Chilled Vegetables in Soybean Purée)

콩즙 냉채

한국에서 한식을 요리해 온 시간을 돌아보면, 한식은 마치 어머니의 품과 같다는 생각이 듭니다. 늘 곁에 있어 익숙하고 당연하게 느껴지지만, 그만큼 소중함을 자주 잊기 때문입니다. 그래서 저는 '콩'이 어머니를 닮았다고 생각합니다. 장의 기본이 되는 재료이면서도, 정작 주인공이 되는 경우는 드물기 때문이죠. 콩국수, 콩탕, 두부처럼 담백한 요리 속에 조용히 자리를 지키지만, 그 가치에 비해 조명을 덜 받는 듯합니다. 늘 묵묵히 가족을 위해 희생하는 어머니의 모습과 많이 닮아 있죠.

여기에서 소개하는 콩즙 냉채는 백태콩을 삶아 진하게 우린 콩물에 뿌리 채소인 우엉을 함께 삶고 이를 곱게 갈아 차갑게 식혀 콩즙 냉채를 만들었습니다. 여기에 영덕 대게 살과 제주 한라봉, 포항초 나물을 감싼 두부피를 올려 완성했습니다.

담백하고 부드러운 콩이 여러 재료를 감싸 안으며 조화롭게 어우러지는 이 한 접시는, 시원한 요리이지만 어머니의 품과 같은 따뜻함을 느낄 수 있습니다.

Looking back on the time I have spent cooking Korean cuisine in Korea, I have come to see that Korean cuisine is like a mother's embrace. Always by our side, it feels so familiar that we often take it for granted and forget how precious it truly is. That is why soybeans remind me of mothers. Soybeans are the foundation of *jangs* (Korean fermented pastes), yet they rarely take the center stage. Quietly present in humble, clean dishes like *kong-guksu*, *kong-tang*, and bean curd, they are often overlooked despite their true value. There is something maternal about them, like a mother who quietly sacrifices herself for her family.

This Soybean Purée *Naengchae* features a delicate soybean purée crafted by blending burdock root into a rich soybean milk broth, extracted from yellow soybeans. It accompanies tofu skin rolls filled with Yeongdeok snow crab, Jeju hallabong, and Pohang spinach.

With the clean, smooth bean purée gently enfolding each ingredient in harmony, it offers comfort as tender and heartwarming as a mother's embrace, despite being a cold dish.

Ingredients

4인 분량
Serves 4

콩즙

백태콩	100g
물 (콩 불리는 용도)	300ml
물 (콩 삶는 용도)	400ml
우엉	70g
땅콩	10g
잣	20g
두유	30ml
생크림	10ml
소금	3g
설탕	7g

냉채

대게	1마리 (1~1.5kg)
손질한 섬초 (포항초)	200g
다진 대파	10g
다진 마늘	5g
소금	5g
한라봉 (250~280g)	1개
두부피 (유바) (20×15 사이즈)	4개

장식

완두콩 순	10g

SOYBEAN PURÉE

100 g	yellow soybeans
300 ml	water (for soaking soybeans)
400 ml	water (for cooking soybeans)
70 g	burdock
10 g	peanuts
20 g	pine nuts
30 ml	soymilk
10 ml	fresh cream
3 g	salt
7 g	sugar

NAENGCHAE (Chilled salad)

1	snow crab (1 to 1.5 kg)
200 g	trimmed winter spinach (Pohang spinach)
10 g	chopped green onion
5 g	minced garlic
5 g	salt
1	hallabong (250 to 280 g)
4 sheets	tofu skin (yuba) (20×15 cm each)

GARNISH

10 g	pea shoots

How to make

  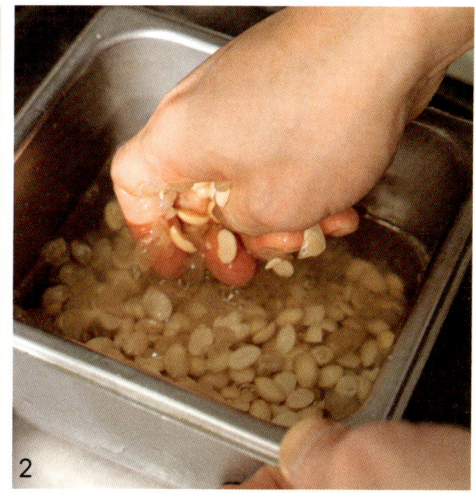

콩즙

1. 냄비에 불린 콩(240g)과 물 400ml를 넣고 가열하다가, 끓기 시작하면 중불에서 약 2분간 익힌 후 얼음물이 담긴 통에 받쳐 식혀줍니다.
- 백태콩 100g을 세척한 후 300ml의 물에 12시간 동안 불려 건지면 약 240g이 됩니다. 콩을 불리는 시간은 계절에 따라 다른데 여름에는 8시간, 봄과 가을에는 10시간, 겨울에는 12시간 불려줍니다.
2. 콩 삶은 물과 삶은 콩을 분리합니다. 삶은 콩은 찬물로 헹군 후 껍질을 제거하고, 콩 삶은 물은 버리지 않고 남겨둡니다.
- 찬물에 여러 번 헹궈가며 껍질을 제거하면 콩의 맛 성분이 빠져나가므로 떠오르는 껍질을 체로 걸러가며 작업하는 것이 좋습니다.

SOYBEAN PURÉE

1. In a pot, combine 240 g of the soaked yellow soybeans with 400 ml of water, and bring to a boil. Once boiling, cook for about 2 minutes over medium heat. Transfer the beans and their cooking liquid into a container, then cool in an ice bath.
- 100 g of yellow soybeans, rinsed, soaked in 300 ml of water for 12 hours, and drained, yields about 240 g. Soaking time may vary depending on the season: 8 hours in summer, 10 hours in spring and autumn, and 12 hours in winter.
2. Separate the yellow soybeans from the cooking liquid. Rinse the yellow soybeans in cold water and remove their skins. Reserve the cooking liquid for later use.
- To prevent loss of flavor from repeated rinsing in cold water, it is recommended to skim off the floating skins using a sieve.

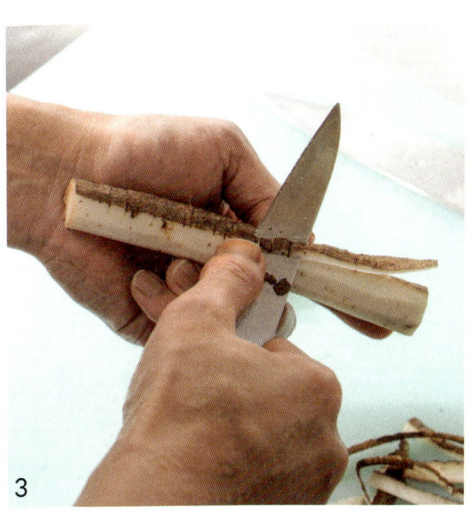  

3. 우엉은 껍질을 벗긴 후 1cm 크기로 잘라줍니다.
- 우엉 70g의 껍질을 벗기면 약 50g이 됩니다.
4. 냄비에 우엉 껍질과 물 500ml를 넣고 차를 우리듯 끓여줍니다.

3. Peel the burdock and slice into 1 cm-thick rounds.
- 70 g of burdock yields about 50 g after peeling.
4. In a pot, combine the burdock skins with 500 ml of water and simmer gently, as if brewing tea.

5. 팬에 우엉을 넣고 타지 않도록 **4**를 적당량 넣어가며 조려줍니다.
- 두꺼운 스테인리스 팬을 사용하면 타지 않고 조리듯 익히기 쉽습니다.
6. 착즙기에 **2**의 껍질 벗긴 백태콩(220g), 땅콩, 잣을 넣고 콩 삶은 물 (220ml)을 추가하며 콩물을 만들어줍니다.
- 이렇게 하면 콩물 350g이 만들어집니다. (이 양은 콩국수 1인 분량이므로 면을 삶아 콩국수로 만들어 드셔도 좋습니다.)
- 착즙기에서 총 3회 걸러주며 진하게 콩물을 만듭니다.
7. 믹서에 **6**과 **5**를 넣고 최대한 곱게 갈아줍니다.

5. In a pan, gently reduce the burdock, gradually adding (**4**) to prevent burning.
- Using a heavy-bottomed stainless steel pan allows gentle reduction without scorching.
6. In a juicer, place 220 g of peeled yellow soybeans from (**2**), along with peanuts and pine nuts. Gradually add 220 g of the reserved soybean cooking liquid to extract the soybean milk broth.
- This yields 350 g of soybean milk broth (enough for one serving of *kong-guksu* when served with noodles).
- Run through the juicer a total of three times to achieve a richer soybean milk broth.
7. In a blender, combine (**6**) and (**5**), then blend until as smooth as possible.

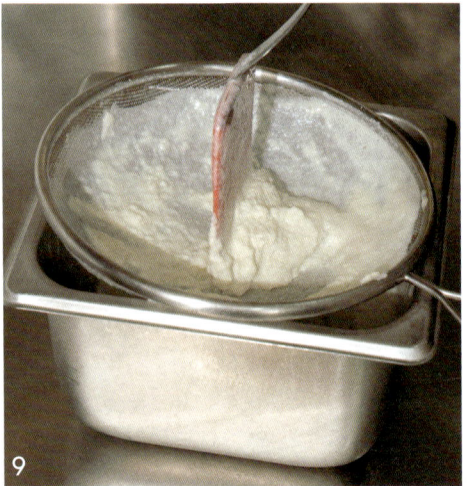

8. 팬으로 옮겨 약불에서 잘 저어가며 끓여줍니다.
9. 고운 체에 두 번 걸러줍니다.
10. 두유와 생크림을 넣고 소금, 설탕으로 간을 맞춘 후 차갑게 식혀 콩즙을 완성합니다.
- 뜨거울 때 체에 거르고 간을 해야 맛의 균형이 잘 잡힙니다.

8. Transfer the mixture to a pan and simmer over low heat, stirring continuously.
9. Strain the mixture twice through a fine-mesh sieve.
10. Add the soymilk and fresh cream, then season with salt and sugar. Let the mixture cool to complete the soybean purée.
- To ensure a balanced flavor, strain and season the mixture while still hot.

대게찜

1. 물이 끓는 찜통에 대게를 넣고 약 12분간 찝니다.
- 대게는 흐르는 물에 깨끗이 씻고 입 부분을 뾰족한 송곳이나 가위로 찔러 입안의 짠물을 제거해 사용합니다.
- 대게 1.5kg 기준으로 오차 100g 내외일 경우 12분간 찌면 적당합니다. 만약 이보다 큰 사이즈라면, 12분간 찐 후 다리를 분리하고 몸통 부분만 추가로 1분 ~ 1분 30초 찌면 다리의 오버 쿡을 막을 수 있습니다.
2. 쪄낸 대게는 다리 부분만 자른 후 얼음물에 30초간 담가 살을 발라냅니다.
- 익힌 대게 다리를 얼음물에 담가 손질하면 붉은색이 선명해져 상품성을 높일 수 있습니다.
3. 손질한 대게 살이 싱겁거나 감칠맛이 약한 경우, 냄비에 몸통 부분의 내장과 대게 껍질을 넣고 약불에서 졸이듯 끓여 소금으로 간을 한 후 대게 살에 발라주거나 버무리면 간도 맞출 수 있고 감칠맛도 더할 수 있습니다.

STEAMED SNOW CRAB

1. Steam the snow crab in a boiling steamer for about 12 minutes.
- Rinse the crab thoroughly under running water, then pierce its mouth with a sharp tool or scissors to drain any salt water before use.
- For a 1.5 kg snow crab (±100 g), 12 minutes is appropriate. For larger snow crabs, steam the whole crab for 12 minutes. Then, detach the legs and continue steaming only the body for 1 to 1.5 more minutes to prevent overcooking the legs.
2. Detach only the legs from the steamed snow crab. Soak them in ice water for 30 seconds, then extract the crab meat.
- Soaking the steamed snow crab legs in ice water during preparation helps enhance their bright red color, making them more commercially valuable.
3. If the snow crab meat tastes bland or lacks *gamchilmat*, combine the innards from snow crab body and the shell in a pot, then gently simmer over low heating. Season the mixture with salt, then coat or toss the crab meat with it to adjust the seasoning and enhance *gamchilmat*.

섬초 나물

1. 섬초는 밑동을 제거한 후 깨끗이 씻어줍니다.
2. 손질한 섬초를 끓는 물에 살짝 데친 후 찬물에 헹궈줍니다.
- 손질한 섬초 200g을 데치면 약 160g이 됩니다.
3. 데친 섬초는 물기를 꼭 짜 다진 대파, 다진 마늘, 소금으로 간을 맞춰 완성합니다.

WINTER SPINACH

1. Remove the stem bases from the winter spinach and wash thoroughly.
2. Gently blanch the trimmed spinach in boiling water, then rinse in ice water.
- 200 g of trimmed spinach yields about 160 g after blanching.
3. Squeeze out the excess water from the blanched spinach, then season with salt, chopped green onion, and minced garlic.

한라봉

1. 한라봉은 칼로 돌려가며 껍질을 벗겨 냅니다.
2. 속 껍질 사이사이 알맹이 부분만 칼로 잘라 준비합니다.

HALLABONG

1. While rotating the hallabong, remove the peel and white pith with a knife.
2. Cut between the membranes to separate the segments, extracting only the flesh.

 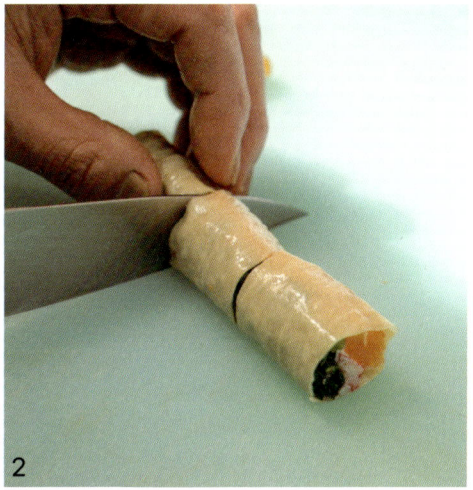 

마무리

1. 두부피를 넓게 펼친 후 대게 살, 한라봉, 섬초 나물을 올리고 빈 공간이 생기지 않도록 타이트하게 말아줍니다.

- 두부피는 끓인 두유(또는 두부)의 표면에 생기는 얇은 막을 걷어 만든 식재료로, 고소하고 부드러운 식감이 특징입니다.
- 두부피 1장 기준 대게 살 30g, 한라봉 30g, 섬초 나물 5g이 적당합니다.

2. 말아 놓은 냉채를 한입 크기로 잘라 접시에 담습니다.
3. 콩즙(1인 기준 80~100g)을 접시 가장자리로 담아 완성합니다.

- 완두콩 순을 곁들여도 좋습니다.

FINISH

1. Lay out the tofu skin, place the crab meat, hallabong, and winter spinach on top. Roll it up tightly, making sure there are no gaps inside.

- Tofu skin is a thin layer that forms on the surface of heated soymilk (or tofu), known for its nutty flavor and tender texture.
- One sheet of tofu skin is best filled with 30 g of crab meat, 30 g of hallabong, and 5 g of winter spinach.

2. Cut the roll into bite-sized pieces and arrange them on a plate.
3. Pour the soybean purée (80 to 100 g per serving) at the edge of the plate.

- Garnish with pea shoots, as desired.

콩즙 냉채 활용 팁

❶ 콩물 활용법

- 콩즙을 만드는 과정에서 콩물을 내리면, 콩국수 한 그릇 분량의 콩물이 만들어집니다. (6번 과정)
- 따라서, 콩즙 레시피에 콩물은 콩국수 1인분 레시피로도 활용할 수 있습니다.

❷ 제철 과일과의 조합

이 레시피에서는 한라봉을 사용했지만 꼭 한라봉이 아니더라도 제철의 과일로 대체해도 좋습니다. 계절별 추천 과일은 다음과 같습니다.

- 봄: 대저 토마토(짭짤이 토마토)
- 여름: 복숭아(잘 익은 백도)
- 가을: 무화과(잘 익고 부드러운 것)
- 겨울: 딸기

이 중에서도 가장 잘 어울리는 조합은 가을의 무화과를 추천 드립니다.

Tips for using the soybean purée *naengchae*

❶ How to use the soybean milk broth

- The process of preparing the soybean purée (Step 6) yields enough soybean milk broth for one serving of *kong-guksu*.
- This soybean milk broth can also be used as the base for one serving of *kong-guksu*.

❷ Pairing with seasonal fruits

This recipe uses hallabong, but it can be substituted with other seasonal fruits. Recommended fruits by season include:

- Spring: Daejeo Tomatoes (Korean salty tomatoes)
- Summer: Peaches (ripe white peach)
- Autumn: Figs (ripe and soft)
- Winter: Strawberries

Among these, figs in autumn are the most highly recommended pairing.

Hanwoo Galbijjim and Abalone

(Braised Korean Beef Short Ribs and Abalone)

활전복 한우 갈비찜

가정식
HOME COOKING

레시피대로 요리했지만 기대와 다른 결과에 실망한 경험, 누구나 한 번쯤은 있을 겁니다. 요리는 단순한 공식이 아니라, 불 조절이나 재료 손질 같은 미묘한 차이가 큰 차이를 만드는 섬세한 작업입니다. 같은 재료를 써도 요리 실력에 따라 맛이 달라지는 이유죠. 볶거나 굽고 튀기는 방식은 순간의 감각이 중요하지만, 찌는 조리법은 정해진 과정을 따르기만 해도 일정한 맛을 낼 수 있어 초보자에게도 적합합니다. 수비드 조리처럼 일정한 온도로 천천히 익히는 방식은 재료의 풍미를 살리는 데 효과적이고, 압력솥 조리는 짧은 시간에 깊은 맛을 끌어내는 데 좋습니다. (이 요리가 바로 그러합니다.)

이 책에서 소개하는 활전복 한우 갈비찜은 양파, 대파, 마늘을 직화로 굽고 간장과 함께 끓인 후 한우 갈비와 전복을 넣어 압력솥에 조리합니다. 재료를 손질하는 과정은 조금 번거로울 수 있지만 그만큼 정성이 담긴 좋은 요리로 완성된다는 점이 제가 걸어온 요리사의 길과 닮아 있습니다.

Everyone has likely felt frustrated when a dish didn't turn out as expected, even after carefully following a recipe. Cooking isn't simply a formula, but a delicate craft where subtle details, like heat control or ingredient preparation, can make a big difference. That is why the final flavor can vary depending on a cook's skill, even with the same ingredients. Some methods, like stir-frying, roasting, or deep-frying, require a cook's sensibility in the moment. Steaming, however, is more approachable, even for beginners, as it yields consistent results when the steps are followed. Slow-cooking at a constant temperature, like in sous-vide cooking, is effective in bringing out the inherent flavors of ingredients. Pressure cooking, on the other hand, is ideal for drawing out deep, concentrated flavor in a shorter time—and this dish is a perfect example.

The *Hanwoo Galbijjim* and Abalone in this book begins with a sauce made by simmering charcoal-grilled onion, green onion and garlic in ganjang. The beef short ribs and abalone are then added to the sauce and cooked together in a pressure cooker. While the preparation process can be somewhat demanding, it yields a heartfelt, satisfying dish—much like my own journey as a chef.

Ingredients

4인 분량
Serves 4

찜용 맛간장*

양파	150g
대파 (흰 줄기)	150g
통마늘	40g
양조간장 (샘표501)	500ml
맛술 (오뚜기 미향)	300ml
쌀 조청	500g
물	1.5L
황설탕	30g
건고추 (사천고추)	5g
통생강	10g
배	1/2개
통후추	10알

활전복 한우 갈비찜

활전복	10미 4마리
표고버섯	10g (약 2개)
인삼	30g
한우 갈비 (찜용)	1.5~2kg
찜용 맛간장*	1L
물	900ml
깐 은행	10개
깐 밤	4개
건대추	10g

SEASONED GANJANG (for braising)*

150 g	onion
150 g	green onion (white part)
40 g	garlic cloves
500 ml	yangjo-ganjang (naturally brewed soy sauce, Sempio 501)
300 ml	matsul (Korean cooking wine, Ottogi Mihyang)
500 g	ssal-jocheong (Korean rice syrup)
1.5 L	water
30 g	brown sugar
5 g	dried chili peppers (Sichuan chili peppers)
10 g	whole ginger
1/2	pear
10	black peppercorns

HANWOO GALBIJJIM AND ABALONE

4	live abalones (about 100 g each)
10 g	shiitake mushrooms (about 2 pieces)
30 g	ginseng
1.5-2 kg	Korean beef short ribs (for braising)
1 L	seasoned ganjang (for braising)*
900 ml	water
10	peeled ginkgo nuts
4	peeled chestnuts
10 g	dried jujubes

How to make

찜용 맛간장

1. 3등분으로 자른 양파, 대파, 통마늘을 석쇠에 올려 직화로 구워줍니다.
- 구운 풍미를 높이기 위해 약간 태우듯 구워줍니다.
- 직화 구이가 어렵다면 200℃의 에어프라이어에서 약 10분간 구운 후 토치나 가스불로 겉면을 태워 사용합니다.
2. 냄비에 모든 재료를 넣고 잘 섞이도록 저은 후 가열합니다.

SEASONED GANJANG (for braising)

1. Cut the onion into thirds, then grill it along with the green onion and garlic cloves over an open flame on a wire rack.
- For a deeper grilled flavor, gently char the vegetables.
- If grilling is not feasible, cook them in an air fryer at 392°F (200°C) for about 10 minutes, then gently char the skins using a blowtorch or gas flame.
2. Place all the ingredients in a pot, stir well to combine, then bring to a boil.

3. 끓기 시작하면 약불로 줄여 약 20분간 가열하고, 실온에 6시간 정도 둔 후 냉장고에서 차갑게 식혀줍니다.
4. 체에 걸러 찜용 맛간장을 완성합니다.

3. Once boiling, reduce the heat to low and simmer for about 20 minutes. Let it sit at room temperature for about 6 hours, then chill in the refrigerator.
4. Strain the liquid to complete the seasoned ganjang.

활전복 한우 갈비찜

1. 전복은 전복 전용 솔을 사용해 흐르는 물에서 깨끗이 닦아줍니다.
2. 표고버섯은 밑동을 제거한 후 윗면에 모양을 내줍니다.
- 모양을 내기 어려운 경우 후 한입 크기로 4등분합니다.
3. 인삼은 흙이 제거될 수 있도록 솔로 깨끗이 씻은 후 껍질을 벗겨 준비합니다.

HANWOO GALBIJJIM AND ABALONE

1. Thoroughly scrub the abalone under running water using an abalone brush.
2. Remove the stems of the shiitake mushrooms, then score the caps for decoration.
- If scoring is not feasible, cut them into bite-sized quarters.
3. Scrub the ginseng with a brush to remove any dirt, then peel the skin.

4. 흐르는 물에 갈비를 씻고 찬물에 1시간 이상 담가 핏물을 제거합니다.
5. 압력솥에 핏물을 제거한 갈비와 찜용 맛간장 1L, 물 700ml를 넣고 가열합니다.
6. 압력솥이 끓으면 약불로 줄여 15분간 가열한 후, 불을 끄고 15분간 김을 빼지 않고 유지합니다. 그 후 김을 빼줍니다.

4. Rinse the short ribs under running water, then soak them in cold water for at least an hour to remove the blood.
5. In a pressure cooker, combine the short ribs with 1 L of seasoned ganjang and 700 ml of water, then bring to a boil.
6. Once boiling, reduce the heat to low and simmer for 15 minutes. Turn off the heat and let it sit for 15 minutes with the pressure sealed, then release the pressure.

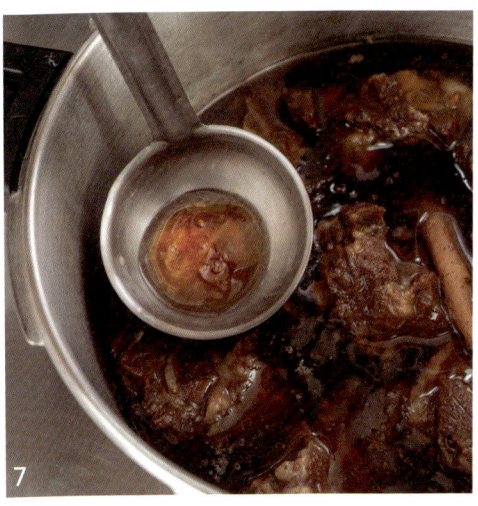

7. 뚜껑을 열고 떠오른 기름을 제거한 후 물 200ml, 전복, 표고버섯, 깐 은행, 깐 밤, 인삼, 건대추를 넣고 뚜껑을 덮어 강불로 가열합니다.
8. 끓기 시작하면 30초간 유지한 후, 불을 끄고 5분간 김을 빼지 않고 유지합니다. 그 다음 압력솥의 김을 빼줍니다.

7. Open the lid and skim off any fat from the surface. Add 200 ml of water along with the abalone, shiitake mushrooms, peeled ginkgo nuts, peeled chestnuts, ginseng, and dried jujubes. Close and seal the lid, then bring to a boil over high heat.
8. Once it comes to a boil, continue boiling for 30 seconds. Turn off the heat and let it sit for 5 minutes with the pressure sealed, then release the pressure.

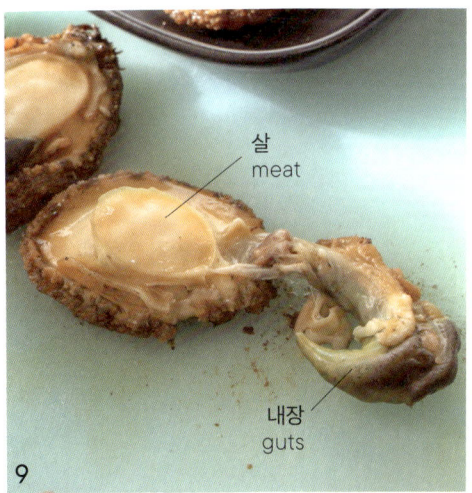

살 meat
내장 guts

9. 숟가락을 사용해 전복 살과 껍질을 분리한 후 내장을 제거합니다.
10. 한 입 크기로 잘라줍니다.
11. 접시 중앙에 갈비와 전복을 담아 중심을 잡고 나머지 재료를 조화롭게 담은 후, 접시의 1/3까지 국물을 채워 완성합니다.
    - 갈비는 1인 기준 3조각(약 450g)이 적당합니다.

9. Using a spoon, separate the abalone meat from the shells and remove the innards.
10. Cut the abalone meat into bite-sized pieces.
11. Place the short ribs and abalone in the center of a plate, and arrange the remaining ingredients around them. Ladle the braising liquid over the dish until it fills one-third of the plate.
    - Three pieces (approximately 450 g) of short ribs are ideal for one serving.

활전복 한우 갈비찜 활용 팁

1. 남은 국물 활용법

활전복 한우 갈비찜을 만들고 남은 국물은 다양한 조림 요리에 활용할 수 있습니다.

❶ 추천 조림 메뉴
- 백태 은행 조림
- 뿌리채소 조림 (특히 우엉이 잘 어울립니다)
- 메추리알 조림

❷ 조림 요리 방법
- 사용하는 재료와 재료가 잠길 정도의 갈비찜 국물을 넣습니다.
- 약불에서 국물이 완전히 졸아들 때까지 끓입니다.
- 마지막에 기호에 따라 소량의 설탕을 추가하면 맛이 더 좋아집니다.

예시

2. 찜용 맛간장 활용법

❶ 소불고기 양념

재료

찜용 맛간장 400ml, 배 1/4개 (약 100g), 양파 100g

만드는 방법
- 믹서에 모든 재료를 넣고 갈아줍니다.
- 슬라이스한 소고기 600g(한 근)에 양념을 붓고 재운 후 조리합니다.
- 양파나 버섯류를 추가하면 더 풍성한 맛을 즐길 수 있습니다.

❷ 숯불구이용 고기 양념

재료

찜용 맛간장 400ml, 배 1/4개 (약 100g), 양파 100g, 대파 50g

만드는 방법
- 믹서에 모든 재료를 넣고 갈아줍니다.
- 구이용 갈비나 채끝살 또는 등심(두께 1cm 이상) 500g에 양념을 붓고 2시간 이상 재웁니다.
- 숯불에 구우면 풍미가 더 뛰어납니다.

Pro tips for using *Hanwoo Galbijjim* and Abalone

1. How to use the remaining braising liquid

The liquid left after braising Korean beef short ribs and abalone can be used in a variety of dishes.

❶ Recommended dishes
- Braised Yellow Soybeans and Ginkgo Nuts
- Braised Root Vegetables (Burdocks pair especially well)
- Braised Quail Eggs

❷ How to make the dishes
- Place the ingredients in a pot and add enough braising liquid to cover.
- Simmer over low heat until the liquid is fully reduced.
- For a better flavor, add a pinch of sugar at the end, if desired.

Example - Photos on the left.

2. How to use the seasoned ganjang

❶ Beef *bulgogi* marinade

Ingredients

400 ml	seasoned ganjang
1/4	pear (about 100 g)
100 g	onion

How to make
- Blend all the ingredients until smooth.
- Pour the marinade over 600 g of the sliced beef, let it marinate, then cook.
- For a richer flavor, add onions and mushrooms.

❷ Marinade for charcoal-grilled meat

Ingredients

400 ml	seasoned ganjang
1/4	pear (about 100 g)
100 g	onion
50 g	green onion

How to make
- Blend all the ingredients until smooth.
- Pour the marinade over 500 g of grilling cuts such as short rib, sirloin, or striploin (cut thicker than 1 cm), and let marinate for at least 2 hours.
- For a deeper flavor, grill the meat over charcoal.

OK DONGSIK

옥동식

屋同食

전통 한식의 단순함 속 깊은 맛에 매료되어 2017년 서울 서교동에 돼지곰탕 전문점 '옥동식'을 열었다. 고기로만 우려낸 맑고 깊은 국물이 특징인 옥동식의 국밥은 기존 국밥의 틀을 벗어난 정제된 한 그릇으로, 미식가들의 주목을 받았다. 그의 요리는 과한 양념 없이도 재료 본연의 맛을 살리는 방식으로, 한식의 새로운 가능성을 제시했다.

2022년에는 뉴욕 맨해튼에 진출하여 현지에서도 큰 반향을 일으켰다. 뉴욕타임스의 음식 칼럼니스트 피트 웰스(Pete Wells)는 "국물을 매일 먹어도 질리지 않을 것"이라며 극찬했으며, 미식 전문 매체 '이터(Eater)'는 옥동식을 '뉴욕에서 가장 핫한 팝업 레스토랑'으로 소개했다. 이후 뉴욕 지점은 정식 매장으로 자리 잡으며, 국밥이라는 한식 소울푸드의 세계화 가능성을 증명했다.

옥동식 셰프는 전통을 기반으로 새로움을 찾는 '온고지신(溫故知新)'의 철학 아래, 최소한의 조리법으로 재료 본연의 맛을 이끌어내는 요리를 지향한다. 한 그릇의 국밥 속에는 단순한 음식 이상의 정성과 균형이 담겨 있으며, 그는 이를 통해 한식의 진정성과 매력을 세계 무대에 전하고자 한다.

Fascinated by the depth in the simplicity of traditional Korean cuisine, Chef Ok Dong-sik opened his eponymous restaurant in Seogyo-dong, Seoul, in 2017, specializing in *dweji-gomtang* (pork and rice soup). His signature dish—a refined, unconventional take on *gukbap*—features a clear yet deeply flavorful broth made by simmering only meat, earning notable attention from epicures. By bringing out the pure, original taste of ingredients without any heavy seasoning, his dish has opened up new possibilities for Korean cuisine.

In 2022, Okdongsik expanded to Manhattan, New York, making waves in the local dining scene. *The New York Times* food columnist Pete Wells praised its broth as "something you could eat every day and not get tired of," while the culinary media outlet *Eater* also spotlighted Okdongsik as "the hottest pop-up restaurant in New York City." What began as a pop-up has since become a permanent establishment, demonstrating the global potential of *gukbap*, one of South Korea's most beloved soul foods.

Under the philosophy of *Ongojisin**—seeking the new through tradition—Chef Ok pursues a style of cooking that brings out the inherent flavors of ingredients through minimal techniques. Each bowl of Okdongsik's *gukbap* reflects his sincerity and a sense of balance that go beyond a simple meal. Through this thoughtful approach, he strives to share the authenticity and appeal of Korean cuisine with the world.

* *Ongojisin* (溫故知新): A four-character idiom meaning "to review the past and learn the new."

옥동식
okdongsik

Gueom Dakgomtang

(Gueom Chicken Soup)

구엄닭곰탕

이야기
STORY

이 메뉴는 우리에게 익숙한 닭곰탕이지만, 케이지에서 사육된 닭이 아닌, 자연에서 건강하게 자란 닭으로 만듭니다. 제주 구엄리에서는 '구엄닭'이라 불리는 재래닭을 자연 방사 방식으로 키우는데, 제주에서는 이 닭을 '날닭'이라 부르기도 합니다. 실제로 100미터 이상 날 수 있을 만큼 원래는 야생성이 강한 종이었고, 국립축산원에서 사육을 시작해 지금은 '구엄닭'이라는 이름으로 온라인에서도 쉽게 구할 수 있습니다. 육질이 단단하고 깊은 풍미를 지닌 이 닭은 특히 곰탕이나 백숙처럼 푹 끓이는 요리에 잘 어울립니다. 옥동식에서 여름 한정으로 판매했던 이 구엄닭곰탕은 진하고 구수한 맛이 일품이며, 보양이 필요한 계절이나 특별한 날 집에서 끓여 드시기에 더없이 좋은 메뉴입니다.

While *dakgomtang* (chicken soup) is a well-known dish in Korea, this version is made with free-range chicken raised in natural surroundings—not in battery cages. In Gueom, a village on Jeju Island, a native chicken called "Gueom chicken," locally known as "*naldak*" (meaning "flying chicken") is raised on pasture. This breed stands out for its strong wild instincts, capable of flying over 100 meters. As the National Institute of Animal Science began raising the breed, it has become available online under the name "Gueom chicken." With its firm flesh and deep flavor, this chicken is ideal for long-simmered dishes like *dakgomtang* and *baeksuk* (whole chicken soup). Once offered as a seasonal dish at Okdongsik, it boasts a rich, savory flavor that is perfect for celebrating special occasions or for boosting energy during the summer season.

Ingredients

4인 분량

Serves 4

구엄닭곰탕

구엄닭	1마리 (1마리 1.6kg기준)
물	2L
소금	16g
두백감자	4개
무우	1/4개
대파	1줄기
양파	1/2개
우엉	50g
생강	20g
마늘	50g
통후추	10g
삼계탕 육수용 재료 (시판용)	1 티백

구엄닭 양념

들기름	2큰술
국간장	2큰술
후춧가루	1작은술

장식

쪽파	적당량

GUEOM DAKGOMTANG
(Gueom chicken soup)

1	Gueom chicken (1.6 kg)
2 L	water
16 g	salt
4	Dubaek potatoes
1/4	Korean radish
1	green onion stalk
1/2	onion
50 g	burdock
20 g	ginger
50 g	garlic
10 g	black peppercorns
1	chicken stock teabag (store-bought)

GUEOM chicken seasoning

2 tbsp	perilla oil
2 tbsp	guk-ganjang (Korean soup soy sauce)
1 tsp	ground black pepper

GARNISH

Q.S	Korean scallion

How to make

  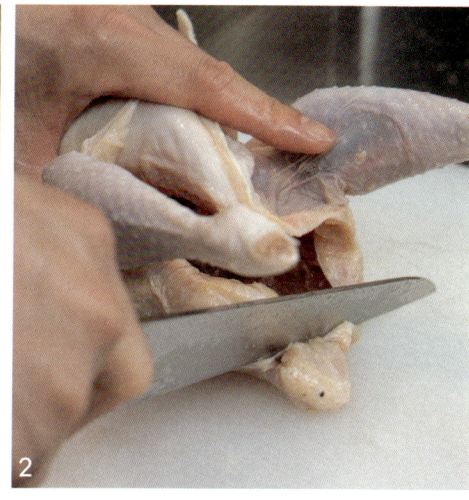

1. 모든 채소는 깨끗이 씻어 적당한 크기로 자릅니다.
- 촬영한 3월에는 두백감자가 없어 사용하지 못했지만, 두백감자가 나오는 철이라면 꼭 사용해보시길 바랍니다. 육수에 두백감자의 맛과 향이 배어 맛이 한층 더 풍부해집니다.
2. 제주구엄닭은 흐르는 물에서 안쪽까지 씻고 꼬리 부분을 잘라 사용합니다. 냉동 제품의 경우 전날 미리 냉장고에 옮겨 천천히 해동한 후 사용합니다.

1. Wash all the vegetables thoroughly and slice them into moderately sized pieces.
- This dish does not include Dubaek potatoes, as it was prepared in March. However, they are highly recommended when in season, as their distinct flavor and aroma enrich the stock.
2. Wash the Gueom chicken thoroughly under running water, including the inner cavity, and remove the tail. If using a frozen chicken, thaw it slowly in the refrigerator one day before use.

3. 압력솥에 모든 재료를 넣고 뚜껑을 닫고 센불로 가열합니다. 압력솥의 추가 울리면(추가 계속 울리는 상태이면) 약불로 줄여 30분간 가열한 후 불을 끕니다.
4. 자연스럽게 압력이 다 빠질 때까지 기다린 후, 압력이 다 빠지면 닭과 두백감자를 꺼내고 육수를 걸러줍니다.
- 거른 육수는 차갑게 식혀 냉동실에 잠시 두고, 떠오른 기름이 굳으면 기름만 걷어내 따로 보관합니다. 구엄닭의 기름은 불포화지방산이 많은 동물성 지방이므로, 감자전 등 전 종류를 부칠 때 사용하면 맛이 아주 좋습니다.

3. Place all the ingredients in a pressure cooker, close and seal the lid, then cook over high heat. When the pressure cooker whistle begins to rattle continuously, lower the heat and cook for 30 minutes, then turn off the heat..
4. Let the pressure is naturally released. Once fully released, remove the chicken and potatoes, then strain the broth.
- Chill the broth in the freezer for a while. When the fat hardens on the surface, skim it off and reserve for later use. Gueom chicken fat is an animal-based fat rich in unsaturated fatty acids—perfect for cooking Korean pancakes like *gamjajeon* (potato pancake).

5. 꺼낸 닭은 한 김 식힌 후 뼈와 살을 분리합니다.
- 발라낸 닭뼈는 닭육수로 재활용할 수 있습니다.
6. 발라낸 살은 적당한 크기로 찢어줍니다.

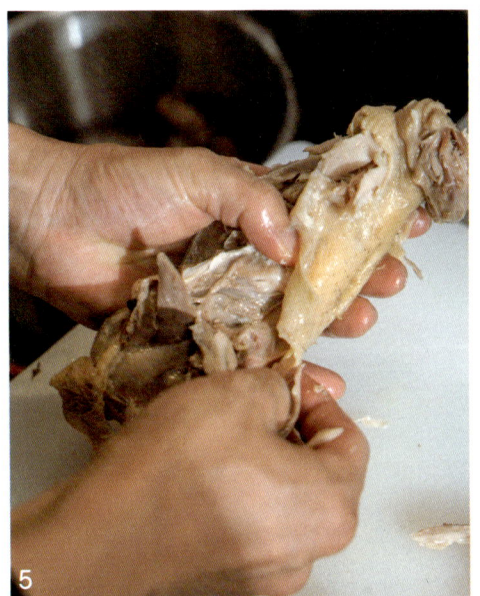 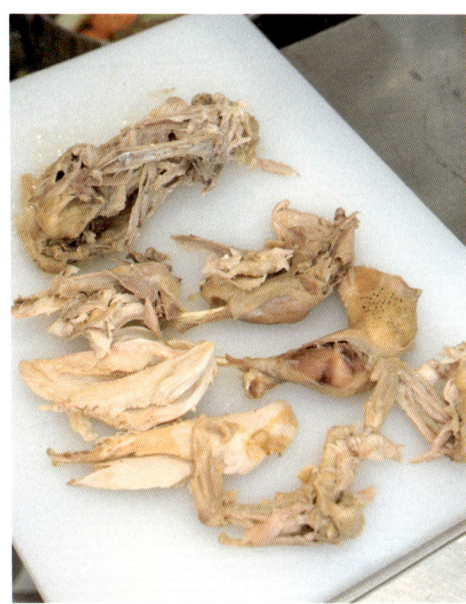 

5. Let the chicken cool slightly, then separate the meat from the bones.
- The bones can be reused to prepare additional chicken broth.
6. Shred the meat into moderately sized pieces.

7. 찢어낸 살은 들기름, 국간장, 후춧가루로 잘 버무려줍니다.

8. 탕기에 양념한 닭고기와 두백감자를 담고 육수를 부어줍니다. 밥을 함께 넣을 경우 탕기에 밥을 먼저 넣고 닭고기와 감자를 올린 후 육수를 부어줍니다. 고명으로 부추를 잘게 다져 내거나 쪽파를 잘라 올려도 좋습니다.

- 곰탕에 넣는 밥은 일반 밥보다 수분을 줄여 고슬고슬하게 짓습니다. 그래야 국물과 함께 먹을 때 더 맛있게 즐길 수 있습니다.

7. Toss the shredded meat with the perilla oil, guk-ganjang, and ground black pepper.

8. Place the seasoned chicken and potatoes into a bowl, then ladle the broth over the dish. When serving with rice, place the rice in the bowl first, followed by the chicken and potatoes, then ladle the broth over the dish. Garnish with chopped garlic chives or Korean scallions, if desired.

- Use slightly less water than usual when cooking the rice to keep it fluffy, which pairs better with the broth.

Yangji-gomtang

(Beef Brisket Soup)

가정식
HOME COOKING

양지곰탕

대학 시절, 지방을 돌며 향토 음식을 맛보던 중 경남 하동 인근 마을에서 '소고기국밥'이라는 메뉴를 접했습니다. 제가 알던 국밥과 달리 맑고 담백한 육수에 얼갈이가 들어간 국밥이었고, 그 특별한 맛이 인상 깊어 '양지곰탕'이라는 이름으로 바꾸어 기억하게 되었습니다. 최근 다시 찾아갔을 때, 아쉽게도 그 식당은 사라졌더군요. 그때의 기억을 되살려 옥동식에서 일주일에 한 번 이 메뉴를 선보이기도 했습니다.

일반적인 소고기국밥이 고춧가루를 푼 얼큰한 국물이라면, 이 양지곰탕은 양지의 진한 감칠맛과 얼갈이의 고소함이 어우러진 시원하고 맑은 국물의 국밥입니다. 얼갈이의 맛이 깊어지는 초가을에 특히 잘 어울립니다.

한식은 고기를 사용하되 채소가 중심이 되는 경우가 많은데, 양지곰탕이 딱 그런 음식이 아닐까요? 여기에 산낙지를 살짝 데쳐 올리면 '양낙탕(양지낙지곰탕)'이 되는데, 해산물을 좋아하는 분들께 특히 추천할 만한 조합입니다. 소고기와 낙지는 전라도 연포탕에서도 볼 수 있는 찰떡궁합이니까요.

During my college years, while traveling across the country and exploring local foods, I came across a dish called *sogogi-gukbap* (beef and rice soup) in a small village near Hadong, in South Gyeongsang Province. Unlike the typical *gukbap*, this version featured eolgari cabbage (young napa cabbage) in a clean, clear broth. The distinctive taste left such an impression that I came to remember it by a different name: *yangji-gomtang*. When I recently revisited the region, I was saddened to find that restaurant had disappeared. Recalling that memory, I offered this dish once a week at Okdongsik.

While traditional *sogogi-gukbap* is known for its spicy broth infused with Korean chili powder, *yangji-gomtang* is defined by a refreshing, clean soup that balances brisket's rich *gamchilmat* with the mellow sweetness of eolgari. It is best enjoyed in early autumn, when eolgari is at its peak.

Korean cuisine often centers around vegetables while still incorporating meat, and *yangji-gomtang* might be one such example. When lightly blanched *san-nakji* (live long-arm octopus) is added, it becomes *yangnak-tang* (beef brisket & long-arm octopus soup). This variation is recommended especially for seafood lovers, as beef and long-arm octopus make a perfect pairing, much like in *yeonpo-tang* (long-arm octopus soup) from Jeolla Province.

Ingredients

4인 분량
Serves 4

양지곰탕

소고기 양지	1kg
물	2L
소금 (정제염)	16g
국간장	2큰술
무	1/4개
대파	1줄기
양파	1/2개
우엉	50g
당근	1/2개
생강	20g
마늘	30g
통후추	5g

얼갈이 무침

얼갈이	2단
(데친 후 무게 200g 기준)	
된장	1큰술
들기름	1큰술
간 마늘	1큰술

YANGJI-GOMTANG (beef brisket soup)

1 kg	yangji (beef brisket)
2 L	water
16 g	refined salt
2 tbsp	guk-ganjang (Korean soup soy sauce)
1/4	Korean radish
1	green onion stalk
1/2	onion
50 g	burdock
1/2	carrot
20 g	ginger
30 g	garlic
5 g	black peppercorns

SEASONED EOLGARI
(Seasoned young napa cabbage)

2	eolgari cabbages (young napa cabbages; 200 g each after blanching)
1 tbsp	doenjang (Korean soybean paste)
1 tbsp	perilla oil
1 tbsp	grated garlic

How to make

1. 양지는 자르지 않고 통으로 준비합니다.
- 핏물은 빼지 않습니다. 양지를 보통 찬물에 담궈 핏물을 뺀다고 하는데 잘못된 상식입니다. 보통 핏물이라고 하는 게 사실은 육즙이라고 할 수 있습니다. 일부 혈관이 보일수도 있는데 그 안에 든 게 피이고, 보통 양지살(근육)에는 피가 들어있지 않습니다. 혈관이 보인다면 흐르는 물에 씻을 때 꾹꾹 눌러 혈관 속 피를 빼주면 됩니다. 찬물에 담그면 맛성분도 빠진다는 사실을 잊지 마세요.
2. 모든 채소는 깨끗이 씻어 엄지손가락 크기로 자릅니다.

1. Prepare the whole yangji without cutting it.
- Do not soak yangji in water to remove the so-called "blood." It is a common misconception that soaking in cold water removes blood. What is often mistaken for "blood" is actually meat juice that appears during cooking. While some visible blood vessels may be present, any actual blood is contained within them. In most cases, however, beef brisket (muscle) contains little to no blood. If blood vessels are visible, simply press them under running water while rinsing to release any remaining blood. Keep in mind that soaking in cold water will draw out the flavor.
2. Wash all the vegetables thoroughly and cut into thumb-sized pieces.

3. 압력솥에 모든 재료를 넣고 뚜껑을 닫고 센불로 가열합니다. 압력솥의 추가 울리면(추가 계속 울리는 상태이면) 약불로 줄여 20분간 가열한 후 불을 끕니다.
- 육수의 간을 보고 기호에 맞게 부족한 간을 합니다. 조미료 맛을 선호한다면 미원이나 소고기 다시다를 1작은술 정도 추가합니다. 담백한 맛을 선호한다면 굳이 조미료를 넣지 않아도 됩니다. 부족한 간은 국간장이나 소금으로 맞춰줍니다.
4. 추를 열어 압력을 다 뺀 후, 양지를 건져내고 육수를 걸러줍니다. 걸러낸 양지는 한 김 식힌 후 적당한 크기로 찢어줍니다.
5. 얼갈이는 한 입 크기로 자른 후 깨끗이 씻어줍니다.

3. Place all the ingredients in a pressure cooker, close and seal the lid, then cook over high heat. When the pressure cooker whistle begins to rattle continuously, lower the heat and cook for 20 minutes, then turn off the heat.
- Taste the broth and adjust the seasoning, as needed. For a deeper savory flavor, you may add 1 teaspoon of Miwon (MSG) or Dashida (beef stock powder). For a cleaner taste, it is recommended to omit them. Adjust the seasoning with guk-ganjang or salt, as needed.
4. Release the pressure completely by opening the pressure cooker whistle, then remove the yangji and strain the broth. Let the meat cool, then shred it into moderately sized pieces.
5. Cut the eolgari cabbages into bite-sized pieces and wash thoroughly.

6. 끓는 물에 살짝 데친 후 손으로 꼭 짜 물기를 제거합니다.

7. 된장, 들기름, 간 마늘로 잘 무쳐줍니다.

- 무친다는 표현은 스며들게 버무린다는 뜻입니다. '사무치다'라는 말이 있는데 '깊이 스며들다'라는 뜻입니다. 아주 멋진 말이지요?

8. 탕기에 잘 무친 얼갈이와 양지살을 넣고 육수 500ml를 넣어 밥과 함께 냅니다. 또는 탕기에 밥을 먼저 담고 얼갈이와 양지살을 올린 후 육수를 넣어도 좋습니다.

- 낙지를 좋아한다면 산낙지 4마리를 준비해 잘 씻은 후 끓는 양지 육수에 10초간 넣어 데칩니다. 육수는 그대로 쓰고 마지막 고명으로 데친 낙지를 먹기 좋게 잘라 올립니다. 냉동 낙지를 사용하면 질길 수 있으므로 산낙지를 사용하는 것을 추천합니다. 산낙지는 너무 큰 것보다 중간 사이즈를 사용하는 게 먹기에 좋습니다.

6. Gently blanch them in boiling water, then squeeze out excess moisture by hand.

7. *Muchida* thoroughly with doenjang, perilla oil, and grated garlic.

- *Muchida* (무치다) is a Korean word that means to toss ingredients until they are fully infused with seasoning. It shares a root with the word *samuchida* (사무치다), which describes something that penetrates deeply—often used to express intense emotion. Isn't that beautiful?

8. Place the seasoned eolgari and shredded yangji in a bowl, ladle 500 ml of broth over the dish, then serve together with rice. Alternatively, place the rice in the bowl first, followed by the eolgari and yangji, then ladle the broth over the dish.

- For long-arm octopus lovers: Prepare 4 *san-nakji* (live long-arm octopuses). Wash them thoroughly, then blanch in the yangji broth for 10 seconds. Use the broth as is, and cut the blanched octopuses into bite-sized pieces for garnish. Live octopuses are recommended, as frozen ones tend to become soggy. Medium-sized octopuses are preferred over extra-large ones, as they are easier to enjoy.

CHOI JIHYUNG

최지형

미술을 전공하며 예술적 감각을 키운 최지형 셰프는 청소년기에 요리에 눈을 뜨며 새로운 길을 걷기 시작했다. 존슨앤웨일즈대학에서 요리와 호텔경영을 배운 후 뉴욕으로 건너가 미쉐린 2스타 레스토랑 '마레아(Marea)'와 세계적인 레스토랑 '일레븐 매디슨 파크(Eleven Madison Park)'에서 경력을 쌓으며 정교한 기술과 깊은 철학을 익혔다.

2017년, 한국으로 돌아온 그는 자신의 뿌리에서 요리의 방향을 찾고자 했다. 어린 시절, 피난민 출신 외할머니와 함께 순대를 만들던 기억은 그에게 깊은 울림으로 남았고, 이북 음식과 순대를 주제로 한 다이닝 '리북방'을 열게 된 계기가 되었다.

순대라는 익숙한 소재에 정제된 감각과 현대적 해석을 더한 '리북방'은 오픈 1년 만에 미쉐린 가이드에 등재되며 주목받았다. 그는 단순히 익숙한 것을 새롭게 포장하는 방법이 아닌, 집안에서 내려오는 맛의 전통을 계승하고 자신의 경험을 더해 익숙한 요리를 완성도 높은 요리로 승화시키기 위해 노력하고 있다.

Majoring in fine arts, Chef Choi Jihyung brought his artistic sensibility to a new path after discovering a passion for cooking during his adolescence. He went on to study culinary arts and hotel management at Johnson & Wales University, then moved to New York, where he gained experience at the two-Michelin-starred Marea, and the world-renowned Eleven Madison Park, honing meticulous techniques and deepening his culinary philosophies.

In 2017, he returned to South Korea and began exploring culinary directions rooted in his heritage. Childhood memories of making *sundae* (Korean blood sausage) with his maternal grandmother, a North Korean refugee, left a profound impression on him, eventually leading him to open Lee Buk Bang, a dining restaurant dedicated to North Korean cuisine and *sundae*.

With a modern take on the familiar dish *sundae*, infused with his refined sensibility, Lee Buk Bang garnered attention by being listed in the MICHELIN Guide just one year after its opening. Rather than simply repackaging the familiar, Chef Choi strives to carry on the tradition of flavor passed down through his family, elevating everyday dishes into high-quality cuisine drawing on his own experience.

리북방
leebukbang

jihyung0401

Cabbage Dish

양배추 디시

이야기
STORY

이북 함경 지역은 척박한 토양과 긴 겨울로 인해 푸른잎 채소를 구하기가 쉽지 않은 환경입니다. 하지만 그런 조건 속에서도 비교적 잘 자라는 채소가 바로 양배추입니다. 배추와는 달리 계절의 제약이 덜하고, 많은 물 없이도 잘 자라기 때문에 이북에서는 자연스럽게 양배추를 활용한 음식이 다양하게 발달해왔습니다. 특히 양배추김치는 그 지역을 대표하는 음식 중 하나로, 독특한 풍미와 담백한 맛으로 사랑받아 왔습니다.

이 책에서 선보이는 요리는 어린 시절부터 이북음식을 접하며 자라온 저의 개인적인 기억과, 사찰음식에서 받은 영감이 더해져 탄생한 메뉴입니다. 세 종류의 양배추를 세 가지 방식으로 조리해 식감과 맛의 대비를 살렸습니다. 고깔 양배추는 겉은 바삭하고 속은 촉촉하게 구워 메인 요리로 만들고, 방울 양배추의 겉잎은 바삭하게 튀기고 속잎은 사찰 김치 양념에 버무려 곁들였습니다. 여기에 적채 양배추로 만든 보랏빛 소스를 함께 곁들여, 시각적으로도 즐거운 한 접시가 되도록 완성했습니다.

Due to its barren soil and long winters, Hamgyong Province in North Korea has limited access to green leafy vegetables. Yet despite these harsh conditions, cabbage grows relatively well compared to other crops. Unlike napa cabbage, cabbage is less sensitive to weather and requires little water to thrive. These environmental factors naturally led to the development of various cabbage-based dishes in North Korean cuisine. Among them, *cabbage kimchi*—one of the representative local dishes—has long been beloved for its distinct flavor and clean finish.

This cabbage dish brings together two key culinary influences: my childhood memories of North Korean cooking, and the inspiration drawn from Korean temple cuisine. Three types of cabbage are prepared in three different ways to highlight the contrast in flavors and textures. Caraflex cabbage is cooked until crisp on the outside and juicy within, serving as the centerpiece. Brussels sprouts are separated: the outer leaves are fried until crisp, while the inner leaves are tossed in Korean temple kimchi paste. A vibrant violet sauce made from red cabbage completes the dish, adding visual appeal to its layered flavors.

Ingredients

🍳 1인 분량
Serves 1

사찰 김치 양념

무우 (흰 부분)	200g
찬밥	125g
배	200g
연두	40g
매실청	40g
생강	15g
고춧가루	130g
다시마 우린 물	200g
호렴	30g
조청	50g

양배추

방울양배추	7개
고깔양배추	1/8개

적채 연두부 퓌레

적채 양배추	300g
건다시마	적당량
연두부	300g
제주도 푸른콩된장	30g
식용유	60g

장식

검은깨	1g
들기름	1큰술

KOREAN TEMPLE KIMCHI PASTE

200 g	Korean radish (white part)
125 g	cooled plain rice
200 g	pear
40 g	Yondu (vegetable umami essence)
40 g	maesil-cheong (Korean plum extract)
15 g	ginger
130 g	Korean chili powder
200 g	kelp-infused water
30 g	horeom (coarse salt)
50 g	jocheong (Korean grain syrup)

CABBAGE

7	Brussels sprouts
1/8	caraflex cabbage

RED CABBAGE AND SILKEN TOFU PURÉE

300 g	red cabbage
Q.S.	dried kelp
300 g	silken tofu
30 g	Jeju Pureun Kong doenjang
60 g	cooking oil

GARNISHES

1 g	black sesame seeds
1 tbsp	perilla oil

How to make

 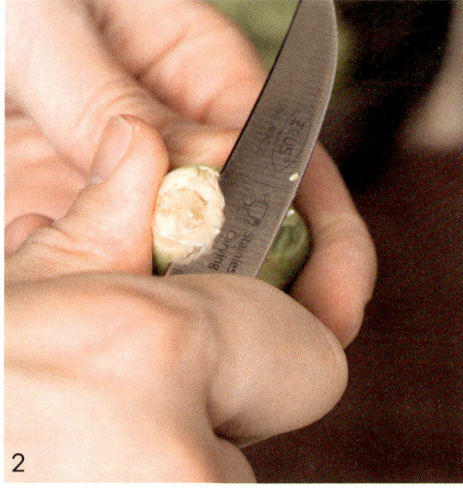 

1. 믹서에 사찰 김치 양념 재료를 모두 넣고 곱게 갈아 준비합니다.
   - 하루 동안 냉장고에 넣어 숙성시킨 후 사용합니다.
2. 방울양배추는 겉잎과 속잎으로 분리합니다. (겉잎은 튀겨내 부각으로, 속잎은 김치로 사용합니다.) 먼저 밑동을 제거한 후 겉잎과 속잎을 떼어냅니다.

1. In a blender, combine all the Korean temple kimchi paste ingredients and blend until smooth.
   - Refrigerate the kimchi paste for one day before use.
2. Separate the Brussels sprouts into outer and inner leaves (Use the outer leaves to make chips, and inner leaves to make kimchi). Remove the base first, then separate the two sets of leaves.

3. 겉잎은 식용유에서 색이 나고 바삭해질 때까지 튀겨줍니다.
4. 속잎은 1과 함께 버무려줍니다.

3. Deep-fry the outer leaves in cooking oil until golden brown and crispy.
4. Toss the inner leaves with (**1**).

5. 고깔양배추는 세로로 8등분해 소금으로 간을 한 후, 식용유를 두른 팬에서 익혀줍니다. 한번 뒤집고 난 후 소량의 물을 붓고 뚜껑을 덮어 중심부까지 익혀줍니다.

6. 적채는 잘게 다진 후 식용유 10g(분량 외)을 넣은 팬에서 볶아줍니다.

5. Cut the caraflex cabbage lengthwise into eight wedges, season with salt, then pan-fry in cooking oil. Flip once, add a dash of water, and cover with a lid to help it cook through the center.

6. Finely chop the red cabbage and stir-fry in a pan with an extra 10 g of cooking oil.

7. 건다시마를 넣고 볶아주다가 연두부를 넣고 으깨가며 볶아줍니다.
8. 물을 붓고 중불에서 적채를 익혀줍니다.

7. Add the dried kelp and continue stir-frying. Stir in the silken tofu, gently breaking it apart.
8. Pour in water and let the mixture cook over medium heat.

9. 믹서에 8과 제주푸른콩된장을 넣고 갈다가 식용유를 넣고 곱게 갈아 적채 연두부 퓌레를 완성합니다.

9. In a blender, combine the Jeju Pureun Kong doenjang and (8), then blend. Add 60 g of cooking oil and continue blending until smooth to make the red cabbage and silken tofu purée.

10. 접시에 적채 연두부 퓌레를 담아줍니다.
11. 그 위에 고깔양배추를 올려줍니다.
12. 두 가지 방울양배추를 올린 후 검은깨와 들기름을 뿌려 완성합니다.

10. Spoon the red cabbage and silken tofu purée onto a plate.
11. Place the caraflex cabbage wedge on top of the purée.
12. Top with the both types of Brussels sprouts, then finish with black sesame seeds and perilla oil.

Nokdujeon

(Mung Bean Pancake)

녹두전

가정식
HOME COOKING

콩을 일상적으로 즐겨 먹는 이북 지역에서 녹두전은 단순한 음식을 넘어, 어린 시절의 기억과 따뜻한 정이 깃든 소울푸드라 할 수 있습니다. '빈대떡'이라는 이름으로도 잘 알려진 이 음식은, 곱게 간 녹두에 다진 고기, 숙주, 김치 등의 속재료를 듬뿍 넣어 반죽한 후 돼지기름에 노릇하게 지져내는 방식으로 만들어집니다. 겉은 바삭하고 속은 촉촉하면서도 고소한 맛이 입안 가득 퍼지며, 씹을수록 녹두 특유의 담백함과 속재료의 풍미가 어우러져 깊은 만족감을 줍니다. 특히 평안도 지역에서는 명절이나 특별한 날 빠지지 않는 대표적인 음식으로, 한 조각만으로도 이북 음식의 진한 정취를 느낄 수 있는 메뉴입니다.

Nokdujeon is more than just a dish in North Korea, where beans are a dietary staple. It is considered a kind of soul food, imbued with childhood memories and heartfelt affection. Also known as *bindae-tteok*, it is made by pan-frying a mixture of finely ground mung beans, chopped pork, mung bean sprouts, and kimchi in pork fat until golden. Crispy on the outside and juicy within, each bite offers a mouthful of a rich, nutty flavor. The more you chew, the clean taste of mung beans and the savory blend of ingredients unfold in a harmonious balance, leaving a deep sense of satisfaction. Especially in Pyongan Province, *nokdujeon* is a dish never absent from the table on national holidays and special occasions. Just one piece is enough to evoke the true essence of North Korean cuisine.

Ingredients

2인 분량
Serves 2

불린 녹두	2컵
불린 멥쌀	1/2컵
느타리버섯	40g
건표고버섯	2개
신김치	20g
대파	20g
부추	15g
숙주나물	70g
두부	120g
돼지고기	30g
소금	적당량
후춧가루	적당량
돼지기름	1/2컵

2 cups	soaked mung beans
1/2 cup	soaked non-glutinous rice
40 g	oyster mushrooms
2	dried shiitake mushrooms
20 g	sin-kimchi (over-fermented kimchi)
20 g	green onion
15 g	garlic chives
70 g	mung bean sprouts
120 g	bean curd
30 g	pork
Q.S.	salt
Q.S.	ground black pepper
1/2 cup	pork fat

How to make

1. 녹두와 멥쌀은 하루 전날 미리 불려 준비합니다.
- 녹두는 상하기 쉬우므로 얼음을 넣고 냉장고에서 불려줍니다.
2. 느타리버섯은 잘게 찢고 건표고버섯은 물에 불린 후 꼭 짜서 얇게 슬라이스합니다.
3. 신김치는 물에 씻은 후 물기를 제거해 잘게 다져줍니다.

1. Soak the mung beans and non-glutinous rice in water a day in advance.
- Since mung beans spoil easily, it is best to soak them in ice water and keep refrigerated.
2. Finely shred the oyster mushrooms, and thinly slice the soaked shiitake mushrooms after squeezing out the excess water.
3. Rinse the sin-kimchi, drain, and finely chop.

4. 대파는 반달 모양으로 자르고, 부추는 적당한 길이로 잘라줍니다.
5. 숙주나물은 끓는 물에 살짝 데쳐 물기를 제거한 후 잘라줍니다.
6. 두부는 칼로 부드럽게 다져줍니다.

4. Slice the green onion into half-moon shapes, and cut the garlic chives into moderately sized pieces.
5. Lightly blanch the mung bean sprouts in boiling water, drain, and cut into moderately sized pieces.
6. Gently crush the bean curd with the side of a knife.

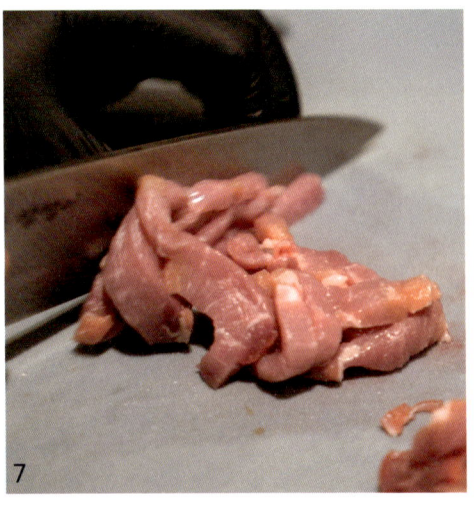  

7. 돼지고기는 적당한 크기로 잘라 소금과 후춧가루로 간을 한 후, 식용유를 두른 팬에 볶고 식혀줍니다.
8. 믹서에 두부, 불린 녹두와 멥쌀을 넣고 곱게 갈아줍니다.

7. Cut the pork into moderate sized strips, season with salt and black pepper. Pan-fry in cooking oil, then let cool.
8. In a blender, combine the bean curd, soaked mung beans, and non-glutinous rice, then blend until smooth.

9. 모든 재료를 볼에 담고 섞은 후, 소금과 후춧가루로 간을 합니다.
- 반죽의 농도가 너무 되직하다면 물을 넣고 농도를 맞춰줍니다.
10. 돼지기름을 넉넉히 두른 팬에 반죽을 떠 넣고 중약불에서 노릇하게 익혀줍니다.
- 익히는 중간중간 돼지기름을 추가해 중심부까지 고르게 익도록 합니다.

9. In a mixing bowl, combine all the ingredients, then mix thoroughly. Season with salt and black pepper.
- If the batter is too thick, adjust the consistency by adding water as needed.
10. In a pan with ample pork fat, ladle in the batter and cook over medium-low heat.
- Add more pork fat as needed to ensure the center cooks through evenly.

SHIN KYESOOK

신계숙

闓香桂

중어중문학과에 진학한 후, 문학 속에 등장하는 다채로운 음식에 매료되어 요리에 대한 관심을 키워갔다. 졸업 후 중국으로 유학을 떠나 현지 음식 문화를 체험하며 중식의 매력에 깊이 빠졌고, 중식 요리사의 길을 걷기로 결심했다.

귀국 후, 1987년 서울 유명 중식당 '향원'에서 주방 보조로 경력을 시작하며 당시 여성으로서는 드물게 중식 주방에 도전했다. 열정과 끈기로 주방의 편견을 이겨내고, 실력을 인정받으며 차곡차곡 경력을 쌓아갔다.

청나라 요리 고서 「수원식단」을 25년간 연구하며 전통 중식의 현대적 재해석에도 힘써온 그녀는, 학문과 실무를 겸비한 보기 드문 중식 전문가로 자리매김했다. 2020년에는 EBS <세계테마기행>과 <신계숙의 맛터사이클 다이어리>를 통해 대중과 소통하며 친근한 이미지로 큰 사랑을 받았고, 이 프로그램은 시즌 4까지 방영되며 화제를 모았다.

2021년, 대학로에 중식당 '계향각'을 오픈해 그간의 오랜 연구와 경험이 녹아든 요리를 선보이고 있다. 계향각은 청나라 고문헌을 바탕으로 한 전통 중식을 현대적으로 풀어낸, 그녀만의 철학이 고스란히 담긴 공간이다.

After studying the Chinese language and literature, she became fascinated by the rich descriptions of food in literature and developed an interest in cooking. After graduation, she traveled to China to study abroad, where she fell in love with Chinese cuisine and decided to pursue a career as a Chinese chef.

After returning to Korea, she began her career as a kitchen hand at Hyangwon, a famous Chinese restaurant in Seoul, in 1987. This decision marked a significant challenge for her, as working in a Chinese kitchen was rare for women at the time. With her passion and persistence, she overcame the prejudices in the kitchen and worked her way up.

She spent 25 years researching the Qing Dynasty culinary classic *Suiyuan Shidan* (Suiyan cuisine) and working on modern interpretations of traditional Chinese cuisine, making her one of the rare Chinese food experts who combine academia and practice. In 2020, she communicated with the public through EBS's *World Theme Travel* and *Shin Kyesook's Tastorcycle Diary* and was loved for her friendly vibe. The latter program aired until 4th season, creating a buzz.

In 2021, she opened a Chinese restaurant, "Kyehyanggak," on Daehak-ro, serving dishes that embody years of research and experience. Kyehyanggak is a modernized version of traditional Chinese food based on ancient texts from the Qing Dynasty, a space that reflects her own philosophy.

계향각
@ gaehyanggak

Tangsu Galbi
(Sweet and Sour Ribs)

탕수갈비

이야기
STORY

남녀노소를 불문하고 모두가 좋아하는 계향각의 인기 메뉴를 소개합니다. 이 요리의 핵심은 누구나 좋아할 만한 익숙한 맛과 빠른 조리에 있습니다. 케첩을 넣어 만든 새콤달콤한 탕수 소스는 누구에게나 친숙한 맛으로 다가가며, 등갈비는 반으로 잘라 핏물을 빼 준비해두면 언제든 빠르게 조리가 가능합니다. 소스를 미리 만들어두고 보관하면, 주문이 들어왔을 때 바로 가열해 서빙할 수 있어 조리 효율성도 뛰어납니다. 쉽고 빠르게 만들 수 있으면서도 맛있는, 그래서 더 사랑받는 계향각의 대표 메뉴입니다.

This is the signature dish at Gyehayanggak, beloved by people of all ages and backgrounds. The keys to *Tangsu Galbi* lie in its quick cooking and a familiar flavor that appeals to everyone. True to its name *tangsu*, this ketchup-based sauce delivers a sweet and sour flavor that is universally approachable. Once the back ribs are halved and the blood removed, the dish can be cooked quickly at any time. With the sauce is prepped in advance, it only needs to be reheated and served to order, making the process highly efficient. Easy and quick to prepare yet flavorful, this dish has become the signature dish at Gyehyanggak.

Ingredients

2인 분량
Serves 2

돼지등갈비

돼지등갈비	500g
간장	1작은술
청주	1작은술
녹말가루	적당량
식용유	적당량

소스

흰설탕	70g
2배사과식초	20g
케첩	40g
간장	20g
소금	적당량

PORK BACK RIBS

500 g	pork back ribs
1 tsp	soy sauce
1 tsp	cheongju (Korean refined rice wine)
Q.S.	starch
Q.S.	cooking oil

SAUCE

70 g	white sugar
20 g	Double Strength apple vinegar
40 g	ketchup
20 g	soy sauce
Q.S.	salt

How to make

1. 돼지등갈비는 뼈 방향으로 자른 후 찬물에 약 4시간 담가 핏물을 뺍니다.
2. 물기를 제거한 등갈비에 간장과 청주로 밑간을 한 후 녹말가루를 묻혀줍니다.
3. 예열된 식용유에 넣고 등갈비가 노릇하게 익을 때까지 튀겨줍니다.

1. Cut the pork back ribs along the bones, and soak in cold water for about 4 hours to draw out any blood.
2. Drain thoroughly, season the ribs with soy sauce and cheongju, then lightly coat with starch.
3. Deep-fry the ribs in preheated oil until golden brown.

4. 소스 재료를 모두 섞은 후 팬에 넣고 소스 농도가 될 때까지 졸여줍니다.
5. 소스에 등갈비를 넣고 버무려줍니다.

4. Combine all the sauce ingredients, transfer to a pan, then cook until reduced to a sauce consistency.
5. Add the fried ribs to the sauce and toss until evenly coated.

Nanja Wans

(Stir-fried Chinese Meatballs)

난자완스

가정식
HOME COOKING

난자완스는 본래 '완자를 지지기 어려운 음식'이라는 뜻의 '난전완자(難煎丸子)'에서 유래된 요리입니다. 전통 방식은 여러 재료를 썰어 넣는 등 손이 많이 가는 음식이지만, 여기에서는 가정에서도 쉽게 만들 수 있도록 다진 고기를 활용한 방식으로 재해석하였습니다.

완자는 어렵지 않게 지져 익힐 수 있도록 하였고, 다진 고기를 사용해 남녀노소 누구나 부담 없이 즐길 수 있는 요리로 완성했습니다. 특히 보성녹돈을 사용해 돼지고기와 비계의 비율을 7:3으로 맞춰, 고소하면서도 부드러운 맛을 살렸습니다.

Nanja Wans originates from a Chinese dish *Nan Jian Wan Zi*, which literally means "a dish whose meatballs are difficult to shallow-fry." While the traditional method involves meticulous slicing of a variety of ingredients, this version simplifies the process by using minced meat for easier home cooking.

The meatballs are designed to fry easily and are made with minced meat, making them approachable for everyone. In particular, this reimagined recipe uses *Boseong Nokdon*, a specialty pork from pigs fed green tea in Korea's renowned Boseong County, blended in a 7:3 ratio of lean to fat to enhance both flavor and tenderness.

Ingredients

4인 분량
Serves 4

돼지고기 완자

대파 (초록 부분)	20g
생강	3g
간 돼지고기 (보성녹돈)	500g
달걀	25g
감자전분	15g
간장	1작은술
후춧가루	1g
식용유	적당량

소스

식용유	적당량
대파 (흰 부분)	40g
마늘	3알
불린 건표고	50g
죽순	40g
간장	1큰술
닭육수 또는 물	400ml
소금	적당량
물에 푼 감자전분	2큰술
참기름	적당량

PORK MEATBALLS

20 g	green onion (green part)
3 g	ginger
500 g	minced pork (*Boseong Nokdon*)
25 g	whole egg
15 g	potato starch
1 tsp	soy sauce
1 g	ground black pepper
Q.S.	cooking oil

SAUCE

Q.S.	cooking oil
40 g	green onion (white part)
3	garlic cloves
50 g	rehydrated shiitake mushrooms
40 g	bamboo shoots
1 tbsp	soy sauce
400 ml	chicken stock or water
Q.S.	salt
2 tbsp	potato starch slurry
Q.S.	sesame oil

How to make

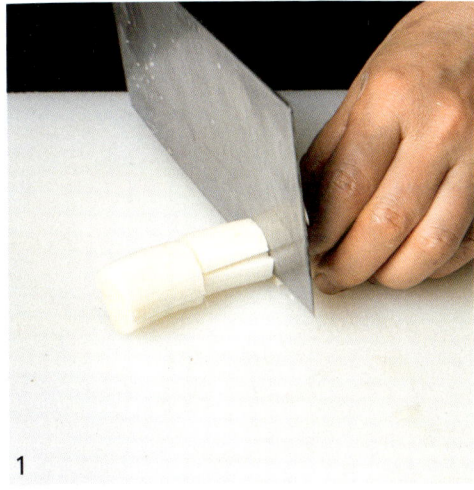  

1. 대파 흰 부분은 큼직하게 썰고, 대파 초록 부분과 생강은 잘게 다져줍니다.
2. 마늘은 얇게 썰어줍니다.
3. 소스에 사용할 불린 건표고, 죽순은 한입 크기로 썰어 준비합니다.

1. Cut the white part of green onion into large pieces, and finely chop the green part and ginger.
2. Thinly slice the garlic.
3. For use in the sauce, cut the rehydrated shiitake mushrooms and bamboo shoots into bite-sized pieces.

  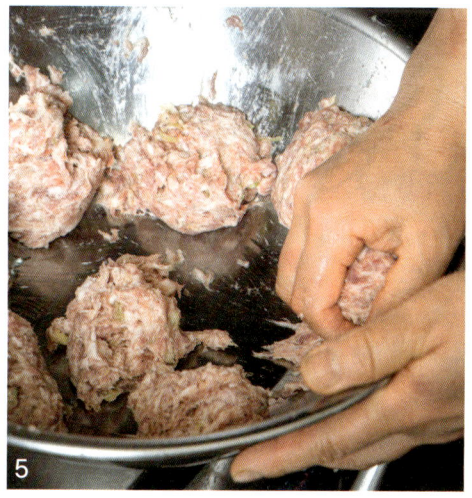

4. 볼에 식용유를 제외한 돼지고기 완자 재료를 모두 넣고 섞은 후 반죽을 던지듯 치대줍니다.
5. 완자 반죽을 8등분한 후 동그랗게 만들어줍니다.

4. In a mixing bowl, combine all the pork meatball ingredients except cooking oil, and mix well. Knead the mixture by slapping it against the bowl several times.
5. Divide the mixture into eight equal portions and shape into round meatballs.

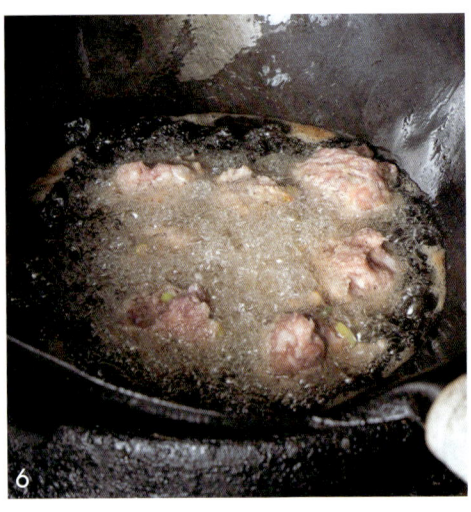

6. 식용유를 넉넉하게 두른 팬에 완자를 넣고 튀기듯 지집니다. 이때 국자로 완자를 눌러 넓적하게 모양을 잡아주며 익힙니다.
7. 다른 팬에 식용유 약 3큰술을 두르고, 대파 흰 부분과 마늘을 넣어 향을 낸 후 불린 건표고와 죽순, 간장을 넣고 익혀줍니다.

6. Pan-fry the meatballs in a generous amount of cooking oil, as if shallow-frying. Gently press them down as they cook to form a wider shape.
7. In a separate pan, heat about 3 tablespoons of cooking oil. Add the white part of the green onion and garlic to infuse the oil with their aroma, then stir in the rehydrated shiitake mushrooms, bamboo shoots, and soy sauce.

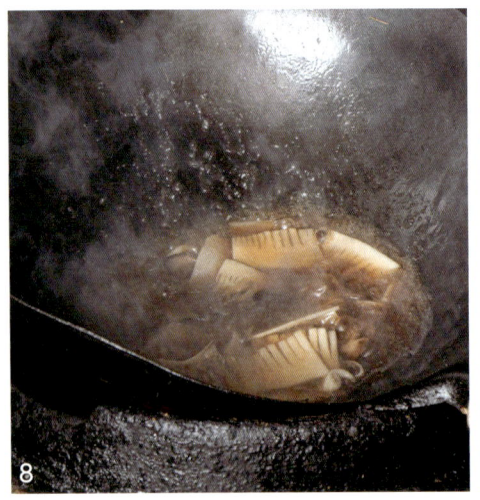

8. 닭육수를 붓고 소금으로 간을 한 후, 물에 푼 감자전분을 넣어 소스 농도로 맞춰줍니다.
   - 계향각에서는 노계를 4시간 동안 고은 것을 육수로 사용합니다. 가정에서는 시판 치킨 스톡을 사용하거나 닭날개 2개를 넣고 끓인 육수, 또는 물을 사용합니다.
9. 익힌 완자를 넣고 소스로 버무린 후 소금으로 간을 합니다.
10. 참기름을 뿌려 마무리합니다.

8. Pour in the chicken stock and season with salt. Stir in the settled potato starch until the liquid thickens to a sauce consistency.
   - The recipe at Gyehyanggak uses a rich stock made by simmering a stewing hen for 4 hours. For home cooking, you may use store-bought chicken stock, a quick broth from two chicken wings, or even water.
9. Add the meatballs to the sauce and toss until evenly coated. Adjust seasoning with salt.
10. Finish with sesame oil.

LIM TAEHOON

임 태 훈

어려운 가정 형편으로 인해 어린 시절을 고아원에서 보내고, 이후 할머니와 함께 지내며 신문 배달, 전단지 배포, 음식 배달 등 다양한 일을 경험했다. 이러한 성장 환경은 그의 책임감과 성실함을 단련시켰다.

고등학교 1학년 때 중식당에서 배달 아르바이트를 하며 요리에 흥미를 느꼈고, 요리에 대한 열정 하나로 스승 없이 독학으로 기술을 익히며 요리사로서의 길을 닦아 나갔다.

30세가 되던 해에 경복궁역 인근에 본인의 첫 중식당 '아량'을 열었다. 오픈 초반에는 손님이 없어 큰 어려움을 겪었지만 꾸준한 노력 끝에 입소문이 퍼지기 시작했고, 이후 서촌에 '도량'을 오픈하며 오너 셰프로서의 입지도 다졌다. '도량'은 그의 요리 철학과 진심이 담긴 중식을 선보이며 많은 이들의 사랑을 받고 있다.

2024년에는 넷플릭스 요리 서바이벌 프로그램 <흑백요리사: 요리 계급 전쟁>에 출연하여 '철가방 요리사'라는 별명으로 주목받았고, 그의 진솔한 인생 이야기와 뛰어난 요리 실력은 대중에게 큰 감동을 주었다.

최근 도량과는 또 다른 콘셉트의 중식당, '감개무량'을 오픈한 그는, 현재도 중식 셰프로서 끊임없이 성장 중이며, 언젠가는 자신의 경험을 바탕으로 젊은 요리사들을 육성할 수 있는 아카데미를 설립하는 것을 목표로 하고 있다.

Chef Lim spent his childhood in an orphanage due to his family's difficult circumstances. Later, he stayed with his grandmother, where he held various jobs, including delivering newspapers, handing out flyers, and delivering food. This upbringing honed his sense of responsibility and integrity.

During his first year of high school, he became intrigued by cooking while working as a delivery driver for a Chinese restaurant. His passion for cooking led him to self-teach the skills without a formal teacher, paving the way for his career as a chef.

At the age of 30, he opened his first Chinese restaurant 'Aryang,' near Gyeongbokgung Palace Station. Initially, he struggled with a lack of customers. Still, with persistent efforts, word of mouth began to spread, which led him to open 'Doryang' in Seochon, solidifying his position as both owner and chef. Doryang is loved by many people for its cuisine, which embodies his culinary philosophy and heartfelt Chinese food.

In 2024, he starred in the Netflix cooking survival show *Culinary Class Wars*, where he was known as the "Self-made Chef," and his authentic life story and culinary skills impressed the public.

He recently opened Gamgye Muryang, a Chinese restaurant with a different concept from Doryang, and is still growing as a Chinese chef. He aims to establish an academy one day to train young chefs based on his experience.

도량
doryang_restaurant

chulgabangchef

Eight Treasures Meatball

이야기
STORY

팔보완자

팔보완자는 그 이름처럼 완자 안에 여덟 가지 재료가 들어가는 음식입니다. 중국에서 숫자 '8'은 발음이 '바(八)'로, '부(發, 부유하다)'와 유사하게 들려 재물과 번영을 뜻하는 길한 숫자입니다. 따라서 팔보 요리는 '재물과 행운이 넘친다'는 상징성을 갖습니다.

저만의 방식으로 풀어본 이 요리는, <흑백요리사 : 요리 계급 전쟁> 첫 라운드에서 선보인 특별한 메뉴였습니다. 방송에서 보여드릴 마지막 요리가 될 수도 있다는 마음으로, 가장 저다운 음식을 만들고 싶었고, 그래서 직접 연구하고 개발한 이 메뉴를 선택하게 되었습니다. 전통적인 조리법은 따르지 않았지만, 그 안에 담긴 진심이 닿았는지 심사위원들로부터 극찬을 받을 수 있었던, 제게도 의미 깊은 요리입니다.

Named Eight Treasures Meatball, the dish literally contains eight distinct ingredients enclosed within the meatball. In Chinese, the number eight (8), pronounced "*ba* (八)", sounds similar to "*fa* (發)," meaning "to prosper," making it an auspicious number associated with wealth and prosperity. Accordingly, Eight Treasures dishes traditionally symbolize "overflowing wealth and good fortune."

This special version, created in my own style, was featured in the first round of the culinary survival show *Culinary Class Wars*. Imagining it as the final dish I might present, I chose something that best reflected who I am—a dish thoughtfully developed through personal exploration. While it departs from traditional methods, it embodies my sincerity. Perhaps that sincerity came through, earning the judges' praise and making the dish even more meaningful to me.

팔보 완자는 이름 그대로 완자 안에 여덟 가지 재료가 들어가는 요리입니다. 양파에 다진 고기를 입혀 튀기고, 양파를 꺼내 속을 비워낸 다음 청경채, 새우, 버섯 등 다양한 해산물과 채소를 특제 소스로 볶아 넣어 만듭니다.

이 레시피는 제가 오랜 시간 연구하며 완성한 특제 소스를 사용하는데, 고추기름, 굴소스, 두반장, 몽고간장, 설탕 등이 어우러져 깊고 풍부한 맛을 냅니다. 정확한 배합은 공개할 수 없지만, 방송을 통해 소개된 뒤 많은 분들이 이 요리의 형태를 만드는 방법을 궁금해하셔서 이 책에 담게 되었습니다.

조리 과정이 독특하고 흥미로워 보는 것만으로도 이 요리의 매력을 충분히 느낄 수 있을 것입니다. 만드는 즐거움과 함께, 자신만의 맛으로 완성해보시길 바랍니다.

Eight Treasures Meatball literally includes eight ingredients encased within the meatball. The dish is made by coating an onion with minced meat and frying it, after which the onion is removed to create a hollow shell of meat. The shell is then filled with a variety of seafood and vegetables, such as bok choy, shrimp, and mushrooms.

The filling is stir-fried in a special sauce—a deep, rich blend of chili oil, oyster sauce, doubanjiang, Monggo soy sauce, and sugar—that I developed through extensive exploration. While the exact proportions remain confidential, I've decided to share the recipe in this book, as many have shown interest in how to shape the meatball after it was featured on the show.

The preparation itself is so unique and engaging that its charm comes through simply by watching the process unfold. I hope you enjoy making it and adding your own touch.

How to make

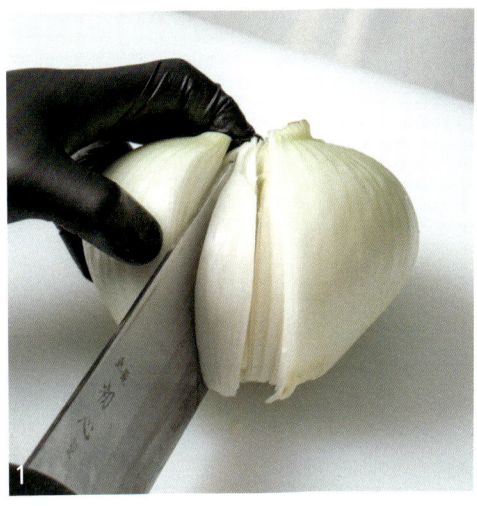
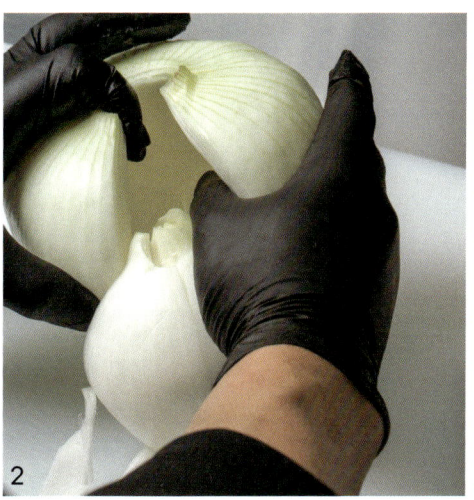
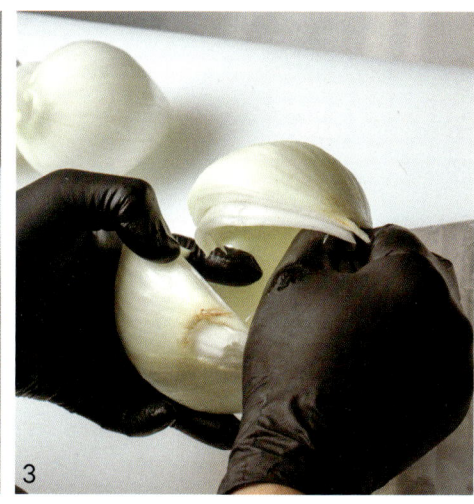

1. 양파는 중심부를 기준으로 사진처럼 잘라줍니다.
2. 잘라진 틈으로 안쪽의 양파를 조심스럽게 빼냅니다.
3. 빼낸 양파도 칼집이 나 있는 상태입니다. 겉껍질과 심지를 제거해 큰 양파에 잘 들어갈 수 있게 만들어줍니다.
- 양파 안이 비어 있으면 튀길 때 떠올라 고르게 익히기 어렵습니다. 큰 양파 안에 작은 양파가 잘 들어갈 수 있도록 크기를 잘 맞춰줍니다.

1. Make a cut at the center of onion as shown in photo (**1**).
2. Carefully remove the inner section of the onion through the cut.
3. From the inner section, discard both the outer layers and core, leaving a piece that fits easily inside the large onion.
- If the onion is too hollow, it may float during frying, which can prevent it from cooking evenly. Adjust the size of the small onion so that it fits easily inside the large onion.

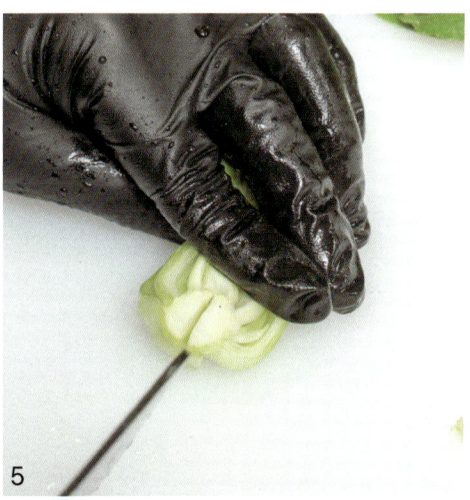

4. 큰 양파 안에 작은 양파를 넣어줍니다.
- 6월부터 나오는 양파는 2겹만 남겨두어도 됩니다. 촬영 시기에는 햇양파여서 4겹으로 남겨두었습니다.
5. 청경채는 반으로 자른 후 밑동에 칼집을 내줍니다.
6. 사용하는 다른 채소들은 모두 한입 크기로 썰어줍니다.

4. Place the small onion inside the large one.
- If using onions harvested after June, leave only two layers on the small onion. In this recipe, four layers were left, since freshly harvested onions were in season at the time of the photo shoot.
5. Halve bok choy and score the base.
6. Cut the remaining vegetables into bite-sized pieces.

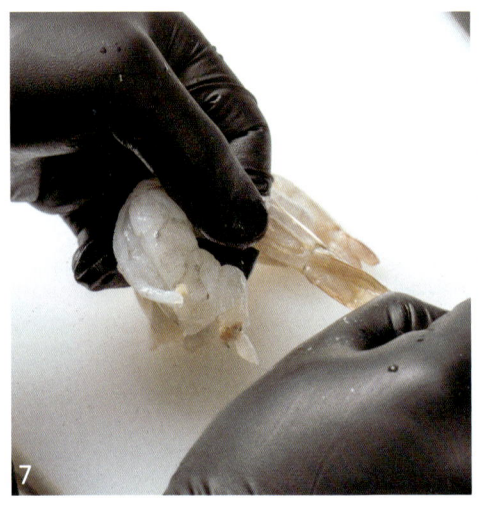  

7. 새우는 등에 있는 내장을 제거하고 머리와 꼬리를 잘라줍니다.
8. 사용하는 다른 해산물 재료는 칼집을 낸 후 한입 크기로 썰어줍니다.
9. 돼지고기 민찌는 칼로 곱게 다집니다.

7. Devein shrimp and cut off the head and tail.
8. Score the remaining seafood and cut into bite-sized pieces.
9. Finely chop the minced pork with a knife.

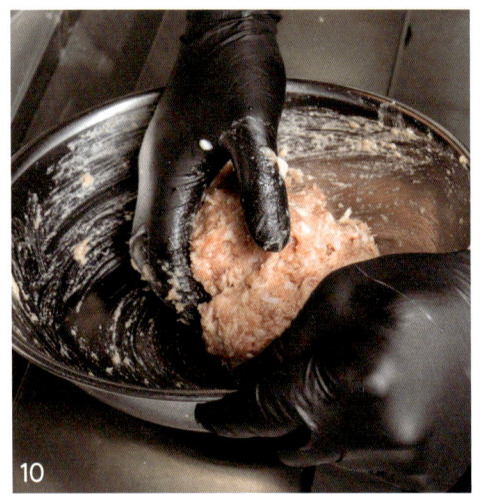  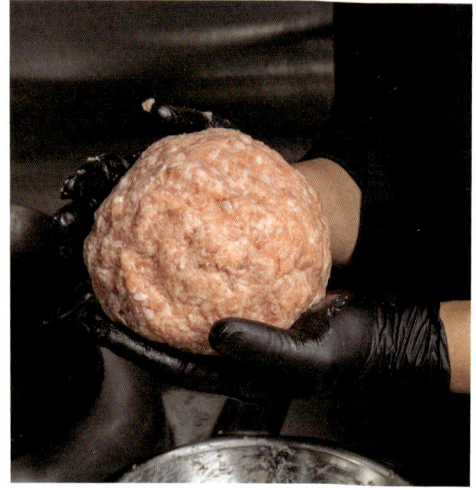

10. 볼에 9와 소금, 후춧가루, 감자전분, 달걀물을 넣고 고르게 섞은 후 반죽을 여러 번 던져가며 치댑니다.
11. 준비한 양파 표면에 10을 고르게 붙여줍니다.

10. In a mixing bowl, combine potato starch, beaten eggs, salt, black pepper, and (9), then mix well. Knead the mixture by slapping it against the bowl several times.
11. Evenly coat the assembled onion with (10).

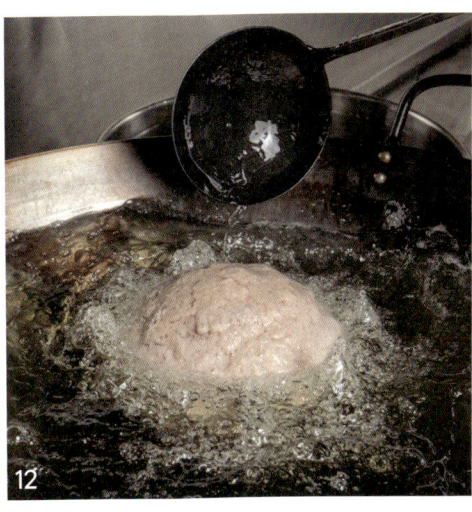  

12. 170℃로 예열된 식용유에 넣고 약 10분간 튀겨 고기를 완전히 익혀줍니다.
    - 초반에는 국자를 이용해 고기 윗면에 뜨거운 식용유를 계속 부어줍니다. 이 작업을 하지 않으면 식용유에 잠긴 아랫부분과 잠기지 않은 윗면의 온도 차로 인해 고기가 갈라지게 됩니다. 고기가 고르게 익은 후에도 국자를 이용해 계속 돌려가며 모든 면을 고르게 익혀주세요.
13. 손질한 청경채는 끓는 물에서 가볍게 데친 후 체반에 받쳐 물기를 제거합니다. 중간에 잠시 뚜껑을 덮어 빠르게 데쳐줍니다.

12. Deep-fry in cooking oil preheated to 338°F (170°C) for about 10 minutes to cook through.
    - At the beginning, continuously ladle hot oil over the meat. Skipping this step may cause the meat to crack due to temperature difference between the submerged and exposed sides. Even after the meat is cooked through, keep turning it gently with the ladle to ensure even cooking on all sides.
13. Lightly blanch the bok choy in boiling water, then drain in a sieve. Briefly cover with a lid halfway through to speed up the blanching.

14. 나머지 채소와 해산물도 가볍게 데친 후 체반에 받쳐 물기를 제거합니다.
15. 식용유를 두른 웍에 청경채를 제외한 채소 재료, 해산물 재료를 넣고 볶다가 굴소스, 두반장, 중화미원, 설탕, 고추기름, 식용유, 몽고간장 등으로 만든 소스를 넣고 강한 불에서 빠르게 볶아줍니다.

14. Gently blanch the remaining vegetables and seafood, then strain them through the sieve.
15. In a wok with cooking oil, stir-fry all the vegetables except the bok choy together with the seafood. Add the sauce made with oyster sauce, doubanjiang (Chinese broad bean paste), Chinese MSG, sugar, chili oil, cooking oil, and Monggo soy sauce. Stir-fry briskly over high heat.

16. 물에 푼 감자전분을 넣어 소스 농도로 맞춰줍니다.
17. 다른 웍에 고추기름, 식용유, 다진 대파 등을 넣고 가열해 고추기름 소스를 만듭니다.
- 마지막에 여분의 물을 넣어 농도를 맞춰줍니다.

16. Stir in the starch slurry and cook until the sauce thickens.
17. In a separate wok, heat chili oil, cooking oil, and chopped green onion to make chili oil sauce.
- Stir in extra water at the end to adjust the consistency.

18. 익힌 돼지고기의 윗면을 칼로 잘라줍니다.
19. 가위를 이용해 안쪽 양파를 잘라 빼내기 좋게 만듭니다.

18. Cut a small round lid from the top of the meat shell using a knife.
19. Through the opening, cut the onion inside the meat shell with scissors to make it easier to remove.

LIM TAEHOON

20. 집게를 이용해 안쪽 양파를 모두 꺼냅니다.
21. 볶은 채소와 해산물을 넣어줍니다.

20. Use tongs to pull out all of the onion from the meat shell.
21. Fill the cavity with the stir-fried vegetables and seafood.

22. 뚜껑을 닫아줍니다.
23. 고추기름 소스를 붓고 금박을 올려 마무리합니다.

22. Cover with the meat lid.
23. Ladle the chili oil sauce over the dish and garnish with gold leaf.

Pipa Tofu

비파두부

가정식
HOME COOKING

비파 두부는 중국 가정에서도 자주 즐기는 반찬 같은 음식으로, 옛 악기인 비파와 닮은 모양 때문에 이런 이름이 붙여졌습니다. 우리나라의 동그랑땡과도 비슷한 요리로 볼 수 있는데요. 겉은 노릇하게 구워 바삭하고, 속은 부드러우면서도 촉촉한 식감을 자랑합니다. 두부의 담백함에 채소와 고기의 풍미가 함께 느껴지는 것이 특징이죠. 특별한 재료 없이도 손쉽게 만들 수 있고, 어렵지 않게 완성할 수 있어 많은 분들께 소개하고 싶은 음식입니다.

Pipa Tofu, a dish often enjoyed as a side dish in Chinese households, is named for its resemblance to the *pipa*, a traditional Chinese string instrument. It can also be regarded as the Chinese equivalent of Korean *donggeurangttaeng* (meat fritters). Pan-fried until golden, it boasts a crispy crust with a tender, juicy center. The dish highlights the clean flavor of tofu, complemented by the savory notes of vegetables and meat. Easy to make and requiring no special ingredients, it's a dish I would gladly recommend to many.

Ingredients

1접시 분량
Makes 1 plate

반죽

돼지민찌	100g
새우살	100g
두부	100g
죽순과 동고버섯	60g
백후추	두 꼬집
꽃소금	1작은술
달걀흰자	달걀 1개 분량
감자전분	5작은술

소스

물	200g
굴소스	10g
해선장	10g
간장	1작은술
노추◆	2작은술
백후추	2꼬집
물에 푼 감자전분	20g

◆ 노추는 중식에서 음식에 짙은 색과 윤기를 더하기 위해 사용하는 진한 간장입니다.

장식

다진 대파	적당량

COATING

100 g	minced pork
100 g	shrimp meat
100 g	tofu
60 g in total	bamboo shoots and shiitake mushrooms
2 pinches	ground white pepper
1 tsp	fine sea salt
Q.S.	egg white (from 1 egg)
5 tsp	potato starch

SAUCE

200 g	water
10 g	oyster sauce
10 g	hoisin sauce
1 tsp	soy sauce
2 tsp	lao chou ◆ (Chinese dark soy sauce)
2 pinches	ground white pepper
20 g	potato starch slurry

◆ Lao chou is a dark soy sauce used in Chinese cuisine to add deeper color and glossy finish.

GARNISH

Q.S.	chopped green onion

How to make

1

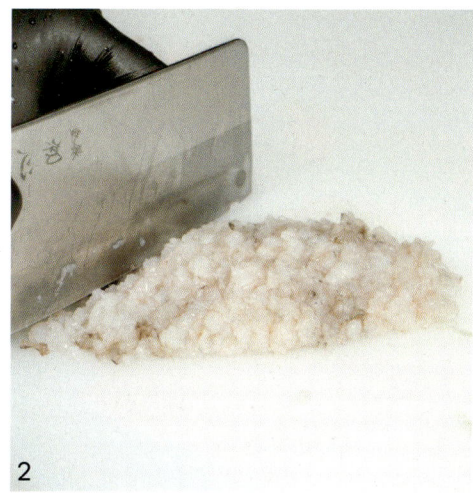
2

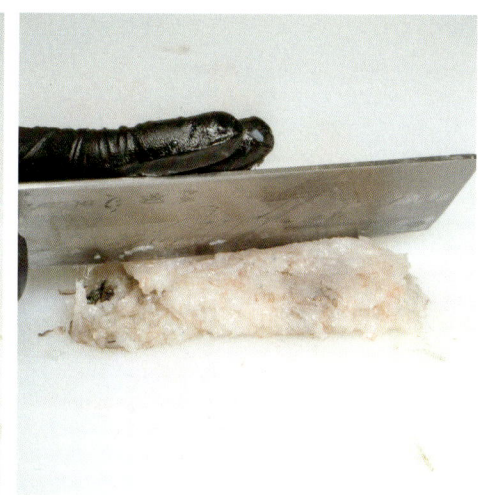

1. 돼지고기 민찌는 칼로 곱게 다집니다.
2. 새우살은 칼날로 다지고 칼등으로 밀어가며 곱게 다집니다.

1. Finely chop the minced pork with a knife.
2. Chop the shrimp meat, then finely scrape it with the back of the knife.

3

4

3. 두부도 칼날로 다지고 칼등으로 밀어가며 곱게 다집니다.
4. 죽순과 동고버섯도 곱게 다집니다.

3. Chop the tofu, then finely mash it with the back of the knife.
4. Finely chop the bamboo shoots and shiitake mushrooms.

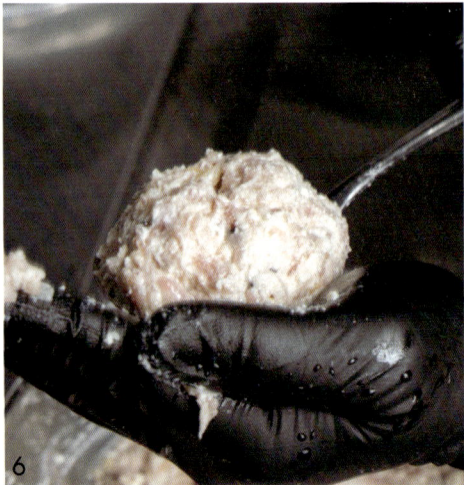

5. 볼에 반죽 재료를 모두 넣고 고르게 섞은 후, 반죽을 여러 번 던져가며 치댑니다.
6. 큰 숟가락 또는 작은 국자를 이용해 반죽을 비파 모양으로 만들어줍니다.
7. 160~170℃로 예열된 식용유에서 튀겨줍니다.

5. In a mixing bowl, combine all the coating ingredients and mix well. Knead the mixture by slapping it against the bowl several times.
6. Using a large spoon or small ladle, scoop portions of the mixture and shape them into a *pipa*-like shapes.
7. Deep-fry in cooking oil preheated to 320 to 338°F (160 to 170°C).

8. 웍에 물에 푼 감자전분을 제외한 소스 재료를 모두 넣고 가열한 후, 물에 푼 감자전분으로 농도를 맞춰 마무리합니다.
9. 7 위에 8을 부려줍니다.
10. 다진 대파를 올려 완성합니다.

8. In a wok, heat all the sauce ingredients except the starch slurry. Stir in the starch slurry at the end to adjust the sauce consistency.
9. Pour (**8**) over (**7**).
10. Garnish with chopped green onion.

LIM TAEHOON

조광효

CHO KWANGHYO

조광효

만화책 한 권에서 시작된 꿈을 현실로 만든 독학 중식 셰프. 자전거 회사에서 디자이너로 일하던 그는, 우연히 친구와 함께 시작한 만화방에서 인생의 전환점을 맞이한다. 만화방에 놓인 요리 만화 속 음식들을 직접 따라 만들어보며, 요리에 대한 열정이 차오르기 시작했다. 그는 요리 학원 한 번 다니지 않고 중국 요리책을 사서 스스로 번역하고, 실험과 실패를 반복하며 기술을 익혔다. 그러다 사천요리에 매료되어 현지로 가 맛의 경험을 쌓고, 그 경험을 토대로 자신만의 스타일을 다듬어 나갔다.

2019년, 첫 중식당 '조광101'을 열며 셰프로서의 첫 발을 내딛었다. 이후 2022년, 장지동에 '조광201'을 오픈하며 더 깊은 사천요리의 세계를 펼치고 있다. 2024년에는, 요리 서바이벌 프로그램 <흑백요리사: 요리 계급 전쟁>에 출연해, 만화책에서 튀어나온 듯한 열정으로 '만찢남'이라는 별명을 얻으며 화제를 모았다. 심사위원 중 한 명은 '독학으로 이 정도 요리를 한다는 건 말도 안 된다'고 호평했고, 그의 실력은 대중과 심사위원 모두에게 깊은 인상을 남겼다.

A self-taught Chinese chef whose dream began with a comic book and turned into a reality. He was working as a designer for a bicycle company when his life changed at a comics cafe he started with a friend. His passion for cooking was sparked by his attempt to recreate the food in comic books, and he began to develop a genuine interest in cooking. He never attended a cooking school; instead, he bought Chinese cookbooks, translated them himself, and experimented and failed to perfect his skills. Then, one day, he became fascinated by Sichuan cuisine and traveled to the region to experience its unique flavors, which he used to refine his own style.

In 2019, he took his first step as a chef by opening his first Chinese restaurant, ChoKwang101. In 2022, he opened ChoKwang201 in Jangji-dong to further explore the world of Sichuan cuisine. In 2024, he appeared on the culinary survival show *Culinary Class Wars*, where he was nicknamed "Comic Book Chef" for his enthusiastic approach to cooking, which seemed to jump out of a comic book. His skills impressed the public and the judges alike, with one of the judges commenting, "It's unbelievable that a self-taught chef can cook this well."

조광101
chokwang101

조광201
chokwang2o1

cho__kwang

Biryong Tteokbokki

(Biryong Stir-Fried Rice Cake)

비룡 떡볶이 & 볶음밥

이야기
STORY

비룡 떡볶이는 친구와 함께 만화방을 운영하던 시절에 처음 만들었던 요리입니다. 당시는 요리에 대한 전문 지식도 장비도 부족했지만, 만화 속 요리를 따라 만들어보는 재미에 푹 빠져 있었죠. 특히 만화 『요리왕 비룡』의 주인공 '비룡'이 선보였던 떡볶이 장면에서 영감을 받아 만든 요리였는데, 그때는 시판 떡볶이 소스를 활용해 간단하게 완성했었습니다.

오랜 시간이 흐른 지금, 그때의 맛을 최대한 떠올려 다시 비슷한 소스를 직접 만들어보았습니다. 매콤하면서도 달콤한 맛의 균형을 맞추는 데 중점을 두었고, 입안에 오래 남는 양념의 감칠맛이 인상적인 레시피입니다. 맵기의 정도만 조절하면 아이들도 부담 없이 맛있게 먹을 수 있어, 온 가족이 함께 즐기기에도 좋은 메뉴입니다.

비룡 떡볶이는 단순한 간식 그 이상으로, 추억과 상상력에서 출발한 요리입니다. 만화 속 요리가 현실의 접시 위에 올라온 순간의 즐거움을 여러분도 느껴보시길 바랍니다.

Biryong Tteokbokki is a dish I first created when I was running a comic book store with a friend. Although I had little culinary knowledge and lacked proper equipment at the time, I was fascinated by trying to make dishes featured in comic books. In particular, this recipe was inspired by the *tteokbokki* (stir-fried rice cake) made by Biryong, the main character in **Cooking King Biryong**. Back then, I made it simply using store-bought sauce.

Now, many years later, I've recreated a sauce similar to the one I once made, doing my best to bring back those early memories. The sauce features a well-balanced sweet and spicy flavor with a savory finish that lingers on the palate. When prepared less spicy, it becomes a perfect dish that the whole family can enjoy, even children.

More than just a snack, *Biryong Tteokbokki* was born from nostalgia and imagination. I hope you also find joy in bringing a recipe from the pages of a comic book to life.

Ingredients

1인 분량
Serves 1

떡볶이 떡 (쌀떡)	200g
물	100ml

떡볶이 소스

고운 고춧가루	30g
양조간장	15ml
다시다	15g
설탕	30g
요리당	30g

볶음밥

햄	적당량
식용유	적당량
밥	1공기 분량
마요네즈	15g

장식

깻잎	2장
건조 파슬리	적당량

200 g	rice cake sticks
100 ml	water

TTEOKBOKKI SAUCE

30 g	fine Korean chili powder
15 ml	yangjo-ganjang (naturally brewed soy sauce)
15 g	Dashida (beef stock powder)
30 g	sugar
30 g	Yoridang (cooking syrup)

FRIED RICE

Q.S.	ham
Q.S.	cooking oil
1 bowl	plain rice
15 g	mayonnaise

GARNISHES

2	perilla leaves
Q.S.	dried parsley

How to make

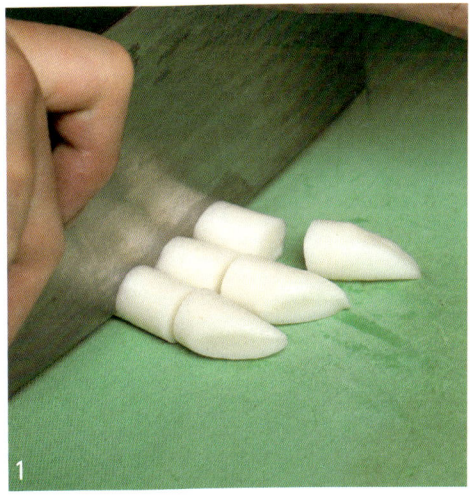  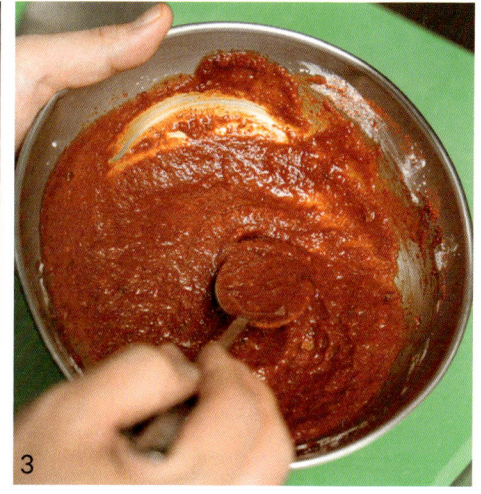

떡볶이

1. 떡볶이 떡은 한입 크기로 잘라줍니다.
2. 냄비에 물과 떡볶이 떡을 넣고 가열합니다.
3. 볼에 고운 고춧가루, 양조간장, 다시다, 설탕, 요리당을 넣고 섞어 떡볶이 소스를 만듭니다.

TTEOKBOKKI

1. Cut the rice cake sticks into bite-sized pieces.
2. Place them in a pot with the water and bring to a boil.
3. In a mixing bowl, combine the fine Korean chili powder, yangjo-ganjang, Dashida, sugar, and Yoridang to make the *tteokbokki* sauce.

4. 물이 끓으면 **3**을 넣고 풀어준 후 졸여줍니다.

4. Once the water comes to a boil, stir in (**3**), then simmer until reduced.

 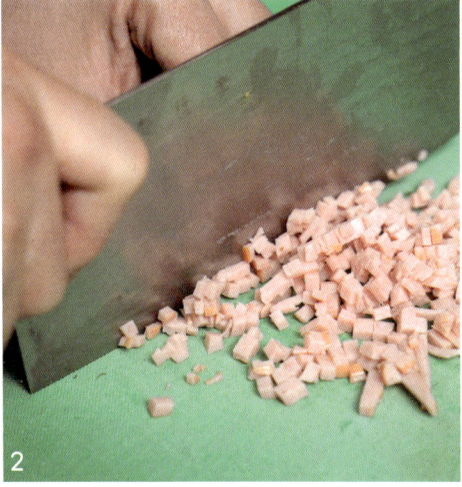

볶음밥

1. 깻잎은 잘게 채 썰어 준비합니다.
2. 햄은 작게 깍둑썰어줍니다.

FRIED RICE

1. Finely slice the perilla leaves.
2. Dice the ham into small cubes.

3. 식용유를 두른 팬에 밥, 햄, 마요네즈를 넣고 주걱으로 섞어가며 볶아줍니다.

3. In a pan with cooking oil, stir-fry the plain rice, ham, and mayonnaise with a spatula.

마무리

볶음밥을 밥공기에 담고 뒤집어 그릇 중앙에 담은 후, 볶음밥 주위로 떡볶이를 담고 채 썬 깻잎을 올려줍니다. 볶음밥 위에 다진 파슬리를 뿌려도 좋습니다.

볶음밥과 떡볶이 소스를 비벼 밥과 떡, 깻잎을 한입에 먹으면 더 맛있습니다.

FINISH

Pack the fried rice into a rice bowl and invert it onto the center of a plate. Arrange the *tteokbokki* around it and top with sliced perilla leaves. If desired, sprinkle chopped parsley over the fried rice.

It is best enjoyed by mixing the fried rice with the *tteokbokki* sauce, and taking a bite that includes the rice, rice cake, and perilla leaf together.

Mapo Tofu

마파두부

가정식
HOME COOKING

여기에서 소개하는 마파두부는 매장에서 판매하는 방식에서 불필요한 재료를 덜어내고, 가정에서도 쉽게 따라 할 수 있도록 간소화한 레시피입니다. 복잡한 공정이나 어려운 재료 없이도 마파두부 특유의 얼큰하고 감칠맛 나는 풍미를 충분히 즐길 수 있도록 구성했습니다.

이 레시피에서 가장 중요한 포인트는 두반장과 설탕의 비율입니다. 두반장의 깊은 풍미와 함께 설탕이 적절히 들어가야 간이 맞고 자극적이지 않게 맛의 균형이 잡힙니다. 매장에서는 풍미를 더해주는 채수를 육수로 사용하는데, 가정에서는 일반 물을 사용해도 충분히 깔끔하고 담백하게 완성할 수 있습니다.

또한 두부는 순두부나 연두부처럼 부드러운 질감을 가진 제품을 추천합니다. 몽글몽글하게 풀어지면서도 입안에서 사르르 녹는 식감이 마파두부의 매력을 더욱 잘 살려주기 때문입니다. 단단한 부침용 두부도 가능하긴 하지만, 이 레시피에서는 부드러운 두부가 훨씬 더 잘 어울립니다.

복잡한 테크닉 없이도 맛을 살릴 수 있도록 구성한 이 마파두부는 그 자체로도 훌륭한 요리이며, 밥을 곁들여 덮밥처럼 즐겨도 좋습니다.

This *mapo tofu* recipe removes any unnecessary elements from the restaurant version, making it more streamlined and accessible for home cooking. It is designed to capture the dish's signature spicy and savory flavors without relying on complex techniques or hard-to-find ingredients.

The key to this recipe lies in the ratio of doubanjiang to sugar. The savory depth of doubanjiang, balanced with just the right amount of sugar, results in a well-seasoned dish that is flavorful without being overly intense. While vegetable stock adds depth in the original version, using plain water at home can create a clean and delicate flavor.

For the tofu, a soft variety such as extra-soft or silken tofu is recommended. Its gentle, melt-in-your-mouth texture enhances the dish's appeal. While firm tofu for pan-frying can also be used, soft tofu works much better in this recipe.

Designed to deliver full flavor without complicated steps, this *mapo tofu* is excellent on its own, or served over rice like a Korean *deopbap* (rice bowl dish).

Ingredients

3인 분량
Serves 3

두부	1모
두치◆ (솔티드 블랙 빈스)	50g
두반장	130g
채수 또는 물	적당량
두태기름	적당량
소민찌	500g
노추◆	10g
고추기름	적당량
설탕	17g
산초	10알
베트남고추	3개
물	150ml
전분물	적당량
마라유	30ml

◆ 두치(豆豉)는 발효시킨 검은콩을 소금에 절인 것으로, 구하기 어려운 경우 시판 고추기름(라오간마)로 대체합니다.

◆ 노추는 중식에서 음식에 짙은 색과 윤기를 더하기 위해 사용하는 진한 간장입니다.

1	tofu block
50 g	douchi (salted black beans) ◆
130 g	doubanjiang (Chinese broad bean paste)
Q.S.	vegetable stock or water
Q.S.	suet
500 g	minced beef
10 g	lao chou (Chinese dark soy sauce) ◆
Q.S.	chili oil
17 g	sugar
10	Sichuan peppercorns
3	Vietnamese chili peppers
150 ml	water
Q.S.	starch slurry
30 ml	mala oil

◆ Douchi (豆豉) is a type of fermented and salted black soybeans. If unavailable, substitute with store-bought chili oil (Lao Gan Ma).

◆ Lao chou is a dark soy sauce used in Chinese cuisine to add deeper color and glossy finish.

How to make

1. 두부는 한입 크기로 깍둑썬 후 끓는 물에서 데쳐줍니다.
2. 두치는 작게 다집니다.
3. 두반장은 시판 두반장 제품에 채수 또는 물로 농도를 맞춘 후 블렌더로 곱게 갈아줍니다.
- 블렌더로 갈지 않으면 콩이 씹히면서 짠맛이 강하게 느껴집니다.

1. Dice the tofu into bite-sized cubes and blanch in boiling water.
2. Finely chop the douchi.
3. Add vegetable stock or water to the doubanjiang to adjust the consistency, then blend until smooth.
- Skipping this step may leave coarse bean bits in the sauce, making it overly salty.

4. 달궈진 웍에 두태기름을 넣고 볶아줍니다.
5. 두태기름이 녹으면 소민찌를 넣고 튀기듯 볶아줍니다.
- 소민찌는 가급적 기름이 많은 부위가 좋습니다. 기름이 적은 부위라면 소민찌의 양을 300g 정도 추가해 줍니다.
6. 우민찌가 익으면 노추를 넣어 짙은 색을 내줍니다.

4. In a preheated wok, stir-fry the suet.
5. Once the suet has rendered, add the minced beef and stir-fry as if deep-frying.
- Use fatty minced beef, if possible. If using lean minced beef, increase the amount by about 300 g.
6. Once the minced beef is cooked, add the lao chou to deepen the color.

7. 다른 웍에 고추기름을 한 바퀴 정도 두른 후 **6**과 설탕, 산초, 베트남고추를 넣고 가열합니다.
8. 두치를 넣고 가열합니다.
9. 물을 넣고 가열합니다.

7. In a separate wok, heat a swirl of chili oil, then add (**6**), sugar, Sichuan peppercorns, and Vietnamese chili peppers.
8. Add the douchi and continue heating.
9. Pour in the water and simmer.

10. 소스 농도로 졸아들면 데친 두부를 넣고 으깨지지 않도록 저어가며 가열합니다.
11. 전분물을 넣어 농도를 맞춘 후 마라유를 두 바퀴 정도 두르고 섞어 마무리합니다.
- 전분물은 전분과 물을 1:1 비율로 섞어 사용합니다.

10. When the mixture has reduced to a sauce consistency, add the blanched tofu. Gently stir to avoid breaking the tofu, and continue simmering.
11. Stir in the starch slurry to thicken the sauce. Finish with two swirls of mala oil and mix well.
- To make the starch slurry, mix starch and water in a 1:1 ratio.

HWANG JINSEON

황진선

어릴 적부터 태권도를 좋아해 시범단 활동과 대회 출전을 이어갔고, 대학에선 경호학을 전공하며 장학금을 받을 만큼 실력을 인정받았다. 하지만 무릎 부상으로 운동을 그만두게 되면서 요리에 관심을 갖게 됐다.

요리사가 되기로 마음먹고 코리아나호텔 중식당 '대상해'에 입사했다. 그곳에서 중식 대가 왕육성 셰프를 만났고, 약 10년 동안 요리 기술과 운영 노하우를 전수받았다. 정식 교육을 받지 않았기에 부족한 기본기를 채우기 위해 밤낮없이 연습에 매달렸고, 그 결과 젊은 나이에 부주방장 자리까지 올랐다.

2015년, 스승인 왕육성 셰프와 함께 서울 서교동에 중식당 '진진'을 열었다. 호텔에서만 접할 수 있던 고급 중식을 일상에서도 즐길 수 있게 하겠다는 목표로, 자장면이나 탕수육 같은 익숙한 메뉴 대신 멘보샤, 대게살 볶음처럼 색다른 요리를 선보였다. 그 결과 '진진'은 2017년부터 3년 연속 미쉐린 1스타를 받았고, 이후엔 '빕 구르망'에 이름을 올리며 꾸준한 인기를 이어갔다.

그는 요리를 '반복과 숙달의 연속'이라고 말하며, '맛은 세월이 만든다'는 신념으로 지금도 고급 중식의 대중화를 위해 노력하고 있다.

He loved taekwondo from a young age, participating in demonstrations and competing in competitions, and was good enough to earn a scholarship to major in Security Management at university. But a knee injury forced him to stop physical activity, and he turned his attention to cooking.

When he decided to become a chef, he joined the Chinese restaurant 'Great Shang Hai' at the Hotel Koreana. There, he met Chinese food master Chef Wang Yuk-sung, who taught him cooking techniques and management know-how over the course of about 10 years. Since he had no formal education, he practiced day and night to fill in the gaps, and as a result, he rose to the position of sous chef at a young age.

In 2015, he opened JinJin, a Chinese restaurant in Seogyo-dong, Seoul, with his mentor, Chef Wang yu cheng, to make high-end Chinese food, which was once only available in hotels, accessible to everyday diners. They introduced unconventional dishes such as *Mianbaoxia* and stir-fried snow crab meat instead of familiar favorites like *jajangmyeon* and sweet and sour pork (*tangsuyuk*). As a result, JinJin has been awarded one Michelin star for three consecutive years since 2017 and continued to be popular, being listed on Bib Gourmand.

He describes cooking as "a series of repetition and mastery" and believes that "taste comes with time" and is still working to popularize high-end Chinese food.

진진
JINJIN

jinseon.hwang

Egg-Wrapped Spring Rolls

이야기
STORY

작춘권

달걀로 만든 얇은 피에 채소와 해산물 볶음을 돌돌 말아 기름에 바삭하게 튀겨낸 '작춘권'은, 제가 요리사로서 첫걸음을 뗄 때 가장 애를 먹었던 메뉴 중 하나입니다. 막내 시절, 불판 앞에 처음 서서 달걀피를 만들던 순간이 아직도 생생합니다. 얇게 부쳐야 하는 달걀피는 자주 찢어지기 일쑤였고, 그럴 때마다 혼나고 또 연습하며 점점 손에 익혀갔습니다. 어렵사리 달걀피를 성공적으로 부쳐도, 그 안에 볶아놓은 재료를 넣고 말다가 다시 찢어져 속상했던 기억도 납니다. 수없이 실패하고 반복하며 익혔던 요리라 애증이 담겨 있는 메뉴이기도 합니다. 그렇게 공들여 만든 작춘권은 바삭한 식감과 고소하고 풍부한 속재료의 조화로 정말 맛있는 요리입니다.

그래서 진진 오픈 당시, 이 요리를 시그니처메뉴로 선보이고 싶다는 마음으로 메뉴에 올렸습니다. 하지만 멘보샤의 인기에 가려져 아쉽게도 그 존재가 잘 드러나지 못했지요. 한때는 예약 메뉴로만 제공했지만, 지금은 이 메뉴를 제대로 만들 줄 아는 셰프가 부족해 더 이상 판매하지 않고 있습니다. 그럼에도 불구하고 저는 지금도 다른 중식당에 가서 작춘권이 있으면 꼭 주문해 먹습니다. 제게는 그 시절의 땀과 추억이 고스란히 담겨 있는, 잊을 수 없는 메뉴이기 때문입니다.

Wrapped stir-fried vegetables and seafood in a thin egg roll wrapper, then deep-fried until crispy, these spring rolls were one of the most challenging dishes I faced as a rookie chef. I still vividly remember standing by the fire for the first time, making egg roll wrappers as the most junior member of the team. The thin wrappers tore so easily and often. Every mistake meant starting over, and even when I finally managed to make one, rolling it with the filling would often cause it to break again, which left me frustrated. This dish holds both love and hate for me, as it took countless failures and repeated attempts to finally get it right.

These meticulously wrapped spring rolls boast a crispy texture and a rich, savory filling in perfect harmony. When opening Jinjin, I added this dish to the menu with the hope of making it as a signature dish. Unfortunately, it was soon overshadowed by the popularity of *Mian Bao Xia*, the fried shrimp sandwich. Once offered as a reservation-only dish, it is no longer available, as few chefs are able to make it properly. Still, whenever I see egg-wrapped spring rolls on the menu at another Chinese restaurant, I can't help but order them a dish that holds the sweat and memories of my early days in the kitchen and remains unforgettable.

Ingredients

2접시 분량
Makes 2 plates

달걀 지단

달걀	12개
소금	적당량
물감자전분 ◆	2큰술
양파	작은 것 1개
배춧잎	3장
슬라이스한 당근	3쪽
슬라이스한 애호박	3쪽
불린 목이버섯	5개
호부추	30g
숙주나물	100g
알새우	20개
소흥주	1작은술
달걀물	1큰술
감자전분	1큰술
참기름	1큰술
잡채용 돼지고기	50g
간장	1작은술
미원	1/5작은술
노추 ◆ 또는 간장	1작은술
소흥주	1작은술
달걀물	1큰술
감자전분	1큰술
참기름	1큰술
식용유	적당량
작게 자른 대파	10g
다진 생강	5g
슬라이스한 마늘	5쪽
간장	2큰술
소흥주	3큰술
해삼채	50g
굴소스 (이금기 프리미엄)	1.5큰술
미원	2작은술
후춧가루	1작은술
참기름	2큰술

◆ 물감자전분은 감자전분을 물에 담근 후 가라앉으면 감자전분만 걸러내 물기를 꼭 짜낸 것을 말합니다.

◆ 노추는 오래 숙성시킨 간장으로, 색이 짙고 풍미가 깊습니다.

EGG ROLL WRAPPERS

12	eggs
Q.S.	salt
2 tbsp	settled potato starch ◆
1	onion (small)
3	napa cabbage leaves
3	carrot slices
3	zucchini slices
5	soaked wood ear mushrooms
30 g	Chinese chives
100 g	mung bean sprouts
20	shrimps
1 tsp	Shaoxing wine
1 tbsp	beaten egg
1 tbsp	potato starch
1 tbsp	sesame oil
50 g	julienned pork (for *japchae*)
1 tsp	soy sauce
1/5 tsp	Miwon (MSG)
1 tsp	lǎo chōu (Chinese dark soy sauce) ◆ or soy sauce
1 tsp	Shaoxing wine
1 tbsp	beaten egg
1 tbsp	potato starch
1 tbsp	sesame oil
Q.S.	cooking oil
10 g	chopped green onion
5 g	minced ginger
5	sliced garlics
2 tbsp	soy sauce
3 tbsp	Shaoxing wine
50 g	sea cucumber slices
1.5 tbsp	oyster sauce (Lee Kum Kee Premium)
2 tsp	Miwon
1 tsp	ground black pepper
2 tbsp	sesame oil

◆ Settled potato starch refers to the starch that settles at the bottom of a potato starch slurry, which is then strained and squeezed to remove excess moisture.

◆ Lǎo chōu is a longer-aged soy sauce with a darker color and deeper flavor.

How to make

1. 볼에 달걀, 소금, 물감자전분을 넣고 알끈이 풀릴 때까지 섞은 후 거품을 걷어내 준비합니다.
2. 양파, 배춧잎, 당근, 애호박, 불린 목이버섯은 0.5cm 두께로 채 썰어 준비합니다.
- 길이는 양파 길이에 맞춰줍니다.

1. In a mixing bowl, combine the eggs, salt, and settled potato starch. Mix until the chalazas are broken up, then skim off any foam.
2. Slice the onion, napa cabbage leaves, carrot, zucchini, and soaked wood ear mushrooms into 0.5 cm-thick pieces.
- Adjust the length of all vegetables to match the onion slices.

3. 호부추, 숙주나물은 3.5cm 간격으로 잘라 준비합니다.
4. 알새우는 반으로 자른 후 소흥주 1작은술, 달걀물 1큰술을 넣고 치대다가, 새우에 달걀이 스며들면 감자전분 1큰술과 참기름 1큰술을 넣고 골고루 비벼 준비합니다.

3. Cut the Chinese chives and mung bean sprouts into 3.5 cm lengths.
4. Halve the shrimp widthwise, then toss with 1 teaspoon of Shaoxing wine and 1 tablespoon of beaten egg. Once the shrimp have absorbed the egg, coat evenly with 1 tablespoon each of potato starch and sesame oil.

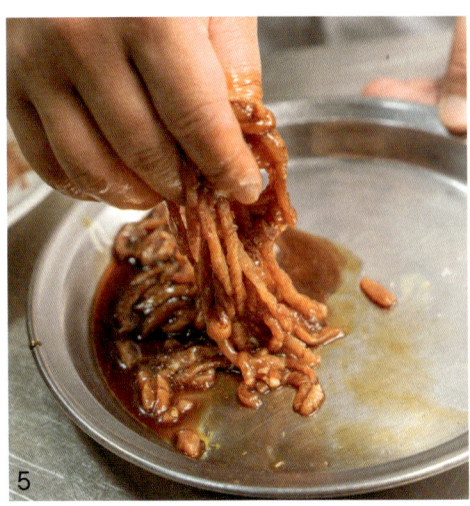  

5. 잡채용 돼지고기는 면포에 올려 핏물을 제거한 후 간장 1작은술, 미원 1/5 작은술, 노추 1작은술, 소흥주 1작은술, 달걀물 1큰술과 함께 치대다가, 고기에 달걀이 스며들어서 통통해지면 감자전분 1큰술과 참기름 1큰술을 비벼 준비합니다.

6. 팬에 식용유를 둘러 코팅합니다. 식용유 한 국자(약 200ml)를 넣고 130℃까지 온도를 올린 후, **4**를 넣고 기름에 삶듯 익혀 건져냅니다. 동일한 방식으로 **5**를 넣고 익혀 건져냅니다.

5. Pat the julienned pork with muslin (cheesecloth) to remove any blood. Toss with 1 tablespoon of beaten egg, and 1/5 teaspoon of Miwon, along with 1 teaspoon each of soy sauce, lao chou, and Shaoxing wine. Once the pork has absorbed the egg and become slightly plump, coat it with 1 tablespoon each of potato starch and sesame oil.

6. Lightly coat the pan with cooking oil. Add about one ladle (approximately 200 ml) of oil and heat to 266°F (130°C). Cook (**4**) in the oil as if blanching, then remove. Add (**5**) and cook in the same way.

7. 같은 팬에 식용유(약 5큰술)와 작게 자른 대파를 넣고 향을 내 파기름을 만든 후, 다진 생강, 슬라이스한 마늘을 넣고 낮은 온도에서 높은 온도까지 온도를 올려가며 서서히 볶아 향을 우려냅니다.

8. 팬 주위에 연기가 나기 시작하면 간장 2큰술, 소흥주 3큰술, **2**와 해삼채를 넣고 가장 센불로 볶아줍니다.

7. In the same pan, add about 5 tablespoons of cooking oil and the chopped green onion to make the green onion oil. Add the minced ginger and sliced garlic, then gradually increase the heat from low to high to gently infuse the oil with their aromas.

8. Once the pan begins to smoke, add 2 tablespoons of soy sauce, 3 tablespoons of Shaoxing wine, (**2**), and the sea cucumber slices. Stir-fry over the highest heat.

9. 재료에 향이 입혀지면, 굴소스 1.5큰술, 미원 2작은술을 넣고 빠르게 볶다가 3과 8을 넣고 골고루 잘 섞어줍니다. 그 다음 후춧가루 1작은술, 참기름 2큰술을 넣고 볶은 후 접시에 펼쳐 식혀줍니다.
- 채소가 숨이 죽지 않게 빠르게 볶는 것이 중요합니다.
10. 다른 팬에 식용유를 둘러 코팅합니다. 키친타월로 식용유를 닦아 팬에 소량의 기름만 스며들어 있는 상태로 만듭니다.

9. Once the ingredients have absorbed the aroma, add 1.5 tablespoons of oyster sauce, 2 teaspoons of Miwon, then stir-fry quickly. Add (3) and (8), then toss to combine. Stir in 1 teaspoon of black pepper and 2 tablespoons of sesame oil. Spread everything out on a plate and let cool.
- Be sure to stir-fry quickly to prevent the vegetables from wilting.
10. Lightly coat a separate pan with cooking oil, then wipe off the excess oil with a kitchen towel, leaving only a thin layer of oil.

11. 코팅된 팬에 1을 넣어 얇고 평평한 달걀피를 만들어줍니다.
- 달걀물 한 국자를 팬에 넣고 팬을 돌려 달걀피를 얇게 만든 후 여분의 달걀물은 덜어냅니다. 큰 웍이 없는 가정이라면 일반 팬의 크기에 맞춰 달걀 지단을 부치듯 만들면 됩니다.

11. Add (1) to the prepared pan to make the thin, even egg roll wrappers.
- Ladle in some of the beaten egg, swirl the pan to spread it thinly, then pour out any excess. If a large wok is unavailable, use a regular pan and make wrappers to fit its size, as you would when preparing egg garnish.

12. 완성한 달걀피를 반으로 접고 절반을 잘라줍니다.
13. 달걀피 가장자리에 밀가루 풀을 발라줍니다.
- 밀가루 풀은 밀가루와 물을 섞어 만듭니다. 달걀피를 고정시키는 용도이므로 밀가루의 점성이 느껴지는 정도로 묽게 만들어주면 됩니다.

12. Fold the egg roll wrapper in half, and cut it into two equal pieces.
13. Apply flour paste along the edge of the wrapper.
- Flour paste is made by mixing flour and water. Since it is used to secure the wrapper, make it thin but with enough flour-based viscosity to hold the edges.

14. 팬에 닿은 쪽이 위로 가도록 달걀피를 도마에 놓은 후 **9**를 펼쳐 돌돌 말아줍니다.
- 달걀피가 찢어지지 않을 정도의 힘을 주며 타이트하게 말아줍니다. 너무 헐겁게 말아 빈 공간이 생기지 않도록 주의합니다.
15. 거의 다 말아지면 양옆 달걀피를 안으로 넣고 말아줍니다.

14. Lay each piece on a cutting board with the pan-fried side facing up. Arrange (**9**) evenly in a line along the wrapper, then roll it up.
- Roll it tightly, firm enough not to tear the wrapper, and snug enough to prevent any gaps inside.
15. As you near the end of rolling, fold both sides of the wrapper inward, then finish rolling.

16. 만들고 남은 밀가루 풀, 물감자전분 1큰술, 달걀물 적당량을 섞어 묽은 튀김옷을 만들어 **15**에 펴 발라줍니다. (분량 외)

17. 팬에 식용유를 넣고 185℃까지 온도를 올린 후 **16**을 넣고 튀깁니다.

16. In a mixing bowl, combine the remaining flour paste, 1 tablespoon of settled potato starch, and a small amount of beaten egg to make a thin coating. Spread it over (**15**). (Note: This coating mixture is not listed in the ingredients section.)

17. Heat cooking oil in a pan to 365°F (185°C), then deep-fry (**16**).

18. 노르스름하게 잘 튀겨지면 건져낸 후 한입 크기로 잘라 접시에 담습니다.
- 속재료는 다 익은 것이므로 겉에 묻힌 튀김옷만 익으면 건져냅니다.

18. Once golden brown, remove from the oil, cut into bite-sized pieces, then plate.
- Since the filling is already cooked, remove as soon as the coating is done.

Hong Shao Cod
(Soy-Braised Cod)

가정식
HOME COOKING

홍쇼대구

'홍믄생선(紅燜生鮮)'은 생선을 통째로 조리해 진한 풍미를 끌어내는 중국식 요리인데요. '홍믄'은 간장, 설탕, 향신료를 사용해 붉은빛의 진한 소스로 은근하게 조려내는 방식을 말합니다. 여기에서 소개하는 홍쇼대구는 그 조리법을 응용해, 도톰한 대구살만을 발라내어 만든 생선 요리입니다.

대구살에 밀가루를 묻혀 기름에 노릇하게 지진 후, 진한 맛의 소스와 함께 어우러지면 고소한 향과 함께 입안에서 살살 녹는 부드러움이 살아납니다. 통생선을 쓰지 않아 조리도 간편하고, 살만 즐길 수 있어 누구나 편하게 즐길 수 있는 한 접시입니다.

Hong Men Fish is a Chinese-style dish in which a whole fish is cooked to bring out its inherent richness. *Hong Men* (*hóngmèn*) refers to a braising method where ingredients are gently reduced in a reddish-brown, rich sauce made with soy sauce, sugar, and spices. In this version, *Hong Shao Cod*, the same method is applied using only thick slices of cod fillet.

The cod fillet is coated with flour and pan-fried in oil until golden brown, then gently simmered in the savory sauce, where it develops a melt-in-your-mouth texture and a subtle nutty aroma. By using fillets instead of a whole fish, the dish is easy to prepare and enjoyable for everyone.

Ingredients

2접시 분량

Makes 2 plates

배추	큰 잎 3장		3	napa cabbage leaves (large)
표고버섯	3개		3	shiitake mushrooms
죽순	1/4개		1/4	bamboo shoot
청피망	1/4개		1/4	green bell pepper
홍피망	1/4개		1/4	red bell pepper
호부추	30g		30 g	Chinese chives
대구살	500g		500 g	cod fillets
소흥주	1큰술		1 tbsp	Shaoxing wine
간장	1작은술		1 tsp	soy sauce
중력분	적당량		Q.S.	all-purpose flour
식용유	적당량		Q.S.	cooking oil
파 기름	1큰술		1 tbsp	green onion oil
돼지비계	50g		50 g	pork fat
잘게 썬 대파	10g		10 g	finely chopped green onion
슬라이스한 마늘	5g		5 g	sliced garlic
다진 생강	5g		5 g	minced ginger
간장	2큰술		2 tbsp	soy sauce
소흥주	3큰술		3 tbsp	Shaoxing wine
굴소스 (이금기 프리미엄)	2큰술		2 tbsp	oyster sauce (Lee Kum Kee Premium)
미원	2작은술		2 tsp	Miwon (MSG)
닭육수 또는 물	400ml		400 ml	chicken stock or water
후춧가루	1작은술		1 tsp	ground black pepper
물감자전분 ◆	2큰술		2 tbsp	settled potato starch ◆
참기름	1작은술		1 tsp	sesame oil

◆ 물감자전분은 감자전분을 물에 담근 후 가라앉으면 감자전분만 걸러내 물기를 꼭 짜낸 것을 말합니다.

◆ Settled potato starch refers to the starch that settles at the bottom of a potato starch slurry, which is then strained and squeezed to remove excess moisture.

How to make

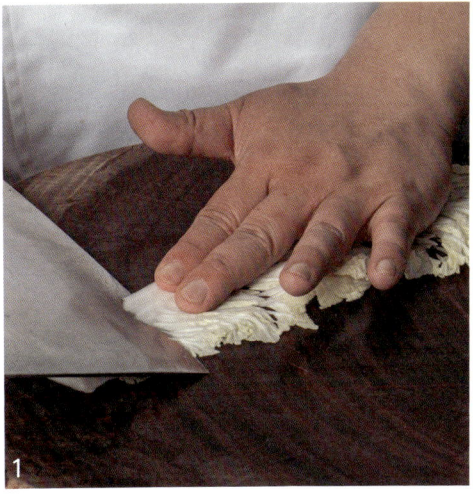  

1. 배추는 이파리를 제거하고 하얀 줄기 부분만 3cm 간격으로 잘라 준비합니다. 표고버섯, 죽순도 같은 크기로 잘라 준비합니다.
2. 청피망, 홍피망은 꼭지와 씨를 제거한 후 3cm 간격으로 잘라 준비합니다.

1. Remove the leafy parts from the napa cabbage, and cut only the white stems into 3 cm pieces. Cut the shiitake mushrooms and bamboo shoot into pieces of the same size.
2. Remove the stems and seeds from the red and green bell peppers, then cut into 3 cm pieces.

3. 호부추는 2cm 간격으로 잘라 준비합니다.
4. 대구살을 두께 약 2cm, 사방 5cm 크기로 편을 떠 준비합니다.
- 가정에서는 대구 필렛을 사용해도 좋습니다.

3. Cut the Chinese chives into 2 cm lengths.
4. Slice the cod fillets into pieces about 2 cm thick, 5 cm wide, and 5 cm long.
- For home cooking, pre-filleted cod can be used.

5. 볼에 **4**와 소흥주 1큰술, 간장 1작은술을 넣고 버무려줍니다.
6. **5**에 중력분을 묻힌 후 손으로 꾹 눌러 준비합니다.
7. 팬에 식용유를 자박하게 두른 후 **6**을 넣고 센불에서 양면을 노릇하게 익혀줍니다.
- 완전히 익히지 않아도 됩니다.

5. In a mixing bowl, combine (**4**) with 1 tablespoon of Shaoxing wine, and 1 teaspoon of soy sauce, then toss gently.
6. Lightly coat (**5**) in all-purpose flour and press firmly by hand.
7. In a pan with an ample amount of cooking oil, add (**6**) and cook over high heat until both sides are golden brown.
- It does not need to be fully cooked at this stage.

8. 다른 팬에 파 기름을 두른 후 돼지비계를 넣고 약불에서 천천히 가열합니다.
- 파 기름은 식용유에 잘게 썬 파를 볶아 향을 우려내 사용합니다.
- 돼지비계는 1cm 간격으로 잘라 사용합니다.
9. 돼지비계가 갈색으로 변하면서 기름이 나오면 잘게 썬 대파, 슬라이스한 마늘, 다진 생강을 넣고 볶으면서 서서히 향을 우려냅니다.
10. 팬 주위에 연기가 올라오면, 간장 2큰술, 소흥주 3큰술, 1을 넣고 센불에서 볶아줍니다.

8. In a separate pan with green onion oil, add the pork fat and slowly heat over low heat.
- To make green onion oil, stir-fry finely chopped green onion in cooking oil until fragrant.
- Cut the pork fat into 1 cm pieces before use.
9. When the pork fat turns brown and renders its oil, add finely chopped green onion, sliced garlic, and minced ginger. Stir-fry to gently infuse the oil with their aromas.
10. Once the pan begins to smoke, add 2 tablespoons of soy sauce, 3 tablespoons of Shaoxing wine, and (**1**), then stir-fry over high heat.

11. 10에 굴소스 2큰술, 미원 2작은술, 닭육수를 넣습니다. 끓어오르면 대구살을 넣고 중불로 줄여 간이 배도록 조려줍니다.
    - 닭육수가 없다면 물로 대체하거나 시판 치킨스톡을 활용합니다.
12. 대구살이 익으면 건져내 접시에 담습니다.

11. Add 2 tablespoons of oyster sauce, 2 teaspoons of Miwon, and chicken stock to (**10**). Once it comes to a boil, add the cod fillets, reduce the heat to medium, and simmer until well seasoned.
    - If chicken stock is unavailable, use water or store-bought chicken stock.
12. Once the cod is cooked, remove and arrange it in a plate.

13. 대구살을 건져내고 남은 소스에 **2**와 **3**을 넣고 한소끔 끓인 후, 후춧가루를 넣고 물감자전분을 넣어 점성이 있게 만듭니다.
14. 참기름을 넣고 섞어줍니다.
15. 대구살이 담긴 접시에 뿌려 마무리합니다.

13. Add (**2**) and (**3**) to the remaining sauce, then bring to a boil. Stir in the black pepper and settled potato starch to slightly thicken the sauce.
14. Add a dash of sesame oil and toss well.
15. Ladle the sauce over the dish.

KIM SEUNGMIN

김승민

도쿄 조리사 전문학교에서 일본 요리를 전공한 뒤, 2000년부터 2002년까지 일본 'Ra Sendai'에서 차장으로 일하며 요리사의 기초를 다졌다. 전통과 절제의 가치를 몸에 익힌 그는, 2010년 서울에 '아루요'를 열고 정갈한 일본 가정식으로 단골들의 신뢰를 얻었다.

2012년, <마스터셰프코리아 시즌 1>에서 우승한 그는 상금으로 제주에 삶의 터전을 마련하고 도시를 떠나기로 결심했다. 자연과 가까운 삶을 택한 그는, 2014년 제주 애월의 숲속에 '모리노아루요'를 열었다. 2024년에는, 넷플릭스 <흑백요리사: 요리 계급 전쟁>에 출연하며 다시 한번 대중의 주목을 받았다.

'모리노아루요'는 오늘도 조용히 제주의 시간에 맞춰 식탁을 차려낸다. '숲 속에 있다'라는 뜻을 지닌 이곳은, 계절의 재료로 차린 단정한 한 끼를 통해 위로와 감동을 전하는 공간이다. 그는 요리를 통해 자연을 이해하고, 사람을 위로하며, 자신만의 방식으로 삶을 기록해나가고 있다.

After majoring in Japanese cuisine at the Tokyo Culinary Institute, Chef Kim Seungmin worked as a sous chef at Ra Sendai in Japan from 2000 to 2002, where he solidified his culinary foundation. Having learned the value of tradition and moderation, he opened Aruyo in Seoul in 2010 and gained the trust of his loyal customers with his refined Japanese home-style cooking.

After winning the first season of MasterChef Korea in 2012, he used his prize money to make a home on Jeju Island and decided to leave the city. Choosing to live close to nature, he opened Morino Aruyo in 2014 in the forest of Aewol, Jeju. In 2024, he appeared in Netflix's *"Culinary Class Wars,"* which brought him back into the public eye.

Morino Aruyo quietly sets the table every day according to the rhythm of Jeju. With the name meaning "exist in the forest," it's a place where a simple meal prepared with seasonal ingredients brings comfort and affection. He uses cooking to understand nature, comfort people, and document life in his own way.

모리노아루요
morino_aruyo

Mackerel Balls

이야기
STORY

고등어 완자

어린 시절부터 우리 집 식탁에 가장 자주 올라온 생선은 단연 고등어였습니다. 저도 좋아했고 가족 모두가 잘 먹는 익숙하고 편안한 음식이었죠. 하지만 중학교 2학년 무렵, 요리사의 꿈을 품기 시작하면서 문득 이런 의문이 들었습니다. '왜 고등어 요리는 늘 구이나 조림뿐일까?' 이 질문은 제게 하나의 숙제로 남았고, 언젠가 요리사가 되면 고등어를 좀 더 다양하고 새로운 방식으로 요리해보고 싶다는 다짐으로 이어졌습니다.

이 책에서 소개하는 요리는 바로 그 다짐에서 시작된 고등어 요리 중 하나입니다. 고등어 살을 곱게 다져 반죽한 후 동그랗게 빚어, 다시마와 미역으로 바다의 향을 살린 국물에 넣고 천천히 익혀낸 국물 요리입니다. 국물에 토마토를 더해 산뜻한 산미를 더한 것도 이 요리의 포인트입니다. 우리에게 너무나도 익숙한 재료인 고등어를 색다른 조리법으로 풀어낸 이 요리가 여러분들에게 새로운 경험이 되기를 바랍니다.

During my childhood, mackerel was the fish most often served at home. I loved it, and my whole family enjoyed this familiar and comforting dish. But in my second year of middle school, as I began dreaming of becoming a chef, I found myself questioning: *Why is mackerel always served either grilled or braised?* That question stayed with me like a piece of unfinished homework and eventually led to a resolution to explore more diverse and creative ways of preparing it once I became a chef.

Mackerel Balls is one of the dishes born from that very resolution. Finely chopped mackerel is formed into balls and gently simmered in a soup infused with kelp and sea mustard, drawing out a subtle marine aroma. A key element is the addition of a tomato, which imparts a bright tartness to the soup. I hope this unexpected take on a familiar fish offers you a refreshing experience.

Ingredients

1그릇 분량
Makes 1 bowl

고등어	1마리		1	mackerel
소금	50g		50 g	salt
된장	15ml		15 ml	doenjang (Korean soybean paste)
마늘	4알		4	garlic cloves
생강	10g		10 g	ginger
대파	1줄기		1	green onion stalk
달걀	1개		1	egg
중력분	50ml		50 ml	all-purpose flour
건미역	10g		10 g	dried sea mustard
건다시마	10g		10 g	dried kelp
토마토	1/2개		1/2	tomato
양조간장	적당량		Q.S.	yangjo-ganjang (naturally brewed soy sauce)
무	적당량		Q.S.	Korean radish
전분	1/2컵		1/2 cup	starch
참나물 줄기	적당량		Q.S.	chamnamul stems

How to make

  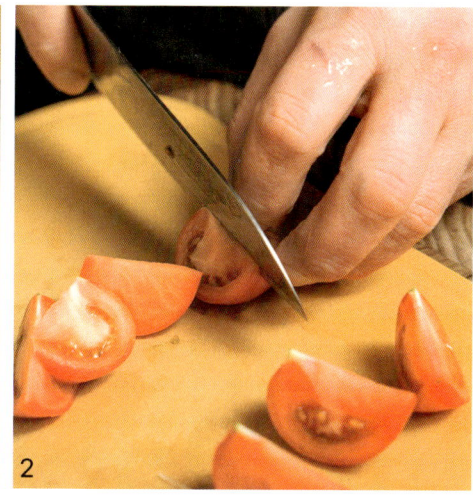

1. 대파 줄기 안쪽은 잘게 다지고, 겉부분은 채 썰어 찬물에 담가둡니다.
2. 토마토는 한입 크기로 썰어둡니다.

1. Finely chop the inner part of the green onion stalk. Thinly slice the outer part and soak it in cold water.
2. Cut the tomato into wedges.

3. 고등어를 3장 뜨기로 손질합니다.
4. 손질한 고등어 앞뒤로 소금을 뿌려 약 15분간 둡니다.
- 계절에 따라 다르지만 고등어에 소금을 뿌린 상태로 15분 정도 두면 삼투압에 의해 수분이 빠지고, 비린내가 제거되며 살에 탄력도 생깁니다.
5. 살을 발라내고 남은 고등어 머리와 뼈는 직화로 굽습니다.
- 토치를 사용해도 되지만 직화로 굽게 되면 고등어의 기름이 불로 떨어지면서 올라오는 직화 특유의 향을 담을 수 있기 때문에 추천합니다.

3. Fillet the mackerel into three pieces.
4. Sprinkle salt over both sides of the mackerel and let it sit for about 15 minutes.
- While the timing may vary depending on the weather, salting mackerel for about 15 minutes draws out moisture through osmosis, reducing unpleasant fishy odors and giving the flesh a springier texture.
5. Grill the head and bones of the mackerel left after filleting over an open flame.
- While a blowtorch works, grilling over an open flame is recommended, as the dripping mackerel oil creates a distinctive smoky aroma.

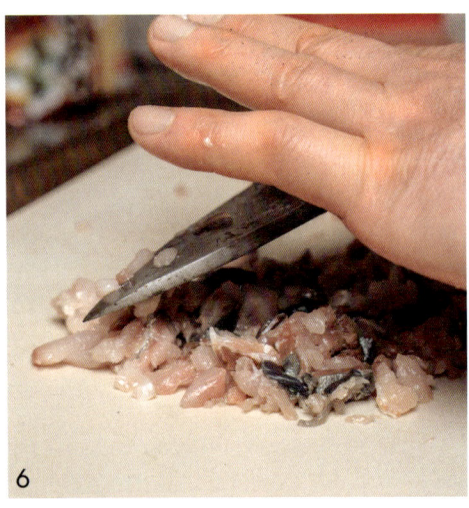  

6. 손질한 고등어를 다집니다.
7. 다진 고등어에 된장, 마늘, 생강을 놓고 잘게 다지며 골고루 섞습니다.
8. 7에 흰자를 넣고 섞습니다.
- 남은 노른자는 20번 과정에서 국물에 풀어 사용합니다.

6. Chop the mackerel flesh into small pieces.
7. Finely chop the garlic, ginger, and doenjang together with the mackerel until evenly combined.
8. Add the egg white to (**7**) and mix well.
- The remaining egg yolk will be added to the soup in (**20**).

9. 중력분을 넣고 치대듯 섞습니다.
10. 다진 대파를 넣고 섞습니다.

9. Add the flour and mix and knead the mixture until well combined.
10. Mix in the chopped green onion.

11. 냄비에 찬물과 건다시마를 넣고 8시간 두어 맑고 깔끔한 국물로 우려냅니다.
12. 직화로 구운 고등어 머리와 뼈, 무를 넣고 가열해 국물을 우려냅니다.

11. Place the kelp in a pot of cold water and let it sit for 8 hours to draw out a clean, clear liquid.
12. Add the grilled mackerel head and bones along with Korean radish, then bring to a boil to make a broth.

13. 건미역은 푸드프로세서를 이용해 곱게 갈아줍니다.

13. Finely grind the dried sea mustard using a food processor.

14. 12가 끓어오르면 곱게 간 건미역을 넣고 불을 끈 후 잠시 둡니다.
- 국물에서 바다의 향을 느낄 수 있도록 하기 위한 작업입니다.
15. 체로 걸러낸 후 다시 가열합니다.

14. Once the broth comes to a boil, add the ground sea mustard. Turn off the heat and let it steep for a while.
- This step helps to infuse the broth with a marine aroma.
15. Strain through a sieve, then bring the broth back to a boil.

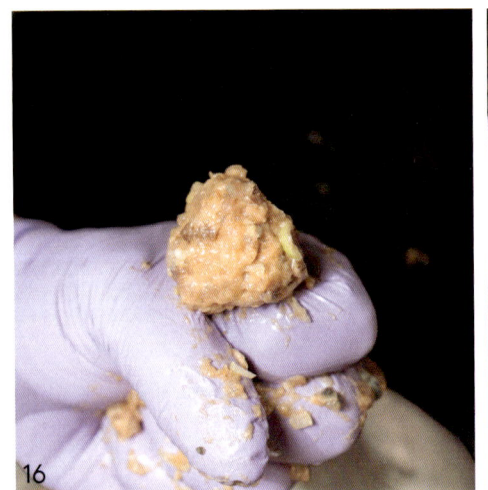  

16. 끓기 시작하면 완자의 모양을 내 넣습니다.
17. 반쯤 익힌 후 건집니다.

16. Once boiling, gently shape the mixture into fish balls and drop them into the broth.
17. When halfway cooked, remove them from the broth.

18. 양조간장, 강판에 간 무, 토마토, 전분 푼 물을 넣고 국물이 약간 걸쭉해지도록 농도를 맞춰줍니다.
- 양조간장은 국물 800ml 기준 약 10ml를 사용합니다. 단, 간장마다 염도나 맛이 다르므로 조금씩 넣어가며 간을 맞춰줍니다.
19. 완자를 넣고 익힙니다.

18. Add the grated radish, tomato, and yangjo-ganjang. Stir in the starch slurry to slightly thicken the broth.
- Season with 10 ml of yangjo-ganjang per 800 ml of broth. Meanwhile, adjust the amount gradually, as the saltiness and flavor may vary depending on the ganjang.
19. Return the half-cooked fish balls to the soup, and continue cooking.

20. 완자가 다 익으면 노른자를 풀어 넣고 불을 끕니다.
- 노른자를 넣으면서 가볍게 섞어줍니다.
21. 접시에 옮겨 담아 썬 파, 참나물 줄기를 올려 마무리합니다.

20. Once fully cooked, stir the beaten egg yolk into the soup, then turn off the heat.
- Gently stir while adding the egg yolk.
21. Transfer to a bowl and garnish with the sliced green onion, and chamnamul stems.

Doubanjiang Karaage

(Doubanjiang Fried Chicken)

가정식
HOME COOKING

두반장 가라아게

'가라아게'는 일본어로 '가라(から, 비어 있음)'와 '아게(あげ, 튀김)'가 합쳐진 말로, 튀김옷 없이 튀긴 요리를 뜻합니다. 물론 실제로는 재료를 그대로 튀길 수 없기 때문에, 보통 전분만 살짝 입혀 바삭하게 튀겨내는 방식으로 조리합니다. 튀김집마다 닭에 밑간을 하는 방법은 다양하지만, 장이나 소금을 사용하는 것이 일반적입니다. 저는 이보다 조금 더 강렬하고 이국적인 맛을 표현하고 싶어 중국식 고추된장인 '두반장'을 사용했습니다. 그래서 한 입 베어무는 순간 짭조름하고 깊은 감칠맛이 입안 가득 퍼져 가라아게에 색다른 매력을 더해줍니다. 이 메뉴는 제가 운영하는 '모리노아루요'에서 실제로 판매되고 있는 인기 메뉴이기도 합니다.

The term *karaage* combines *kara* (から, meaning "empty") and *age* (あげ, meaning "fry"), originally referring to ingredients that are deep-fried without a batter coating. In practice, however, they are typically dusted with a light coating of starch before frying, as moist ingredients do not deep-fry well without a protective layer. Though each tempura restaurant has its own way of seasoning chicken, salt or *jangs* (Korean fermented pastes) are commonly used. For this dish, however, I used doubanjiang (Chinese broad bean paste) to bring a more intense and intriguing flavor. With each bite, the sauce offers a burst of saltiness and deep umami, lending the *karaage* its unique character. It is also one of the popular dishes at our restaurant, Morino Aruyo.

Ingredients

1접시 분량

Makes 1 plate

닭다리살	2덩이	2	chicken legs	
간장	50ml	50 ml	soy sauce	
마늘	2알	2	garlic cloves	
생강	10g	10 g	ginger	
두반장	15ml	15 ml	doubanjiang (Chinese broad bean paste)	
미림	50ml	50 ml	mirin	
정종	50ml	50 ml	sake	
감자전분	4컵	4 cups	potato starch	
식용유	2L	2 L	cooking oil	
파래김가루	적당량	Q.S.	roasted green laver flakes	

How to make

1. 믹서에 간장, 마늘, 생강, 두반장, 미림, 정종을 넣고 갈아줍니다.
2. 닭다리살을 한입 크기로 자릅니다.
3. 2에 1을 담고 최소 2시간 재워둡니다.
- 가능한 하루 전날 작업해 냉장고에 넣어두면 확실한 두반장의 풍미를 느낄 수 있습니다.

1. In a blender, blend the soy sauce, garlic, ginger, doubanjiang, mirin, and sake.
2. Cut the chicken legs into bite-sized pieces.
3. Pour (**1**) over (**2**) and let it marinate for at least 2 hours.
- For deeper flavor from the doubanjiang, let marinate a day in advance and refrigerate, if possible.

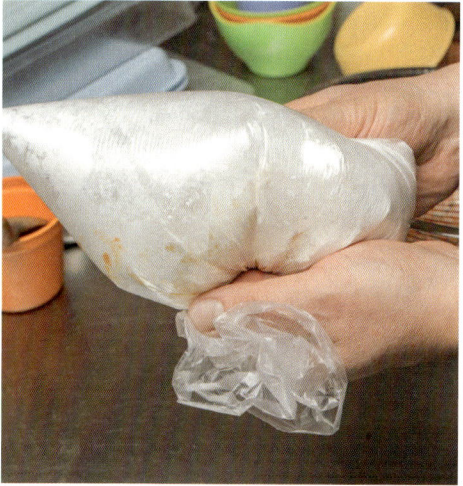

4. 체에 걸러줍니다.
5. 감자전분이 담긴 비닐에 넣고 고르게 묻도록 비닐을 흔들어줍니다.

4. Strain the marinade through a sieve.
5. Place the marinated chicken legs in a plastic bag with the potato starch, and shake until evenly coated.

냉장 전
before refrigeration

냉장 후
after refrigeration

6. 감자전분을 묻힌 닭다리살은 냉장고에서 30분간 둔 후 다시 한 번 전분을 묻혀줍니다.
- 전분을 한 번만 묻혀 튀겨도 되지만 좀 더 바삭한 식감을 위해서는 시간차를 두고 두 번 묻히는 것이 좋습니다.
7. 170°C로 예열된 식용유에서 튀깁니다.

6. Refrigerate the chicken legs for 30 minutes, then coat with potato starch once more.
- While a single coating works, double coating with a resting period creates a crispier texture.
7. Deep-fry in cooking oil preheated to 338°F (170°C).

8. 파래김가루를 뿌려 마무리합니다.

8. Finish with a sprinkle of roasted green laver flakes.

LEE JINGON
이 진 곤

SIM SUNGOH
심 성 오

서울 신당동에 자리한 '시미베'는 소박한 외관과는 달리, 안으로 들어서면 두 셰프의 손길이 담긴 정갈한 요리를 온전히 느낄 수 있는 공간이다. 닮은 듯 서로 다른 감각을 지닌 두 셰프는 같은 주방에서 호흡을 맞추며, 날것의 긴장감과 익숙한 온기를 함께 요리하고 있다.

시미베의 요리는 계절의 흐름을 따라 자연스럽게 구성된다. 사시미는 제철 생선을 중심으로 매일 조금씩 달라지고, 그에 맞춰 항정살 구이나 유부 도로 같은 따뜻한 요리가 곁을 채운다. 메뉴는 많지 않지만, 그날 준비된 재료에 가장 잘 어울리는 방식으로 다듬어 낸다. 오픈 초기부터 이어져 온 대표 메뉴인 '사시미 케이크'는 익숙한 재료를 낯선 방식으로 풀어내는 시미베의 시선을 고스란히 담고 있다.

이진곤 셰프는 주방에서 쌓은 오랜 경험을 바탕으로, 정갈한 손질과 재료 본연의 맛을 살리는 요리를 이어가고 있다. 함께 호흡을 맞추고 있는 심성오 셰프는 언젠가 동네 어귀에서 따뜻한 밥 한 끼를 나눌 수 있는, 정이 넘치는 식당을 여는 것을 꿈꾼다. 지금의 시미베는 그 마음을 조금 앞당겨 보여주는 공간이다.

시미베는 많은 말보다 요리로 감정을 전하는 곳이다. 이곳에서 두 셰프는 오늘도 자신들의 방식으로 하루를 요리하고, 기억에 남는 한 끼를 조용히 차려낸다.

Simibe, located in Sindang-dong, Seoul, has an unassuming, simple exterior, but once you step inside, you can fully appreciate the refined cuisine of the two chefs. The two chefs, with similar yet distinct sensibilities, work together in the same kitchen, cooking side by side with raw tension and familiar warmth.

Simibe offers cuisine that is composed naturally with the flow of the seasons. The sashimi varies slightly from day to day, centered around seasonal fish, and is accompanied by warm dishes such as grilled pork shoulder or yubu-toro. The menu isn't extensive, but it's prepared to what works best with what's available that day. The sashimi cake, a signature dish that has been on the menu since the restaurant's inception, epitomizes Simibe's knack for taking familiar ingredients and presenting them in innovative ways.

With his years of experience in the kitchen, Chef Lee Jingon continues to cook with a focus on cleanliness and bringing out the natural flavors of the ingredients. He and Chef Sim Sungoh dream of one day opening a restaurant where people can share a warm meal at the entrance of a neighborhood. For now, Simibe is a space that brings that dream a little closer to reality.

Simibe is a place where emotions are conveyed through food rather than words. Here, the two chefs work their way through the day, and quietly prepare a memorable meal.

시미베
simibe__

jingon1221
simsungoh__

심성오
SIM SUNGOH

Blue-Backed Fish Sashimi with Romesco

등푸른 생선 사시미와 로메스코 소스

이야기
STORY

등푸른 생선을 활용한 새로운 요리를 고민하던 중, 평소 즐겨 먹던 멕시칸 타코에서 아이디어를 얻어 탄생한 메뉴입니다. 타코에 자주 쓰이는 로메스코 소스를 접목해, 익숙하면서도 전혀 다른 방식으로 등푸른 생선 사시미를 즐길 수 있도록 구성해보았습니다.

로메스코 소스는 견과류의 고소함, 식초의 산미, 훈제 파프리카의 깊은 풍미가 어우러진 소스로, 등푸른 생선 특유의 비릿함을 부드럽게 눌러줄 뿐만 아니라 고등어나 전갱이, 정어리처럼 기름진 생선과도 특히 좋은 궁합을 이룹니다. 사시미에 은은한 훈연 향을 더하면, 생선의 풍미가 입체적으로 살아나 훨씬 복합적인 맛을 경험하실 수 있습니다.

While exploring new dishes featuring blue-backed fish, I got the idea from one of my favorite dishes—Mexican tacos. This dish combines romesco, a sauce often used in tacos, with blue-backed sashimi, offering a familiar yet unexpected way to enjoy it.

Balanced with savory nuts, tangy vinegar, and the deep, smoky flavor of roasted bell peppers, the romesco not only softens the fishy notes typical of blue-backed fish but also pairs exceptionally well with oily varieties like mackerel, horse mackerel, and sardine. A subtle touch of smoke enriches the sashimi's flavor profile, bringing out deeper layers and greater complexity.

Ingredients

3인 분량

Serves 3

횟감용 고등어	1마리

로메스코 소스

적색 파프리카	3개
소금	22g
설탕	70g
화이트와인 비네거	110ml
아몬드	50g
엑스트라버진 올리브오일	30ml
훈제 파프리카 파우더	적당량
건조 아르볼 칠리	적당량

장식

허브	적당량
엑스트라버진 올리브오일	적당량

1	sashimi-grade mackerel

ROMESCO

3	red bell peppers
22 g	salt
70 g	sugar
110 ml	white wine vinegar
50 g	almonds
30 ml	extra virgin olive oil
Q.S.	smoked paprika powder
Q.S.	dried chile de árbol (dried Mexican chilies)

GARNISHES

Q.S.	fresh herbs
Q.S.	extra virgin olive oil

How to make

1. 파프리카는 직화로 겉면을 완전히 태운 후 얼음물에 식혀줍니다.
2. 숟가락을 이용해 겉면의 탄 부분을 제거합니다.

1. Char the skin of the red bell peppers completely using a blowtorch, then transfer them to ice water to cool.
2. Scrape off the charred skin with a spoon.

3. 파프리가의 꼭지와 심지, 안쪽의 하얀 부분을 제거한 후 큼직하게 잘라줍니다.
4. 믹서기에 3과 나머지 소스 재료를 모두 넣고 곱게 갈아줍니다.
- 건조 아르볼 칠리를 넣을 경우 씨를 제거하고 따뜻한 물에 미리 불려 사용합니다. 없는 경우 생략해도 좋습니다.

3. Remove the stem, core, and inner white membrane, then roughly chop into pieces.
4. Combine (**3**) with the remaining romesco ingredients in a blender and blend until smooth.
- If using dried chile de árbol, remove the seeds and soak in warm water before use. If unavailable, it can be omitted.

5. 완성된 소스는 냉장고에 두고 차갑게 식혀줍니다.
6. 횟감으로 사용할 등푸른 생선을 손질합니다.
- 여기에서는 고등어를 사용했습니다. 훈제향을 입힌 시메사바를 사용하면 더 복합적인 맛을 느낄 수 있습니다.

5. Chill the romesco in the refrigerator.
6. Thinly slice the fillet of sashimi-grade blue-backed fish.
- This recipe uses mackerel. Smoked *shime-saba* (Japanese cured mackerel) offers a more complex flavor.

7. 접시에 소스를 담고 펼쳐줍니다.
8. 준비한 사시미를 올려줍니다.
9. 허브를 올리고 올리브오일을 뿌려 마무리합니다.

7. Spoon the romesco onto a plate and spread it evenly.
8. Arrange the sliced sashimi over the romesco.
9. Top with fresh herbs and a drizzle of olive oil.

심성오
SIM SUNGOH

가정식
HOME COOKING

Soy-Braised Tai Kama

(Japanese Soy-Braised Snapper Collar)

도미 턱살을 이용한 일본식 간장 조림

흰살생선은 담백하고 부드러운 맛이 매력적이지만, 우리나라 가정식에서는 의외로 자주 활용되지 않는 재료입니다. 이번에 소개하는 레시피는 그런 흰살생선을 조금 더 가깝게 느낄 수 있도록, 집에서도 간편하게 따라 할 수 있는 일본식 간장 조림 요리입니다.

조리법은 어렵지 않지만, 간장과 청주, 생강 등이 어우러져 깊고 풍부한 맛이 살아 있는 것이 특징입니다. 익숙한 재료로 색다른 방식의 조림을 경험할 수 있어, 일본식 가정 요리를 처음 접하는 분들도 편하게 즐기실 수 있습니다.

Although white-fleshed fish has an appealing clean flavor and tender texture, it's surprisingly rarely used in Korean home cooking. To make it feel more approachable, the fish is prepared using a Japanese-style soy braise that is simple enough to try even at home.

Despite its straightforward method, the dish delivers a deep, rich flavor from the harmonious blend of soy sauce, cheongju, and ginger. With an unexpected twist on familiar ingredients, it is enjoyable even for those new to Japanese-style home cooking.

Ingredients

2인 분량
Serves 2

흰살생선	1마리
생강	적당량
꽈리고추	2개
무	4조각
표고버섯	1개
당근	2조각
청경채	약간

조림용 소스

물	400ml
설탕	40g
미림	40ml
정종	40ml
기꼬만 간장	50ml
타마리 간장	1큰술

장식

채 썬 생강	적당량

1	white-fleshed fish
Q.S.	ginger
2	shishito peppers
4 quarter slices	Korean radish
1	shiitake mushroom
2	round slices carrot
Q.S.	bok choy

SAUCE FOR BRAISING

400 ml	water
40 g	sugar
40 ml	mirin
40 ml	sake
50 ml	Kikkoman soy sauce
1 tbsp	Tamari soy sauce

GARNISH

Q.S.	sliced ginger

How to make

1. 채소를 준비합니다. 생강, 무, 당근은 적당한 크기로 자르고, 청경채는 데친 후 물기를 꼭 짜 준비합니다.
2. 냄비에 손질한 흰살생선, 간장을 제외한 소스 재료를 모두 넣고 가열합니다.
- 여기에서는 도미 턱살을 사용했습니다. 생선은 내장을 제거하고 깨끗이 닦아 사용합니다.
3. 끓기 시작하면 중간중간 거품을 걷어내 불순물을 제거합니다.

1. Prepare the vegetables. Cut the Korean radish, carrot, and ginger into moderately sized pieces. Blanch the bok choy and squeeze out any excess water.
2. In a pot, combine the white-fleshed fish with all the sauce ingredients, except for the soy sauce, and bring to a boil.
- This recipe uses snapper collar. If using a whole fish, remove the innards and rinse thoroughly before use.
3. Once it comes to a boil, skim off any scum or impurities as needed.

4. 3에 기꼬만 간장과 타마리 간장, 무, 당근, 생강을 넣고 중불로 가열합니다.
- 너무 강하게 끓이면 생선이 익기 전에 국물이 너무 졸아들 수 있으니 불 조절을 해주며 끓여줍니다. 타마리 간장이 없는 경우 생략해도 좋습니다.

4. Add the Kikkoman and Tamari soy sauces, along with the radish, carrot, and ginger to (**3**). Cook over medium heat.
- Adjust the heat carefully. If it's too high, the cooking liquid may reduce too much before the fish is cooked. Tamari soy sauce may be omitted if unavailable.

5. 국물이 반 정도 졸아들면 표고버섯 꽈리고추를 넣어 완전히 졸여 줍니다.
- 태국 고추를 넣어 함께 조리면 매운맛도 같이 느낄 수 있습니다.
6. 국물이 졸아들면 접시에 생선을 담아줍니다.
7. 익힌 무와 채소, 데친 청경채, 잘게 썬 생강을 담아 완성합니다.

5. Once the liquid is reduced by half, add the shiitake mushroom and shishito peppers. Simmer until the liquid is fully reduced.
- For a spicy flavor, add Thai chili peppers and let them reduce together.
6. When the liquid has reduced, arrange the fish on a plate.
7. Serve with the reduced radish, blanched bok choy, and shredded ginger.

이진곤
LEE JINGON

Sashimi Cake

사시미 케이크

STORY
이야기

시미베의 시그니처메뉴인 '사시미 케이크'는 오이와 박고지를 넣어 만든 김초밥 위에 신선한 제철 사시미를 가득 올린 메뉴입니다. 원래 '야마모리 스시(やまもり すし, 고봉으로 담은 스시)'라는 이름으로 시작했다가 동업자의 지인이 사시미 케이크라고 부르는 것을 듣고 그때부터 사시미 케이크라는 이름으로 자리잡게 된 메뉴죠.

종종 가게에 오신 손님들이나 방송국 관계자 분들이 제게 '셰프님은 왜 요리를 하세요?'라고 물어보실 때마다 저는 늘 '손님들께 맛있는 요리를 만들어 드리면 기분 좋은 선물을 드리는 것 같아 행복하거든요.'라고 말해 왔습니다. 손님들이 우리 가게를 찾아주신 소중한 날 정성을 다해 대접하듯, 늘 그렇게 요리하고 싶은 마음을 담아 만드는 요리입니다.

Sashimi Cake, a signature dish at Simibe, features nori rolls filled with gourd and cucumber, and generously topped with a mound of fresh seasonal sashimi. Its original name was *yamamori sushi* (やまもり すし, meaning "sushi piled high like a mountain"). One of my business partner's friends once called to it a "sashimi cake," and the name eventually became official.

Whenever guests at the restaurant or members of a broadcast crew ask why I cook, I always say, "Making delicious food makes me happy, because it's like giving someone a joyful gift." This dish reflects my desire to cook with the same sincerity as when welcoming guests on their most special occasions.

Ingredients

2인 분량

Serves 2

사시미

참치	50g
도미	40g
광어	50g
방어	60g
가리비 관자	2알

초대리*

적식초 (코하쿠)	180ml
소금	30g
설탕	30g

▸ 볼에 모든 재료를 넣고 소금 설탕이 녹을 때까지 저어 사용합니다.

박고지*

박고지	25g
물	80ml
설탕	25g
간장	25g
미림	13ml

김 초밥

사조 골드 김	1장
흰쌀밥	130g
초대리*	20ml
오이	15g
박고지*	25g

장식

쪽파	10g
와사비	적당량

SASHIMI

50 g	tuna
40 g	snapper
50 g	halibut
60 g	yellowtail
2	scallops

SUSHI VINEGAR*

180 ml	red vinegar (Kohaku)
30 g	salt
30 g	sugar

▸ In a mixing bowl, combine all the ingredients and stir until the salt and sugar dissolve.

BRAISED GOURD SHAVINGS*

25 g	dried gourd shavings
80 ml	water
25 g	sugar
25 g	soy sauce
13 ml	mirin

NORI ROLLS (seaweed-wrapped sushi)

1	roasted seaweed sheet (Sajo Gold roasted laver)
130 g	plain white rice
20 ml	sushi vinegar*
15 g	cucumber
25 g	braised gourd shavings*

GARNISHES

10 g	Korean scallions
Q.S	wasabi

How to make

 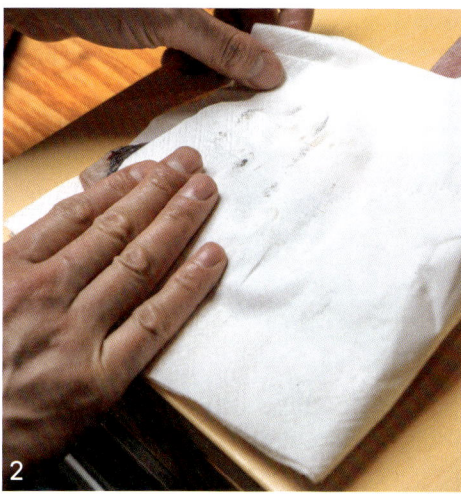 

1. 생선 필렛을 준비합니다.
2. 키친타월을 이용해 생선의 물기를 제거합니다.
3. 한입 크기로 도톰하게 썰어줍니다.

1. Prepare the sashimi fillets.
2. Pat them dry with a kitchen towel to remove any excess moisture.
3. Slice into moderately thick, bite-sized pieces.

4. 냄비에 박고지, 물, 설탕, 간장, 미림을 넣고 약불에서 간장이 거의 없어질 때까지 조려줍니다.
5. 오이는 가운데 심을 제거한 후 길게 채 썰어줍니다.

4. In a pot, combine the dried gourd shavings, water, sugar, soy sauce, and mirin. Simmer over low heat until the liquid is almost completely reduced.
5. Core the cucumber, and thinly slice it into long strips.

6. 흰 쌀밥에 초대리를 섞어 김초밥용 밥을 만듭니다.
- 밥이 뜨거울 때 비비고, 비비고 나서는 부채로 한숨 식혀 줍니다.
7. 김을 반으로 자릅니다.

6. Mix the sushi vinegar into the plain white rice to make sushi rice for nori rolls.
- While the rice is still hot, mix in the vinegar, then gently fan the rice to cool.
7. Cut the roasted seaweed sheet in half.

8. 김발에 김을 놓고 김초밥용 밥 65g, 오이 15g을 올린 후 말아줍니다.
　　 동일한 방법으로 김발에 김을 놓고 김초밥용 밥 65g, 박고지 25g을 올린 후 말아줍니다.

8. Place a half sheet of roasted seaweed on a sushi rolling mat. Evenly spread 65 g of the sushi rice over the seaweed, top with 15 g of cucumber trips, then roll tightly. Repeat with another half sheet, this time topping the rice with 25 g of braised gourd shavings instead of cucumber, then roll in the same way.

9. 두 가지 김초밥을 8등분으로 자른 후 접시에 담습니다.
10. 손질한 생선을 쌓습니다.

9. Cut each nori roll into eight pieces and arrange both types on a plate.
10. Mound the sashimi on top of the rolls.

11. 완성된 사시미 케이크 한쪽에는 와사비를, 위에는 쪽파를 뿌리고 픽을 꽂아 마무리합니다.

11. Serve with wasabi on the side of the sashimi cake. Garnish with chopped Korean scallions and a cake pick.

Miso Chicken

이진곤
LEE JINGON

가정식
HOME COOKING

미소 치킨

'미소 치킨'은 서울에 처음 올라왔을 때 일하던 '카이싱(かいしん, 혁신)'이라는 이자카야에서 판매했던 인기 메뉴입니다. 이 메뉴의 포인트는 소스에 있는데요. 미소 된장에 마늘, 설탕, 미림을 섞어 만든 미소 소스는 여러 요리에 두루두루 사용하기에 좋은 감칠맛 가득한 만능 소스입니다. 이 요리처럼 닭고기와도 잘 어울리지만 돼지고기나 소고기에 사용해도 참 잘 어울려 다양한 요리에 활용하기 좋습니다. 특히 쇼가야끼(しょうがやき, 일본식 돼지고기 요리)처럼 돼지고기 목살에 양념으로 사용해 살짝 볶아 생강과 함께 곁들이거나, 차돌박이에 양념해 구워 먹는 것을 추천합니다.

Miso Chicken was a standout dish at Kaishin (かいしん, meaning "innovation"), the izakaya where I worked after first moving to Seoul. The key to this dish is the umami-rich sauce made from miso, garlic, sugar, and mirin—a blend that works beautifully across a variety of dishes. This versatile sauce pairs well not only with chicken, as in this recipe, but also with pork or beef—especially thinly sliced beef brisket or pork shoulder, as in *shogayaki* (しょうがやき), a Japanese-style pork dish served with ginger.

Ingredients

1인 분량

Serves 1

미소 소스

미소 된장 (마루산 아와세)	100g
마늘	20g
설탕	50g
미림	50ml
양파	1/2개
쪽파	10g
닭다리살	200g
소금	두 꼬집
후춧가루	적당량
식용유	적당량

장식

채 썬 쪽파	적당량

MISO SAUCE

100 g	miso (Marusan Awase)
20 g	garlic
50 g	sugar
50 ml	mirin
1/2	onion
10 g	Korean scallion
200 g	chicken legs
2 pinches	salt
Q.S.	ground black pepper
Q.S.	cooking oil

GARNISH

Q.S	sliced Korean scallion

How to make

1. 믹서기에 미소 된장, 마늘, 설탕, 미림을 넣고 갈아 미소 소스를 만듭니다.
2. 양파 반 개를 얇게 썰어서 물에 20분 정도 담가 매운맛을 빼고 쪽파는 얇게 썰어 준비합니다.

1. In a blender, combine the miso, garlic, sugar, and mirin. Blend until smooth to make the miso sauce.
2. Thinly slice half of the onion and soak it in water for about 20 minutes to remove its sharp flavor. Thinly slice the Korean scallion and set aside.

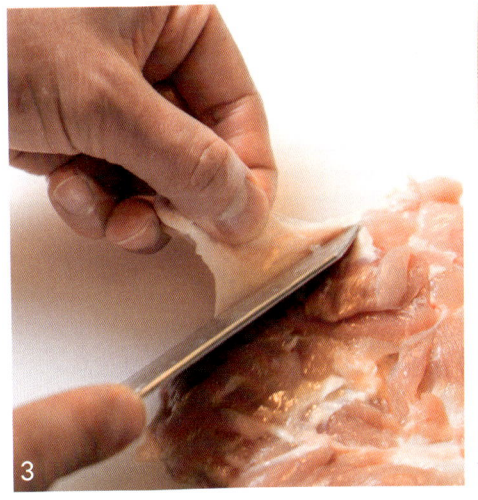
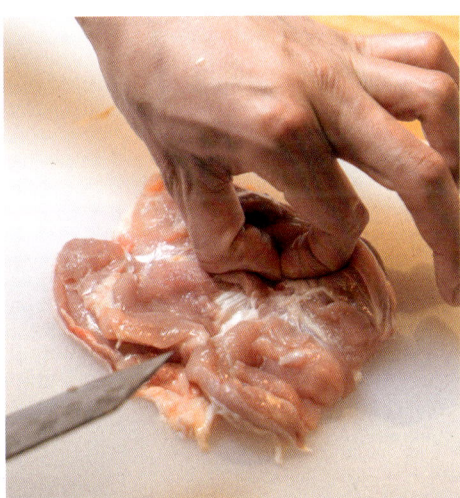

3. 닭다리살을 손질합니다. 지방이 있는 부분을 제거하고, 남아 있는 뼈를 제거합니다.

3. Trim the chicken legs by removing any excess fat and any remaining bones.

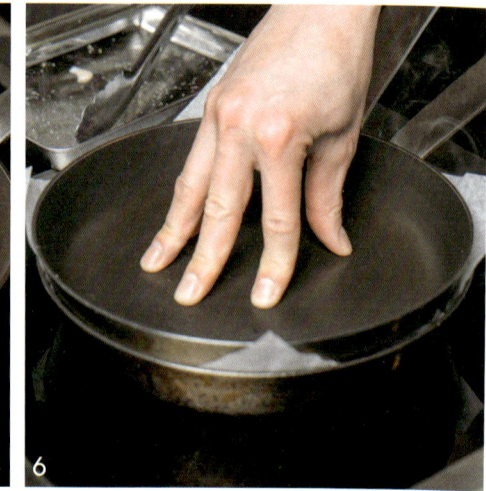

4. 손질한 닭다리살에 소금과 후춧가루로 밑간을 합니다.
5. 식용유를 두른 팬에 닭 다리 살을 올리고 구워줍니다.
6. 닭다리살 위에 기름종이를 올리고 프라이팬이나 무게가 있는 도구를 올려 닭이 평평하게 익을 수 있도록 합니다.

4. Season the chicken legs with salt and black pepper.
5. Pan-fry the seasoned chicken legs in cooking oil.
6. Cover the chicken with a sheet of parchment paper and press down using another pan or a heavy object to ensure even cooking.

7. 닭을 중간중간 뒤집어가며 익힙니다.
8. 80% 정도로 익으면 도마로 옮겨 한입 크기로 자릅니다.

7. Cook the chicken legs, flipping occasionally.
8. When they are about 80% cooked, transfer them to a cutting board and cut into bite-sized pieces.

9. 다시 팬으로 옮겨 미소 소스 30g을 넣고 간이 밸 때까지 볶아줍니다.

9. Return the chicken pieces to the pan, add 30 g of miso sauce, and stir-fry until evenly coated and well seasoned.

10. 물기를 제거한 양파를 접시에 옮겨 닮습니다.
11. 양파 위에 닭을 올립니다.
12. 채 썬 쪽파를 올려 마무리합니다.

10. Drain the onion and arrangeit on a plate.
11. Place the chicken on top of the onion.
12. Garnish with the sliced scallion.

JANG HOJOON

장호준

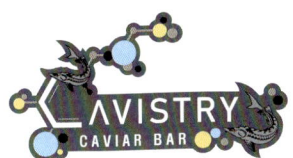

통영에서 태어나고 자란 그는 한때 미용에 흥미를 두기도 했지만, 일식 특유의 정교하고 아름다운 구성에 매료되며 요리사의 길을 선택하게 되었다. 대학에서 호텔조리를 전공하고, 국내 유수의 특급호텔에서 일식 셰프로 경력을 쌓으며 기술과 감각을 다져나갔다.

2015년, 첫 레스토랑 '네기이자카야'를 오픈하며 본격적인 외식업 경영에 뛰어든 그는, 이후 '네기라이브', '모던오뎅', '캐비스트리' 등 기존의 일식 레스토랑과 차별화된 콘셉트를 연이어 선보이며 자신만의 브랜드 세계를 구축해왔다.

그의 요리는 일본 요리를 기반으로 하되, 한식과 중식, 양식의 요소를 유연하게 녹여내는 것이 특징이다. 그는 미각뿐만 아니라 음식의 시각적 완성도를 중시하며, 하나의 접시를 구성하는 그릇, 도구, 플레이팅까지도 '경험'의 일부로 디자인한다.

2024년에는 넷플릭스 요리 서바이벌 프로그램 <흑백요리사: 요리 계급 전쟁>에 출연해, 탄탄한 기술력과 자신감 있는 퍼포먼스로 '일식 끝판왕'이라는 별칭을 얻으며 대중의 주목을 받았다.

요리사이자 경영자, 그리고 브랜드를 만들어가는 사람으로서, 그는 이제 한국을 넘어 동남아를 비롯한 해외에서 한식의 새로운 가능성을 펼쳐 보이려 한다. 익숙하지 않은 문화 속에서도 자신만의 방식으로 한식을 풀어내며, 더 많은 이들과 그 맛을 나누고자 한다.

네기스키야키
◎ negi_sukiyaki_

네기라이브
◎ negi_live

모던오뎅
MODERN ODEN

캐비스트리
◎ cavistry_dining

◎ janghojoon8

Born and raised in Tongyeong, he was once interested in hairdressing, but the elaborate and beautiful composition of Japanese food fascinated him, and he chose to become a chef. He majored in hotel culinary arts at university and worked as a Japanese chef at a leading luxury hotel in Korea, where he honed his skills and refined his sensibilities.

In 2015, he opened his first restaurant, Negi Izakaya. Since then, he has been building his own brand by introducing a series of concepts that are differentiated from traditional Japanese restaurants, including Negi Live, Modern Oden, and Cavistry.

His dishes are based on Japanese cuisine but incorporate elements of Korean, Chinese, and Western cuisine in a flexible manner. He emphasizes the visual completeness of the food as well as the taste. And even the plates, utensils, and plating food that make up a dish are designed as part of the 'experience.'

In 2024, he appeared in Netflix's culinary survival show "*Culinary Class Wars*," where his solid technical skills and confident performances earned him the nickname "King of Japanese cuisine" and brought him to the public's attention.

As a chef, entrepreneur, and brand builder, he is now looking beyond Korea to open up new possibilities for Korean cuisine in Southeast Asia and beyond. He wants to share the flavors of Korean food with a wider audience by creating his own interpretation of Korean food in unfamiliar cultures.

Kuro Damanegi
(Black Onion)

쿠로 다마네기
(くろ たまねぎ)

이야기
STORY

'검은 양파'라는 뜻의 쿠로(くろ, 검은) 다마네기(たまねぎ, 양파). 이자카야 '네기'를 처음 오픈했을 때 시그니처메뉴를 생각하다가 고안하게 된 메뉴입니다. '네기'는 '파'를 의미하는데 '다마네기'는 '동그란 구 모양의 파'라는 의미여서 양파를 선택했고, 여기에 나만의 색깔을 넣을 수 있는 흔하지 않은 방법을 고민하다가 검게 그을린 양파와 된장과 크림을 활용한 소스로 완성했습니다. 덕분에 매장을 방문하는 손님들은 누구나 필수로 주문하는 인기 메뉴이자 시그니처메뉴로 자리 잡았습니다. 작년에 참여했던 요리 경연 프로그램에서도 선보였는데, 그로 인해 네기를 몰랐던 분들에게까지 알리는 계기가 된 뜻깊은 메뉴이기도 합니다.

Kuro Damanegi (くろたまねぎ, meaning "black onion") originated while I was brainstorming a signature dish during the launch of izakaya Negi. With *negi* meaning "green onion" and *damanegi* referring to "a round-shaped green onion," I decided to work with an onion as the main ingredient. To add my own touch, I explored unconventional methods and ultimately charred the onion until it turned black, pairing it with a doenjang-based cream sauce. The dish became a must-try among guests and was recognized as our signature dish. Last year, it was also featured on a culinary survival show, offering a meaningful opportunity to introduce izakaya Negi to a wider audience.

Ingredients

1인 분량
Serves 1

양파	1개 (약 250~300g)
대파	1줄기
감자전분	적당량
식용유	적당량

된장 크림 소스 (양파 약 15개 분량)

니키리 미림◆	120g
니키리 사케 또는 청주◆	50g
물	300g
몽고된장	400g
달걀 (특란 크기)	8개
생크림	500g
설탕	90g
가쓰오부시 가루	12g

◆ '니키리'는 알코올을 날려주는 것을 의미합니다. 미림과 사케는 냄비에서 끓여 알코올을 날린 후 사용합니다.

1	onion (about 250 to 300 g)
1	green onion stalk
Q.S.	potato starch
Q.S.	cooking oil

DOENJANG CREAM SAUCE
(for 15 onions)

120 g	*nikiri* mirin ◆
50 g	*nikiri* sake (or cheongju) ◆
300 g	water
400 g	Monggo doenjang (Korean soybean paste)
8	eggs (extra-large size, 60 to 68 g each)
500 g	fresh cream
90 g	sugar
12 g	kastuobushi powder (dried bonito powder)

◆ *Nikiri* refers to gently boiling to evaporate the alcohol. Boil the mirin and sake in a pot to remove the alcohol before use.

How to make

1. 양파는 겉껍질을 벗기고 190°C로 예열된 오븐에서 50분간 구워줍니다.
2. 대파는 얇게 채 썰어 찬물에 헹군 후 채소 탈수기를 이용해 물기를 제거합니다.

1. Peel the onion and roast it in an oven preheated to 374°F (190°C) for 50 minutes.
2. Thinly slice the green onion, rinse under cold water, and drain using a salad spinner.

3. 2의 2/3 분량을 덜어 감자전분을 살짝만 뿌려 묻혀줍니다.
- 남긴 대파는 고명으로 사용합니다.
4. 160°C로 예열된 기름에서 노릇해질 때까지 튀깁니다.
5. 미림과 사케는 가열해 알코올을 날려줍니다.

3. Transfer two-thirds of (2) to a mixing bowl and lightly coat with potato starch.
- Reserve the remaining green onion for garnish.
4. Deep-fry the green onion in oil preheated to 320°F (160°C) until golden.
5. Gently boil the mirin and sake to evaporate the alcohol.

6. 볼에 물과 몽고된장을 넣고 휘퍼로 풀어준 후 체에 걸러줍니다.
7. 다른 볼에 달걀과 생크림을 넣고 휘퍼로 풀어줍니다.

6. In a mixing bowl, whisk the doenjang and water, then strain through a sieve.
7. In a separate mixing bowl, whisk the eggs and fresh cream.

8. 7을 체에 걸러 6에 넣어줍니다.
9. 8에 5와 설탕을 넣고 약불에서 휘퍼로 잘 섞어가며 가열합니다.
10. 어느 정도 농도가 나면 가쓰오부시 가루를 넣고 가열합니다.

8. Strain (**7**) through a sieve and add it to (**6**).
9. Add (**5**) and sugar to (**8**), then simmer over low heat, whisking continuously until well combined.
10. Once it reaches the desired consistency, add the kastuobushi powder and continue simmering.

  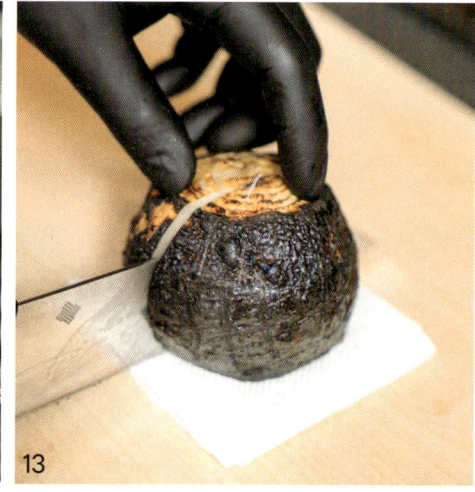

11. 가쓰오부시의 맛과 향이 우러나면 불에서 내리고 블렌더로 곱게 갈아줍니다.
12. 1의 양파를 숯불 또는 토치를 이용해 검게 태워줍니다.
13. 태운 양파를 접시에 담고 열십자로 칼집을 냅니다.

11. When the kastuobushi has released its aroma and flavor, remove from the heat and blend until smooth with a hand mixer.
12. Char the roasted onion from (**1**) with a blowtorch or charcoal until blackened.
13. Place the charred onion on a plate and deeply score a cross.

14. 칼집을 낸 부분을 벌려 채 썬 대파를 넣습니다.
15. 된장 크림 소스를 넉넉하게 부어줍니다.
16. 튀긴 대파를 뿌려 완성합니다.
- 살짝 구운 바게트와 함께 곁들여도 좋습니다.

14. Open the scored sections and fill the center with the sliced green onion.
15. Generously spoon the doenjang cream sauce over the dish.
16. Top with the fried green onion.
- Serve with lightly toasted baguette, if desired.

Beef and Green Onion Udon

가정식
HOME COOKING

소고기 대파 우동

매장 이름이 '네기(ねぎ, 파)'이다 보니, 어떻게 하면 대파를 집약적으로 이용할 수 있을까 고민하며 만든 메뉴입니다. 만드는 공정도 어렵지 않아 가정식으로도 추천하는데요, 만약 우동 육수를 만들기 번거롭다면 시중에 쉽게 구할 수 있는 우동 다시 농축액으로 대체해도 좋고, 차돌박이도 얇게 썰린 냉동 삼겹살로 대체해도 좋습니다. 자극적인 맛이 아니라 아이들과도 함께 먹을 수 있는 온 가족 메뉴입니다.

As a nod to the name of our izakaya, Negi (ねぎ, meaning "green onion"), I created this dish while exploring ways to fully showcase the flavor of green onions. Simple and easy to prepare, it makes a great option for home cooking. If making the stock feels too demanding, store-bought concentrated dashi serves as a convenient alternative; If beef brisket is unavailable, thinly sliced frozen pork belly serves as a good substitute. With its mild, comforting flavor, it is perfect for family meals—even for children.

Ingredients

1인 분량
Serves 1

가쓰오 육수*

물	1200g
건다시마	100g
가쓰오부시	150g

우동 육수 비율

가쓰오 육수* 16 : 미림 1 : 우스구치 1

▶ 우동 육수는 필요한 만큼 위의 비율로 만들어 사용한다.

소고기 대파 우동

대파 (굵은 것)	1줄기
차돌박이	120g
소금	적당량
후춧가루	적당량
냉동 우동면 (시판)	1개

장식

간 생강	적당량
산초가루	적당량

KASTUOBUSHI DASHI* (bonito stock)

1200 g	water
100 g	dried kelp
150 g	kastuobushi (dried bonito flakes)

UDON SOUP RATIO

kastuobushi dashi* 16 : mirin 1 : usukuchi shoyu (Japanese light soy sauce) 1

▶ Mix the ingredients in the given ratio to make as much udon soup as needed.

BEEF AND GREEN ONION UDON

1	thick green onion
120 g	thinly sliced beef brisket
Q.S.	salt
Q.S.	ground black pepper
1	frozen udon noodle block (store-bought)

GARNISHES

Q.S.	grated ginger
Q.S.	sansho powder

How to make

1. 냄비에 물, 건다시마를 넣고 약 80°C의 온도에서 30분간 가열합니다.
- 다시마는 마른 행주로 닦아 사용합니다.
2. 불을 끄고 건다시마를 건진 후 가쓰오부시를 넣고 5~7분간 그대로 두고 우려 가쓰오 육수를 완성합니다.

1. In a pot, combine the dried kelp and water, then simmer at 176°F (80°C) for 30 minutes.
- Wipe the dried kelp clean with a dishtowel before use.
2. Turn off the heat, remove the kelp, and add the kastuobushi. Let it steep for 5 to 7 minutes to make the kastuobushi dashi.

  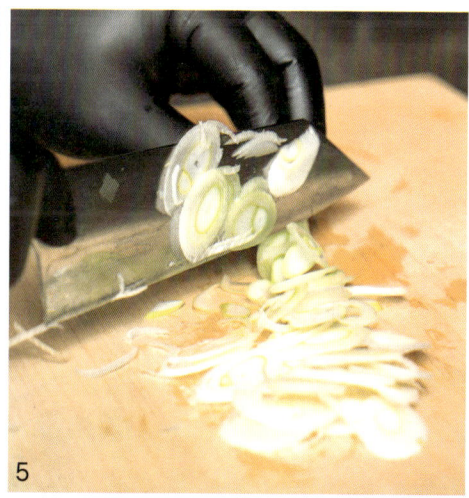

3. 가쓰오 육수를 체에 거릅니다.
4. 냄비에 가쓰오 육수, 미림, 우스구치를 16:1:1 비율로 넣고 한소끔 끓여 우동 육수를 완성합니다.
5. 대파의 초록 부분은 큼직하게 어슷썰고, 흰 부분은 얇게 채 썰어줍니다.

3. Strain the kastuobushi dashi through a sieve.
4. In a separate pot, combine the kastuobushi dashi, mirin, and usukuchi shoyu in a 16:1:1 ratio, then bring to a boil to prepare the udon soup.
5. Slice the green onion: slice the green part on a bias and thinly slice the white part.

6. 달군 팬에 차돌박이를 넣고 볶아 익힙니다.
7. 차돌박이를 볶았던 팬에 어슷썬 대파의 초록 부분을 넣고 익힌 후 소금과 후춧가루로 간을 합니다.
- 대파의 초록 부분이 차돌박이의 기름에 살짝 코팅될 정도로만 센불에서 빠르게 볶은 후 그릇에 옮깁니다.
8. 익힌 대파는 고명으로 남겨둡니다.

6. Stir-fry the thinly sliced beef brisket in a preheated pan.
7. In the same pan, cook only the green part of the green onion, then season with salt and black pepper.
- Pan-fry it over high heat just until lightly coated with the beef fat, then transfer to a separate tray.
8. Set aside for garnish.

9. 끓는 물에 우동면을 넣고 익힙니다.
10. 우동 그릇에 우동면과 우동 육수 500~600ml를 담습니다.

9. Cook the udon noodles in boiling water.
10. Place the noodles in an udon bowl and ladle over 500 to 600 ml of the hot udon soup.

JANG HOJOON

11. 대파의 초록 부분과 흰 부분을 넉넉하게 담고 차돌박이를 올려줍니다.
12. 차돌박이 위에 간 생강을 올려줍니다.
13. 산초가루를 넉넉히 뿌려 완성합니다.

11. Add a generous amount of both the cooked green part and fresh white part of the green onion, along with the beef brisket.
12. Top the beef brisket with grated ginger.
13. Sprinkle generously with sansho powder.

KIM NAKYOUNG

김낙영

실내건축을 전공하고 독일에서 유학 생활을 했다. 요리와는 조금 거리가 있는 삶이었다. 그러다 유럽 여행 중 우연히 마주한 한 접시의 라구 파스타가 삶의 방향을 바꾸었다. 단순한 재료에서 깊은 맛이 나오는 경험, 정성이라는 것이 어떤 식으로 접시에 담길 수 있는지를 처음 깨달은 순간이었다. 그때 처음으로 '이걸 만들고 싶다'는 생각이 들었다.

서른이 넘은 나이에 요리사의 길을 걷기로 결심하고, 이탈리아 I.C.I.F 요리학교에 들어가 정통 이탈리아 요리를 처음부터 배웠다. 생면 파스타, 라구, 치즈, 올리브오일을 숙성과 시간 그 무엇 하나 건너뛰지 않고 직접 손으로 익혔다. 빠르게 요리하는 법보다는 제대로 요리하는 법을 택했다.

그는 요리를 '시간의 결과물'이라 말한다. 숙성된 라구, 손반죽으로 만든 생면, 인위적인 조미료 없이도 충분히 깊은 맛. 재료 본연의 맛을 믿고, 시간이 만들어내는 풍미를 소중히 여긴다.

현재는 서교동에서 카밀로 라자네리아 1호점과 2호점, 그리고 서교난면방을 운영하고 있다. 특히 서교난면방은 그만의 섬세한 해석이 돋보이는 메뉴들로 주목받으며 2025 미쉐린 가이드에 등재되었다.

카밀로 라자네리아
◉ camillo_lasagneria
◉ camillo_lasagneria_italiana

서교난면방
◉ seokyonanmyunbang

◉ camillo_nakyoung_kim

Chef Kim originally studied interior architecture in Germany, keeping a certain distant from the world of cooking. But during a trip through Europe, a single plate of *ragù* pasta became a turning point. Experiencing the depth of flavor drawn from simple ingredients, he realized how sincerity could come through in a dish. It was the first time he ever thought,

In his thirties, he decided to embark on a culinary journey. He enrolled at the Italian Culinary Institute for Foreigners (I.C.I.F), where he learned traditional Italian cooking from the ground up. From fresh pasta to *ragù*, cheese, and olive oil, he studied the craft of aging and timing with his own hands, never skipping a single step. He chose to cook with care rather than haste.

He says cooking is "the result of time." Just like the deep, savory flavor of aged *ragù* and handmade fresh pasta he once tasted, crafted without any artificial MSG. He believes in the natural taste of ingredients and values the flavors nurtured by time.

He now runs three restaurants in Seogyo-dong, including the first and second locations of Camillo Lasagneria, along with Seokyo Nanmyeonbang, which has garnered attention for its dishes that showcase his delicate interpretations and was listed in the 2025 Michelin Guide Seoul & Busan.

Lasagne alla Bolognese

이야기
STORY

라자냐 알라 볼로네제

이탈리아 유학 시절, 라구에 대한 기억은 늘 볼로냐에서 시작됐습니다. 아내가 출장지에서 맛본 한 그릇의 라구 파스타에 대해 이야기해주던 장면은, 내가 요리사의 길을 결심하는 데 큰 영향을 주었습니다. 그리고 볼로냐 근처의 작은 도시 체세나티코에 위치한 레스토랑에서 실습을 하며, 라구라는 요리의 진짜 깊이를 이해하게 됐죠.

라자냐는 말 그대로 시간의 맛을 층층이 쌓아 올린 요리입니다. 고기와 채소, 토마토를 오랜 시간 볶고 끓이며 만든 라구 소스를 생면 사이에 정성스레 얹어 구워냅니다. 그 안엔 그저 고기 소스가 아닌, 제가 볼로냐에서 겪은 시간, 느꼈던 향, 그리고 다짐들이 담겨 있습니다.

친한 요리사인 옥동식 셰프님의 매장을 방문하기 위해 처음 서교동을 찾았을 때, 처음 라자냐를 맛봤던 작은 트라토리아의 공기가 떠올랐습니다. 서교동의 '카밀로 라자네리아'는 그렇게 시작되었습니다. 지금도 이 골목을 지나가면 라구 소스 냄새가 가득합니다. 그 향은 어쩌면, 저를 요리사로 만든 첫 번째 기억일지도 모릅니다.

My memory of *ragù* began in Bologna while I was studying in Italy. It was my wife's story about a bowl of *ragù* pasta she had during her business trip that deeply inspired my decision to pursue a culinary journey. During my apprenticeship at a restaurant in Cesenatico, a small city near Bologna, I came to truly understand the depth of *ragù*.

Lasagna, quite literally, is a dish where the flavor of time is carefully layered. After hours of simmering meat, vegetables, and tomatoes into a rich sauce, the *ragù* is gently nestled between fresh pasta sheets and baked to perfection. What is inside is not mere meat sauce, but the time I lived, the scent I encountered, and the promise I made to myself in Bologna.

When I first visited Seogyo-dong to dine at the restaurant of my close friend, Chef Ok Dong-sik, I was reminded of the air inside the small trattoria where I had my first lasagna. That memory sparked the beginning of Camillo Lasagneria in Seogyo-dong. Even now, this alley is still filled with the scent of *ragù*—perhaps the very first memory that led me to become a chef.

Ingredients

4인 분량
Serves 4

라구 소스*

양파	50g
당근	40g
셀러리	40g
버터	30g
소고기 다짐육 (지방이 없는 부분)	250g
돼지고기 다짐육 (지방이 적당히 있는 부분)	200g
토마토 페이스트 (시리오)	25g
레드와인	100ml
고체 치킨스톡 (스타 다도 델리카토)	1개 (10g)
로즈마리	2줄기
월계수잎	4장
흑후추	10알
타임	4줄기
소금	4g
너트맥가루	적당량

생면*

강력분	200g
중력분	200g
달걀	240g
소금	10g

라자냐

생면* (또는 데체코 건면 라자냐 8장)	400g
라구 소스*	400g
크림치즈 (끼리 또는 필라델피아)	350g
버터	적당량
파르미자노 레자노 치즈	약 150g

장식

이태리파슬리	적당량
엑스트라버진 올리브오일	적당량

RAGÙ*

50 g	onion
40 g	carrot
40 g	celery
30 g	butter
250 g	minced beef (lean)
200 g	minced pork (moderate fatty)
25 g	tomato paste (Cirio)
100 ml	red wine
1	chicken stock cube (Star Dado Delicato)
2	rosemary sprigs
4	bay leaves
10	black peppercorns
4	thyme sprigs
4 g	salt
Q.S.	nutmeg powder

FRESH PASTA*

200 g	bread flour
200 g	all-purpose flour
240 g	whole eggs
10 g	salt

LASAGNA

400 g	fresh pasta* (or 8 De Cecco dried lasagna sheets)
400 g	*ragù**
350 g	cream cheese (Kiri or Philadelphia)
Q.S.	butter
about 150 g	Parmigiano-Reggiano

GARNISHES

Q.S.	Italian parsley
Q.S.	extra virgin olive oil

How to make

라구 소스

1. 양파, 당근, 셀러리를 3mm 정도 큐브로 썰어서 준비합니다.
2. 약 2L 용량의 낮고 넓은 팬에 버터를 넣습니다. 버터가 녹을 때까지 중불을 유지해 줍니다.
3. 중불에서 양파를 볶다가 양파가 투명해지면 당근과 셀러리를 넣고 4~5분간 볶아줍니다.

RAGÙ

1. Dice the onion, carrot, and celery into about 3mm cubes.
2. In a low, wide 2-liter pan, add the butter and heat over medium heat until fully melted.
3. Add the onion and stir-fry over medium heat until translucent. Add the carrot and celery, then continue stir-frying for about 4 to 5 minutes.

4. 강불로 올려 소고기 다짐육, 돼지고기 다짐육을 넣고 덩어리 지지 않게 잘 볶아줍니다.
- 더욱 진한 풍미를 내려면 소고기의 비율을 높여줍니다.
5. 고기 육즙의 수분이 모두 날아가고, 고기가 팬에 살짝 붙는 상태가 되면 토마토 페이스트를 넣고 함께 볶아줍니다.

4. Increase the heat to high, add the minced beef and pork, then stir-fry to prevent the meat from clumping.
- For a richer flavor, increase the proportion of beef to pork.
5. When all the moisture has evaporated from the meat and it begins to stick slightly to the pan, stir in the tomato paste.

6. 골고루 잘 볶아지면 중불로 줄인 후 레드와인을 넣고 알코올이 날아갈 때까지 잘 저어가며 끓여줍니다.
7. 레드와인이 절반으로 졸아들면 약불로 줄인 후 치킨스톡을 넣고 끓여줍니다.
- 좋은 레드와인을 쓸수록 더 깊은 맛이 납니다.
8. 로즈마리, 월계수잎, 흑후추, 타임을 넣은 다시백을 **7**에 넣고 끓여줍니다.

6. Once evenly stir-fried, reduce the heat to medium. Add the red wine and boil while stirring until the alcohol evaporates.
7. When the wine has reduced by half, lower the heat to low, add the chicken stock, and simmer.
- The better the red wine, the deeper the flavor.
8. Add a tea bag filled with bay leaves, black peppercorns, rosemary and thyme sprigs to (**7**), then continue simmering.

9. 2시간 가량 뭉근하게 끓여준 후 소금과 너트맥가루를 넣어 마무리합니다.

9. Let it simmer gently for about 2 hours, and finish with salt and nutmeg powder.

생면 반죽

1. 믹싱볼에 모든 재료를 넣고 날가루와 수분이 보이지 않을 때까지 믹싱합니다.
- 반죽기가 없다면 손으로 반죽해도 좋습니다. 강력분과 중력분은 체에 걸러 사용해주세요.
2. 믹싱볼에서 반죽을 꺼내 덧밀가루(분량 외)를 뿌려가며 손으로 한 번 더 반죽해줍니다.

FRESH PASTA DOUGH

1. In a mixing bowl, combine all the ingredients, then mix until no visible dry flour or moisture remains.
- If a stand mixer is unavailable, knead the dough by hand. Sift the bread flour and all-purpose flour before use.
2. Remove the dough from the mixing bowl and knead it by hand, dusting with extra flour as needed.

3. 반죽이 매끈해지면 타이트하게 랩핑해 실온에서 2시간 휴지시켜줍니다.
4. 제면기 또는 밀대를 이용해 적당한 두께로 반죽을 밀어 폅니다.
5. 사용할 그릇의 크기에 맞춰 반죽을 잘라줍니다.

3. Once the dough is smooth, wrap it tightly and let it rest at room temperature for 2 hours.
4. Roll out the dough to the desired thickness using a pasta machine or rolling pin.
5. Cut the dough sheets to fit the lasagna pan you will use.

라쟈냐

1. 라자냐 면을 약 20초간 삶아 찬물에 식힌 후 물기를 제거합니다.
- 시판 건면을 사용할 경우 설명서에 적힌 시간으로 삶아줍니다.
2. 준비된 라구 소스를 따듯하게 데운 후 크림치즈를 넣고 섞어줍니다.
- 완성된 라구 소스 전량(약 450g) + 크림치즈 350g = 총 800g

LASAGNA

1. Boil the fresh lasagna sheets for about 20 seconds, then soak them in ice water and drain.
- If using store-bought dried lasagna, follow the package instructions for the cooking time.
2. Warm the *ragù*, add the cream cheese, and stir until well combined.
- Entire *ragù* (about 450 g) + cream cheese (350 g) = total 800 g

3. 라자냐 팬에 먼저 버터를 고르게 바릅니다.
4. 라자냐 면을 깔아줍니다.
5. **2**를 160g 넣고 펼쳐줍니다.

3. Evenly butter a lasagna pan.
4. Layer fresh lasagna sheets on the bottom of the pan.
5. Spread 160 g of (**2**) evenly over the sheets.

  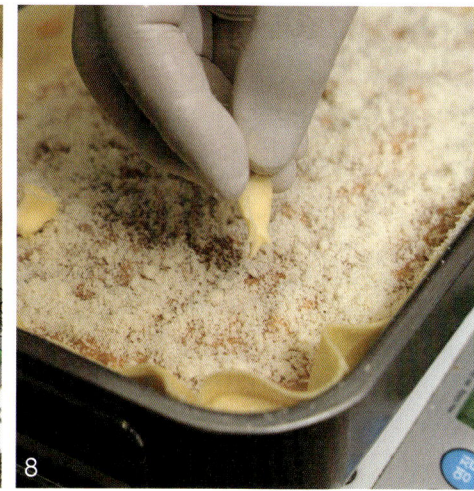

6. 강판에 간 파르미자노 레자노 치즈 20g을 넣고 펼쳐줍니다.
7. 다시 라자냐 면을 깔아줍니다.
8. 5~7 과정을 총 5번 반복한 후 작게 조각 낸 버터 8조각을 군데군데 올려줍니다.

6. Sprinkle 20 g of grated Parmigiano-Reggiano evenly on top.
7. Place another layer of lasagna sheets over the cheese.
8. Repeat steps (5) to (7) five times, and dot the top layer with 8 small pieces of butter.

9. 호일을 덮고 열십자로 칼집을 냅니다. 170°C로 예열된 오븐에 넣고 160°C로 온도를 낮춰 40분간 굽다가 호일을 제거하고 2분간 더 구워줍니다.
 - 바로 드실 경우 그라탕처럼 노릇한 색이 되도록 2분보다 조금 더 구워줍니다. 바로 드시지 않을 경우 잘 식혀 냉장(7일) 또는 냉동 보관합니다.
10. 완성된 라자냐는 적당한 크기로 잘라 접시에 담은 후 파르미자노 레자노 치즈, 올리브오일, 이태리파슬리를 뿌려 마무리합니다.

9. Cover the lasagna pan with foil and score a cross on top. Place it in a preheated oven at 338°F (170°C). Reduce the temperature to 320°F (160°C) and bake for 40 minutes. Remove the foil and bake for 2 more minutes.
 - If serving immediately, bake the lasagna for slightly over 2 minutes until golden, like a gratin. If serving later, let it cool and refrigerate (for up to 7 days) or freeze.
10. Cut the lasagna into moderately sized pieces and place each piece on a plate. Top with grated Parmigiano-Reggiano, chopped Italian parsley, and a dash of olive oil.

Tagliatelle con ragù alla bolognese

가정식
HOME COOKING

탈리아텔레 콘 라구 알라 볼로네제

이탈리아 요리를 배우기 위해 볼로냐에 도착한 첫날, 길을 걷다 우연히 들어간 작은 식당에서 '탈리아텔레 콘 라구 알라 볼로네제'를 처음 맛봤습니다. 그때의 충격은 지금도 생생합니다. 고기와 채소, 토마토가 깊게 녹아든 소스, 넓고 납작한 생면이 그것을 완벽하게 받아내며 주는 밀도 있는 식감. 게다가 치즈의 고소함과 올리브 오일의 풍미까지. 모든 것이 정확하게 맞물리는 느낌이었습니다.

그 한 그릇은 제가 그때까지 알고 있던 파스타의 개념을 완전히 바꾸게 했고, 이 요리를 꼭 제대로 만들고 싶다는 마음이 생겼습니다. 그래서 더 자주 볼로냐를 찾았고, 더 많은 식당을 돌아다니며 맛보고, 관찰하고, 배웠습니다. 그렇게 쌓인 경험은 지금 제 요리 철학의 중심이 되었습니다.

탈리아텔레는 라구 소스를 위해 존재하는 면이라 생각합니다. 넓적한 면이 소스를 감싸 안으며 입안에서 하나로 녹아드는 그 순간, 볼로냐에서의 내 시간과 배움, 그리고 초심이 다시 떠오릅니다. 이 파스타는 단순한 요리가 아닌, 제 인생의 방향을 바꾼 첫 단추와도 같은 존재입니다.

On my first day in Bologna to study Italian cuisine, I came across a restaurant where I had my first *Tagliatelle con ragù alla Bolognese*—a dish whose impact still lingers vividly to this day. The sauce was deeply infused with tomatoes, vegetables and meat; the wide, flat past had just the right density to hold the sauce perfectly. Even the savory cheese and rich olive oil added depth, and I could sense that every component came together with precision.

That pasta completely overturned everything I'd ever known about pasta and made me determined to master the dish properly, at all costs. So I began visiting Bologna more often, going from restaurant to restaurant to taste, observe, and learn. Those experiences now lie at the center of my culinary philosophy.

I believe tagliatelle was made for *ragù*. When the wide pasta embraces the sauce and the two melt into one in the mouth, I brought back to my beginnings—my time, my learning, and the mindset I had when I first set out. To me, this pasta is more than a dish. It is the first button that shifted the direction of my life.

Ingredients

1인 분량
Serves 1

생면 반죽 (249p)	100g
▸ 생면 대신 시판 건면 파스타 1인 분량을 사용해도 좋습니다.	
라구 소스 (247p)	125g
물 또는 치킨 육수	적당량
소금	적당량
후춧가루	적당량
우유 또는 생크림	40g

장식

엑스트라버진 올리브오일	적당량
파르미자노 레자노 치즈	적당량
이태리파슬리	적당량

100 g	fresh pasta (p.249)
▸ One serving of store-bought dried pasta can be used instead of the fresh pasta.	
125 g	*ragù* (p.247)
Q.S.	water or chicken stock
Q.S.	salt
Q.S.	ground black pepper
40 g	milk or fresh cream

GARNISHES

Q.S.	extra virgin olive oil
Q.S.	Parmigiano-Reggiano
Q.S.	Italian parsley

How to make

1. 생면 반죽을 얇게 펴서 탈리아텔레(두께 1~2mm, 너비 8mm 칼국수 사이즈) 크기로 잘라줍니다.
- 시판 건면을 사용할 경우 제품에 따른 조리법과 용량으로 조리합니다.
2. 라구 소스에 물(또는 치킨 육수)을 넣어 농도를 맞추고, 소금과 후춧가루로 간을 합니다.
3. 우유를 넣고 끓여줍니다.

1. Thinly roll out the fresh pasta dough and cut it into tagliatelle (1 to 2 mm thick and 8 mm wide).
- If using store-bought dried pasta, follow the package instructions for the cooking time and quantity.
2. Adjust the consistency of the *ragù* by adding water (or chicken stock), then season with salt and black pepper.
3. Add the milk and bring to a boil.

4. 라구 소스가 준비되면 3L의 물에 1%의 소금(30g)을 넣고 면수를 끓인 후 생면을 넣고 1분 30초간 삶아줍니다.
5. 삶은 생면을 준비된 라구 소스에 넣고 중불에서 고르게 섞어줍니다.
6. 올리브오일을 뿌려줍니다.

4. When the *ragù* is ready, add 1% salt (30 g per 3 liters) of boiling water, then cook the fresh pasta for 1 minute and 30 seconds.
5. Add the cooked pasta to the *ragù*, and toss over medium heat until evenly coated.
6. Drizzle with olive oil.

7. 파스타를 접시에 담고 파르미자노 레자노 치즈, 올리브오일, 이태리파슬리, 후춧가루를 뿌려 마무리합니다.

7. Arrange the pasta on a plate, then top with grated Parmigiano-Reggiano, Italian parsley, black pepper, and a final drizzle of olive oil.

KIM MINSEOK

김민석

요리가 좋아 무작정 이탈리아로 떠났고, 요리학교 '알마(ALMA)'에서 본격적으로 요리를 공부했다. 식재료를 정확히 알고 써야 진짜 감동을 줄 수 있다는 생각에, 재료에 대한 이해와 요리에 대한 탐구를 게을리하지 않았다.

졸업 후에는 밀라노의 미쉐린 2스타 레스토랑에서 모든 파트를 돌며 4년간 일하며 실력을 쌓았다. 이후 자신만의 노하우를 기록하고 공유하고자 유튜브 채널 '김밀란'을 개설했고, 현재 이탈리아에 거주하며 직접 만든 이탈리아 요리를 영상으로 소개하며 구독자들과 소통하고 있다.

그의 요리 영상은 단순한 레시피 영상이 아닌, 한 그릇에 담긴 요리의 과정과 감각, 재료를 다루는 태도까지 전한다. 이따금 한국을 찾아 요리 클래스와 팝업을 열기도 하는데, 특히 한국에 올 때마다 진행하는 요리 클래스는 매번 오픈과 동시에 마감될 정도로 구독자와 팬들에게 인기가 많다.

그는 오늘도 이탈리아와 한국의 주방을 오가며, 단순하지만 깊이 있는 요리를 만들어가고 있다.

His love of cooking led him to Italy, where he studied at the culinary school ALMA. He believes that food is only awe-inspiring if you know what you're using, so he never stopped learning about ingredients and cooking.

After graduating, he worked for four years at a two-Michelin-starred restaurant in Milan, where he was involved in all aspects of the kitchen. He started his YouTube channel, "Kim Milan," to document and share his know-how. He now lives in Italy, where he interacts with his subscribers through videos of his Italian cooking.

His cooking videos are more than just recipes: they convey the process, the sensations, and the attitude of the ingredients on a plate. From time to time, he travels to Korea to hold cooking classes and pop-ups. His cooking classes are so popular with his subscribers and fans that they close as soon as they open.

He continues to travel between his kitchens in Italy and Korea, creating dishes that are both profound and straightforward.

▶ 김밀란 @Kimmilan
◉ milan__kim

Cacio e Pepe Pici with Sea Urchin Roe

이야기
STORY

성게알을 올린 카초 에 페페 소스의 피치

'카초 에 페페'는 제가 가장 좋아하는 파스타 중 하나입니다. 밀라노 나빌리오 운하 근처의 동네 트라토리아에서 처음 맛본 이후, 어느 도시를 가든 이 메뉴가 보이면 꼭 주문할 정도로 애정하는 요리죠. 페코리노 로마노 치즈와 후추만으로 완성되는 이 파스타는 단순함의 미학이 극대화된 요리로, 이탈리아 요리의 본질을 가장 잘 보여주는 음식이라 생각합니다.

피치는 언젠가 토스카나 시에나 근처를 여행하다 우연히 맛보게 된 이후, 제게 스파게티보다 더 매력적인 파스타가 되었습니다. 손으로 투박하게 늘려 만든 피치 특유의 쫄깃하고 묵직한 식감은 그 자체로 강한 존재감을 지니고 있었고, 어느 파스타 요리에 사용해도 잘 어울릴 거라는 확신이 생기게 했죠. 그래서 제가 가장 좋아하는 두 가지 요소인 카초 에 페페와 피치, 그리고 한국에서만 구할 수 있는 고품질의 성게알을 조합해 보았습니다. 특히 소스는 치즈의 엉김을 막기 위해 타피오카 전분을 사용해 벨벳처럼 부드럽고 안정적인 질감으로 완성했습니다. 페코리노 로마노 치즈의 짭조름한 풍미와 산미, 그리고 성게알의 깊고 부드러운 감칠맛이 두툼한 피치 면 사이사이에 고르게 스며들어 주는 강렬한 맛. 이것만큼 이탈리아 요리를 잘 표현한 요리가 있을까요?

Cacio e pepe is one of my favorite pastas. Ever since I had it at a trattoria in a village near the Naviglio Canal, in Milan, I have ordered it whenever I see it on a menu, no matter the city. That is how much I love this dish. Made with nothing more than Pecorino Romano and black pepper, this dish embodies the beauty in simplicity at its finest, and most faithfully captures the essence of Italian cuisine.

Pici has been more appealing to me than spaghetti ever since when I happened to try it near Siena in Tuscany. Hand-rolled into thick strands, pici has its own chewy, substantial texture and a strong presence, which convinces me that it can pair well with any pasta sauce. So I decided to bring together *cacio e pepe* and pici—two of my favorite elements—with the finest sea urchin roe, available only in South Korea. The sauce, in particular, is made velvety and well-balanced by using tapioca starch, which helps prevent the cheese from clumping. It is thick strands of pici, evenly infused with the salty, sharp Pecorino Romano and the gently layered savory depth of sea urchin that bring out the dish's intense flavor. What could better express the essence of Italian cuisine?

Ingredients

2인 분량
Serves 2

피치

세몰리나	200g
(카푸토, 세몰라 리마치나타)	
뜨거운 물	110ml
소금	0.2g
성게알	적당량

소스

페코리노 로마노 치즈	80g
우유	150ml
화이트 타피오카 펄	10g
굵게 빻은 흑후추	3g

PICI

200 g	semolina
	(Caputo, semola rimacinata)
110 ml	hot water
0.2 g	salt
Q.S.	sea urchin roe

SAUCE

80 g	Pecorino Romano
150 ml	milk
10 g	white tapioca pearls
3 g	coarse ground black pepper

How to make

1. 볼에 세몰리나, 뜨거운 물, 소금을 넣고 잘 섞어줍니다.
- 밀가루와 소금이 담긴 볼에 뜨거운 물을 넣고 주걱으로 섞다가 물기가 보이지 않으면 손으로 치대면서 골고루 반죽합니다.
2. 반죽을 한 덩어리로 뭉친 후 5분 정도 휴지시켰다가 다시 손으로 치대면서 매끈해질 때까지 반죽합니다.
- 습도의 영향을 받을 수 있으니 반죽의 상태를 보고 물의 양을 조절합니다.

1. In a mixing bowl, combine the semolina, hot water, and salt, then mix until well combined.
- Add the hot water to a mixing bowl with semolina and salt, then mix with a spatula until no visible moisture remains. Knead the dough by hand until fully incorporated.
2. Bring the mixture together into a single dough, and let it rest for about 5 minutes. Then continue kneading until smooth.
- Adjust the amount of water based on the dough's condition, as it may be affected by humidity.

  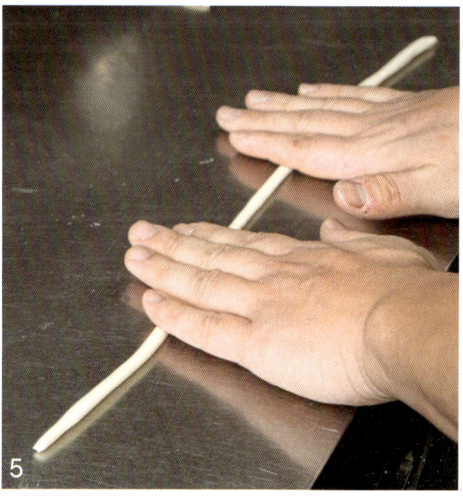

3. 치대는 작업이 끝나면 반죽을 랩으로 감싸 30분 이상 완전히 휴지시킵니다.
4. 휴지가 끝난 반죽은 밀대로 두께 약 2cm, 길이 약 15~20cm가 되도록 밀어 편 후 적당하게 긴 방향으로 잘라냅니다.
5. 잘라낸 반죽은 양손으로 잘 굴리면서 양 끝으로 끊어지지 않게 약 30~40cm 길이로 늘여줍니다.
- 작업하는 동안 사용하지 않는 반죽은 젖은 면포로 덮어두어 마르지 않도록 합니다.

3. Once kneading is complete, wrap the dough in plastic wrap and let it rest completely for at least 30 minutes.
4. Roll out the dough evenly with a rolling pin to about 2 cm thick and 15 to 20 cm long, then cut into long strips.
5. Roll and stretch each strip by hand into a strand about 30 to 40 cm long, being careful not to tear it.
- Cover any unused dough with a damp cloth to prevent it from drying out during the process.

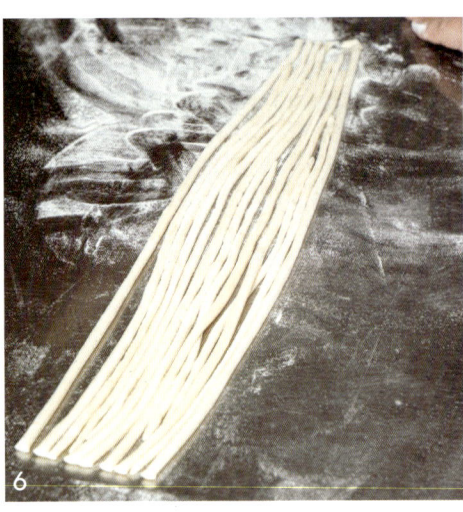  

6. 완성된 피치는 양 끝을 잘라 길이를 맞춰준 후 덧밀가루를 가볍게 뿌려 한쪽으로 치워둡니다.
7. 냄비에 우유와 화이트 타피오카 펄을 넣고 약 85℃를 유지하며 화이트 타피오카 펄이 완전히 호화될 때까지 주걱으로 섞어가며 20~30분간 익힙니다.

6. Trim both ends of the pici to even out the lengths, then dust with extra flour and set aside.
7. In a pot, combine the milk and white tapioca pearls, and stir with a spatula at about 185°F (85°C) for 20 to 30 minutes, until the pearls are fully gelatinized.

8. 화이트 타피오카 펄이 완전히 익으면 곱게 갈아둔 페코리노 로마노 치즈를 넣고 잘 섞은 후 믹서기로 곱게 갈아 체에 걸러줍니다.
9. 통흑후추를 아무것도 두르지 않은 팬에 가볍게 볶아 향을 이끌어 냅니다.

8. Once the pearls are fully cooked, add the finely grated Pecorino Romano and mix well. Blend the mixture with a hand mixer until smooth. Pass it through a sieve with a spatula to make the sauce.
9. Gently toast the black peppercorns in a dry pan to bring out the aroma.

10. 볶은 통흑후추를 굵직하게 빻아줍니다.
11. 끓는 소금물에 피치를 1분 30초간 삶아줍니다.
12. 삶은 피치를 건져내 약간의 면수와 함께 팬으로 옮겨 담은 후 준비한 소스와 **10**을 넣고 잘 섞어 마무리합니다.

10. Grind the toasted black peppercorns into coarse grounds.
11. Cook the pici in boiling water for 1 minute and 30 seconds.
12. Remove the pici and transfer to a pan with a dash of cooking liquid. Toss thoroughly with the sauce and (**10**).

13. 국자와 핀셋을 이용해 면을 말아 접시에 담아줍니다.
14. 성게알을 올리고 흑후추를 살짝 뿌려 완성합니다.

13. Twirl the pici into a nest using a ladle and tweezers, and place it onto a plate.
14. Top with sea urchin roe and finish with a final sprinkle of the coarse ground black pepper.

Homemade Cacio e pepe

가정식
HOME COOKING

가정식 카초 에 페페

카초 에 페페는 이름 그대로 '치즈와 후추'를 의미합니다. '카초(Cacio)'는 치즈를 뜻하는 로마 사투리이며, '페페(Pepe)'는 후추를 뜻하죠. 이 파스타는 단 두 가지 재료, 치즈와 후추만으로 만드는 로마 전통 요리로, 주로 양젖으로 만든 페코리노 로마노 치즈가 사용됩니다.

페코리노 로마노 치즈 특유의 짙고 풍부한 향, 그리고 살짝 도는 산미가 후추의 알싸한 매운맛과 만나 깊고 오묘한 조화를 만들어냅니다. 재료는 단순하지만, 그 조화가 만들어내는 풍미는 결코 단순하지 않은 파스타입니다.

이 메뉴는 제가 앞서 소개한 피치와 성게알을 활용한 카초 에 페페의 가정식 버전으로, 보다 간단한 재료와 방식으로도 충분히 이탈리아 요리의 진수를 경험할 수 있도록 구성했습니다.

Cacio e pepe literally means "cheese and pepper." *Cacio* is the word for cheese in the Roman dialect, and pepe refers to pepper. Made with just these two ingredients, this pasta is a traditional Roman dish that typically features Pecorino Romano, a cheese made from sheep's milk.

The rich flavor and gentle sharpness of Pecorino Romano create a deep, delicate harmony with the pungent heat of black pepper. Despite its humble ingredients, the resulting flavor is anything but modest.

This homemade version of the *Cacio e Pepe Pici*, as introduced earlier, is crafted to showcase the excellence of Italian cuisine through a simpler set of ingredients and a streamlined preparation.

Ingredients

2인 분량
Serves 2

페코리노 로마노 치즈	100g		100 g	Pecorino Romano
통흑후추	3g		3 g	black peppercorns
소금	적당량		Q.S.	salt
스파게티 면	160g		160 g	dried spaghetti

How to make

1. 페코리노 로마노 치즈는 그레이터를 사용해 최대한 곱게 갈아줍니다.
2. 통흑후추를 아무것도 두르지 않은 팬에 가볍게 볶아 향을 이끌어 냅니다.
3. 볶은 통흑후추를 굵직하게 빻아줍니다.

1. Grate the Pecorino Romano as finely as possible using a grater.
2. Gently toast the black peppercorns in a dry pan to bring out the aroma.
3. Coarsely grind the toasted black peppercorns.

4. 소금 간을 한 끓는 물에 스파게티 면을 넣고 삶아줍니다.
- 가급적 포장지에 적힌 조리 시간보다 4분 정도 덜 삶아줍니다.
5. 삶은 스파게티 면은 약간의 면수와 함께 팬으로 옮겨 중불에서 천천히 마저 익혀줍니다.
- 면수는 간에 맞춰 물로 대체할 수 있습니다.
6. 스파게티 면을 익힐 때 면수를 천천히 졸여 최대한 많은 전분이 나와 끈적해지도록 합니다.
- 충분한 양의 물을 남겨두어야 치즈가 들어갔을 때 빠르게 녹일 수 있습니다.

4. Cook the dried spaghetti in boiling salted water.
- If possible, cook it 4 minutes less than the time indicated on the package instructions.
5. Transfer the partially cooked spaghetti to a separate pan with some of its cooking liquid, and finish cooking gradually over medium heat.
- Plain water can be used instead of the cooking liquid to adjust the seasoning.
6. While cooking, let the cooking liquid gradually reduce to draw out as much starch as possible, resulting in a sticky texture.
- Be sure to reserve enough liquid to help melt the cheese quickly.

7. 스파게티 면이 알 덴테(al dente, 면 중심부에 약간의 단단함이 느껴지는 상태) 상태로 익고 면수도 적당한 양으로 졸여지면 불을 끄고 1분여 정도 그대로 두어 잠시 온도를 낮춥니다.

8. 따뜻한 온도로 떨어졌다면 갈아둔 치즈와 **3**을 넣고 잘 섞어줍니다. 치즈가 엉기거나 뭉쳐도 상관없습니다. 원래 그런 요리니까요.

7. When the spaghetti is cooked *al dente* (slightly firm in the center) and the liquid has reduced to the desired consistency, turn off the heat and let it sit for about 1 minute to cool slightly.

8. Once the spaghetti has cooled to a warm temperature, add the grated cheese and (**3**), then toss until evenly coated. It's fine if the cheese clumps or congeals slightly—that's how this dish is meant to be.

9. 완성된 파스타를 접시에 담고 남은 치즈와 여분의 **3**을 뿌려 마무리합니다.

9. Place the pasta on a plate and sprinkle with additional cheese and (**3**).

KIM SEAKYEONG

김 세 경

여수에서 태어나 바다의 맛을 가장 먼저 배웠다. 어린 시절부터 주방에서 가족을 위해 음식을 만들며 요리에 흥미를 느꼈다. 군 제대 후 뉴욕에 있는 이모를 찾아간 것이 전환점이었다. 그곳에서 세계적인 요리학교 CIA를 알게 되었고, 직업이 아닌 삶으로서 요리를 선택했다.

졸업 후 뉴욕 '오리올(Aureole)'에서 커리어를 시작했고, 런던 '더 레드버리(The Ledbury)' 등 유럽의 미쉐린 레스토랑에서 요리의 문법을 익혔다. 이후 찰리 파머 그룹에 합류해 2011년, 동양인 최초로 캘리포니아 지점의 이그제큐티브 셰프로 임명되었다. 이 업적으로 외국인으로는 매우 드물게 미국 EB1 비자*를 취득하고 영주권을 획득했다.

현재 드라이 에이징 스테이크 전문점 '휴135', 솥밥 전문점 '휴135 다온반상', 그리고 다양한 요리와 와인을 함께 즐길 수 있는 '세스타(CESTA)'를 운영하고 있다.

그의 요리는 간결하지만 깊다. 과한 장식을 덜어내고, 재료 본연의 맛을 최대한 끌어올리는 정직한 요리. 누구나 어렵지 않게 즐길 수 있으면서도, 쉽게 잊히지 않는 맛으로 기억되는 것이 요리에 있어서의 그의 목표다.

* EB1 비자
미국 이민 비자 중 가장 높은 우선순위에 속하는 영주권 비자. 특히 전문성과 업적을 갖춘 외국인에게 주어지는 것으로, 심사 기준이 매우 까다롭다.

Chef Kim Seakyeong was born in Yeosu, where he first learned the taste of the sea. He has been interested in cooking since childhood, cooking for his family in the kitchen. A turning point came when he visited his aunt in New York City after being discharged from the military. There, he discovered the world-class culinary school, the CIA, and chose cooking as his life, not a career.

After graduation, he began his career at Aureole in New York City, and he honed his skills at Michelin-starred restaurants in Europe, including The Ledbury in London. He then joined the Charlie Palmer Group, where, in 2011 became the first Asian executive chef of its California location. For this achievement, he was granted a U.S. EB-1 visa*, a very rare case for a foreigner, and acquired permanent residency.

He currently runs Hue135, a dry-aged steak restaurant; Hue135 Daon Bansang, a hot pot rice restaurant; and CESTA, a restaurant where you can enjoy various dishes and wines together.

His cooking is simple yet profound: honest dishes that are free of excessive decoration, bringing out the best in the ingredients. His goal is to create dishes that are accessible to everyone but that are remembered for their unforgettable flavors.

* EB-1 visa
It's a permanent resident visa, the highest priority among U.S. immigrant visas. It is given to foreign nationals with particular expertise and achievements and is highly selective.

세스타
cesta.seoul

휴135
hue135.seoul

다온반상
daonbansang

ockim

Snow Crab Meat and Lemon Bite

이야기
STORY

대게살과 레몬 바이트

크루그(Krug, 프랑스 샹파뉴 지방의 프레스티지 샴페인 브랜드) 엠버서더로 활동하며 선보인 메뉴 가운데 특히 많은 사랑을 받은 요리 중 하나가 바로 '대게살과 레몬 바이트'입니다. 이 메뉴는 매년 크루그가 선정하는 식재료를 주제로 개발하는 요리 중 2023년의 주제였던 '레몬'을 바탕으로 만들어졌습니다.

레몬을 세 가지 방식으로 표현하고자 했고, 각기 다른 조리법을 통해 레몬의 다양한 특징을 풀어냈습니다. 3개월 이상 발효시킨 프리저브드 레몬은 깊고 복합적인 발효의 풍미를, 직접 짜낸 레몬즙으로 만든 레몬 겔은 날카롭고 상큼한 산미를, 그리고 버터를 사용한 레몬 커드는 묵직하고 진한 맛에 약간의 쌉싸름함까지 더해줍니다.

여기에 바다의 향을 더하기 위해 김으로 만든 퍼프와 대게 껍질로 우려낸 다시, 신선한 허브로 만든 젤레를 곁들였습니다. 처음 출시된 이후 지금까지 많은 손님들로부터 꾸준히 사랑받는 세스타의 시그니처메뉴입니다.

Snow Crab Meat and Lemon Bite is one of the most beloved dishes that I presented during my time as an ambassador for Krug, the prestige Champagne brand based in Champagne, France. This dish was created as part of Krug's annual chef collaboration, which centers on a single ingredient selected each year—in 2023, it was lemon.

I sought to express lemon's versatility in three distinct methods, each revealing a different facet of its character: the deep, complex notes of the preserved lemon fermented over three months; the sharp, refreshing tang of lemon gel made with freshly squeezed lemon juice; and a rich, pleasantly bitter lemon curd crafted with butter.

To evoke the scent of the sea, the dish is complemented by a seaweed puff and a snow crab shell dashi, along with a fresh herb gelée. Ever since its launch, it has remained a signature at Cesta, consistently cherished by our guests.

Ingredients

45개 분량
Serves 45

김 퍼프*
찹쌀	100g
찹쌀가루	50g
물	800g
액젓	20g
곱게 간 곱창김	30g
식용유	적당량

대게 다시*
물	4000g
건다시마	20g
구운 대게 껍질	140g
가쓰오부시	65g

다시 젤레*
차이브	6g
처빌	6g
딜	6g
브론즈 펜넬잎	6g
타라곤	6g
대게 다시*	484g
액젓	20g
한천가루	6g
물에 불린 판젤라틴	4장

대게 내장 퓌레*
버터	70g
슬라이스한 대파 (흰 부분)	200g
소금	3g
물	200g
가니미소 (붉은대게장)	30g
엑스트라 버진 올리브오일	30g

레몬 겔*
레몬즙	200g
심플 시럽	60g
잔탄검	4.7g

▶ 심플 시럽은 설탕과 물을 1:1 비율로 끓여 사용합니다.

레몬 커드*
레몬 껍질	10g
레몬즙	140g
노른자	80g
버터	120g
소금	1g
설탕	70g
액젓	24g
기꼬만 간장	6g
레몬 제스트	6g
물에 불린 판젤라틴	3장

프리저브드 레몬*
레몬	3900g
코셔소금 (다이아몬드 크리스탈)	500g
설탕	600g
시나몬 스틱	10g
구운 통후추	10g
구운 주니퍼 베리	4g

대게살과 레몬 바이트 (1개 분량)
익힌 대게살	40g
대게 내장 퓌레*	5g
차이브	3g
타라곤	1g
엑스트라 버진 올리브오일	2g
소금	적당량
후춧가루	적당량
다시 젤레*	1장
레몬 커드*	10g
레몬 겔*	3g
프리저브드 레몬*	2g
허브와 식용꽃	적당량
김 퍼프*	1개

SEAWEED PUFF*
100 g	glutinous rice
50 g	glutinous rice powder
800 g	water
20 g	aekjeot (Korean fish sauce)
30 g	finely ground gopchang dried seaweed (gopchang-gim)
Q.S.	cooking oil

SNOW CRAB DASHI*
4000 g	water
20 g	dried kelp
140 g	roasted snow crab shell
65 g	kastuobushi (dried bonito flakes)

DASHI GELÉE*
6 g	chives
6 g	fresh chervil
6 g	fresh dill
6 g	fresh bronze fennel leaves
6 g	fresh tarragon
484 g	snow crab dashi*
20 g	aekjeot
6 g	agar powder
4	soaked gelatin sheets

SNOW CRAB INNARDS PURÉE*
70 g	butter
200 g	sliced green onion (white part)
3 g	salt
200 g	water
30 g	kani-miso (red snow crab paste)
30 g	extra virgin olive oil

LEMON GEL*
200 g	lemon juice
60 g	simple syrup
4.7 g	xanthan gum

▶ For the simple syrup, use a 1:1 ratio of sugar to water and bring to a boil.

LEMON CURD*
10 g	lemon peel
140 g	lemon juice
80 g	egg yolks
120 g	butter
1 g	salt
70 g	sugar
24 g	aekjeot
6 g	Kikkoman soy sauce
6 g	lemon zest
3	soaked gelatin sheets

PRESERVED LEMON*
3900 g	lemon
500 g	kosher salt (Diamond Crystal)
600 g	sugar
10 g	cinnamon stick
10 g	roasted black peppercorns
4 g	roasted juniper berries

SNOW CRAB MEAT AND LEMON BITE (per bite)
40 g	cooked snow crab meat
5 g	snow crab innards purée*
3 g	chives
1 g	fresh tarragon
2 g	extra virgin olive oil
Q.S.	salt
Q.S.	ground black pepper
1 sheet	dashi gelée*
10 g	lemon curd*
3 g	lemon gel*
2 g	preserved lemon*
Q.S.	fresh herbs and edible flowers
1	seaweed puff*

How to make

김 퍼프

1. 냄비에 찹쌀, 찹쌀가루, 물을 넣고 되직한 상태(죽 농도 정도)가 될 때까지 가열합니다.
2. 1을 블렌더로 곱게 갈아줍니다.
3. 2에 액젓과 곱게 간 곱창김을 넣고 휘퍼를 이용해 뭉치지 않게 섞어줍니다.

SEAWEED PUFF

1. In a pot, combine the glutinous rice, glutinous rice powder, and water. Heat until it thickens to a porridge-like consistency.
2. Blend (**1**) with a hand blender until smooth.
3. Add the aekjeot and finely ground gopchang dried seaweed to (**2**), then whisk to prevent clumping.

4. 실리콘 패드 위에 가로 8.5cm, 세로 5cm, 두께 2mm 몰드를 올린 후 3을 넣고 스패츌러로 평평하게 펼쳐준 다음, 식품 건조기에서 12시간 이상 말려줍니다.
   - 너무 얇지 않게 적당한 두께로 펴 발라줍니다.
5. 분무기를 이용해 표면에 물을 분사해 수분을 머금게 합니다.
   - 물을 뿌리는 이유는 마른 상태로 튀기면 퍼프화(식품 속 수분이 고온에서 순간적으로 증발하며 조직이 부풀어 바삭한 식감을 만드는 현상)가 일어나지 않기 때문입니다.
6. 160~170℃로 예열된 식용유에 넣고 바삭하게 튀겨줍니다.

4. Place a mold measuring 8.5 cm wide, 5 cm high, and 2 cm deep on a silicone pad and evenly spread (**3**) using a spatula. Dry in a dehydrator for at least 12 hours.
   - Spread the mixture to a moderate thickness, rather than making it overly thin.
5. Gently spray the surface with water to help retain moisture.
   - The surface must remain wet during frying; otherwise, puffing will not occur—a process in which the moisture inside the ingredients rapidly evaporates at high temperatures, causing the structure to expand and create a crispy texture.
6. Deep-fry in cooking oil preheated to 320–338°F (160-170°C) until crispy.

7. 튀겨져 나온 김 퍼프는 넓적한 도구를 이용해 평평하게 만들어줍니다.

대게 다시

냄비에 가쓰오부시를 제외한 모든 재료를 넣고 80℃로 온도를 유지하며 재료의 맛을 우려낸 후, 건다시마와 구운 대게 껍질을 제거하고 가쓰오부시를 넣어 15~20분간 우려 거름망에 걸러줍니다.

7. Gently press the fried seaweed puff with a flat tool to shape it evenly.

SNOW CRAB DASHI

In a pot, combine all the dashi ingredients except the kastuobushi, and simmer at 176°F (80°C) until infusing the flavors. Remove the kelp and roasted snow crab shell, then add the kastuobushi. Continue simmering for 15 to 20 minutes, then strain through a sieve.

다시 젤레

1. 허브 재료를 잘게 다진 후 고르게 섞어 준비합니다.
2. 냄비에 차가운 상태의 대게 다시, 액젓, 한천가루를 넣고 3분 동안 휘퍼로 저어가며 가열합니다.
- 차가운 상태의 대게 다시에 한천가루를 넣고 섞어야 뭉치지 않습니다.
3. 물에 불린 판젤라틴을 넣고 섞어줍니다.

DASHI GELÉE

1. Finely chop the fresh herbs and mix thoroughly.
2. In a pot, combine the cold snow crab dashi, aekjeot, and agar powder. Countinuously whisk the mixture over heat for 3 minutes.
- Be sure to add the agar powder to the cold snow crab dashi to prevent clumping.
3. Stir in the soaked gelatin sheets.

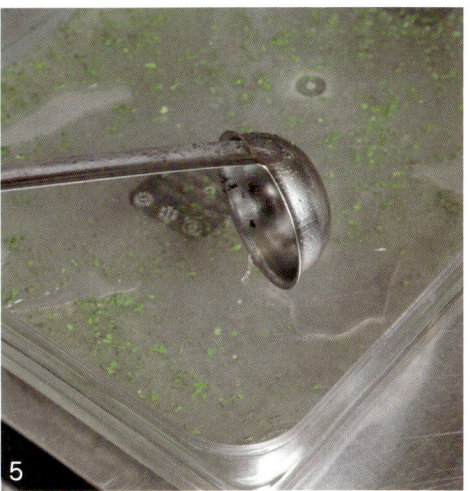

4. 다진 허브 절반을 넣고 섞어줍니다.
5. 넓은 용기에 붓고 평평하게 펼쳐줍니다.

4. Stir in half of the chopped herbs.
5. Pour the mixture evenly into a wide container.

6. 허브가 비어 보이는 곳을 중심으로 남은 다진 허브를 뿌린 후, 실온에 두고 살짝 굳힌 다음 냉장고로 옮겨 완전히 굳혀줍니다.
7. 김 퍼프 몰드보다 좀 더 작은 사이즈의 틀로 잘라줍니다.

6. Scatter the remaining herbs over any empty areas. Let it set slightly at room temperature, then transfer to the refrigerator to fully set.
7. Cut out the set mixture using a mold slightly smaller than the one used for the seaweed puff.

대게 내장 퓌레

냄비에 버터, 슬라이스한 대파, 소금, 물을 넣고 180g이 될 때까지 졸인 후 가니미소를 넣고 가볍게 끓여줍니다. 믹서로 옮겨 중간중간 올리브오일을 넣고 곱게 간 후 식혀줍니다.

SNOW CRAB INNARDS PURÉE

In a pot, combine the butter, sliced green onion, salt, and water, then simmer until reduced to 180 g. Add the kani-miso and gently bring to a boil. Transfer the mixture to a blender and gradually blend in olive oil until smooth, then let cool.

레몬 겔

1. 믹서에 레몬즙과 심플 시럽을 넣고 갈아줍니다.
2. 가는 중간에 잔탄검을 넣고 갈아 마무리합니다.
3. 통에 옮겨 담고 진공 머신을 이용해 공기를 완전히 제거한 후 소스통에 담아 사용합니다.

LEMON GEL

1. In a blender, blend the lemon juice and simple syrup until well combined.
2. Add the xanthan gum and continue blending.
3. Pour the liquid into a container, vacuum out the air completely using a vacuum machine, then transfer to a squeeze bottle.

레몬 커드

1. 냄비에 레몬 껍질과 찬물을 담고 가열합니다. 끓어오르면 물을 버리고 다시 찬물을 담아 끓여줍니다. 이 과정을 총 3회 반복합니다.

- 레몬 껍질을 익힘과 동시에 쓴맛을 제거하기 위한 과정입니다.

2. 진공백에 **1**과 남은 재료를 모두 넣고 75°C에서 1시간 동안 수비드합니다.

LEMON CURD

1. In a pot, combine the lemon peel and cold water, then bring to a boil. Once it comes to a boil, discard the water, add fresh cold water, then bring to a boil again. Repeat this process a total of three times.

- This step helps cook the lemon peel and remove its bitterness.

2. Combine (**1**) and the remaining ingredients in a vacuum bag, then sous-vide at 167°F (75°C) for 1 hour.

3. 수비드가 끝나면 믹서에서 곱게 간 후 얼음물이 담긴 볼에 받쳐 빠르게 식혀줍니다.

- 너무 오랜 시간 갈게 되면 온도가 올라가 노른자가 익어버릴 수 있으니 주의합니다.

4. 완성한 레몬 커드는 냉장고에 보관하고, 사용하기 직전 체에 걸러줍니다.

3. After sous-vide cooking, blend the mixture until smooth, then transfer to an ice bath to cool immediately.

- Be careful not to blend for too long, as it may raise the temperature and cause the egg yolk to cook.

4. Store the lemon curd in the refrigerator, and press it through a sieve just before use.

프리저브드 레몬

1. 깨끗이 씻은 레몬의 정가운데에 십자 모양으로 칼집을 낸 후, 칼집 사이에 코셔소금을 채워줍니다.
2. 병 안에 소금을 채운 레몬과 나머지 재료를 모두 넣고 실온에서 2주 동안 보관합니다.
- 삼투압에 의해 수분이 흘러나오게 됩니다. 실온에 보관하는 동안 매일 한 번씩 병을 뒤집어줍니다.
3. 진공팩에 **2**를 넣고 진공 상태로 만들어 냉장 보관합니다.
- 이때 삼투압으로 흘러나온 수분도 진공팩에 함께 넣어줍니다.
4. 사용할 때는 사진과 같이 레몬의 꼭지 부분과 채워진 소금, 레몬 안쪽의 흰 부분을 제거한 후 적당한 크기로 잘라 사용합니다.

PRESERVED LEMON

1. Wash the lemon thoroughly, score a cross at the center, then pack the cuts with kosher salt.
2. Place the salt-packed lemon and the remaining ingredients in a jar. Seal and store at room temperature for 2 weeks.
- This process releases moisture through osmosis. Turn the jar upside down once a day while storing at room temperature.
3. Transfer (**2**) to a vacuum bag, seal under vacuum, and store in the refrigerator.
- Include the juice released through osmosis in the vacuum bag.
4. Before using the lemon, remove the packed salt, the top, and the white pith, then cut into moderately sized pieces, as shown in the photo.

대게살과 레몬 바이트

1. 볼에 익힌 대게살, 대게 내장 퓌레, 다진 차이브와 타라곤, 올리브오일, 소금, 후춧가루를 넣고 고르게 섞어줍니다.
2. 다시 젤레와 동일한 사이즈의 틀에 넣고 평평하게 펼쳐줍니다.
3. **2** 위에 다시 젤레를 올려줍니다.

SNOW CRAB MEAT AND LEMON BITE

1. In a mixing bowl, combine the snow crab meat, snow crab innards purée, chopped chives, tarragon, olive oil, salt, and black pepper. Mix thoroughly.
2. Place the mixture into a mold the same size as the dashi gelée, and spread evenly.
3. Top (**2**) with the dashi gelée.

 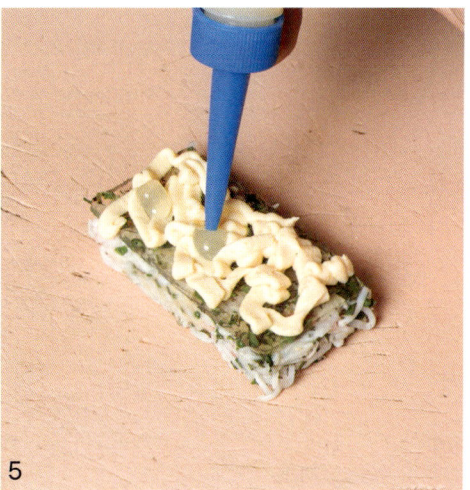 

4. 다시 젤레 위에 레몬 커드를 파이핑합니다.
5. 레몬 겔을 군데군데 파이핑합니다.
6. 작게 자른 프리저브드 레몬을 군데군데 올려줍니다.

4. Pipe the lemon curd over the dashi gelée.
5. Pipe the lemon gel in small dots.
6. Dot with finely chopped preserved lemon.

7. 허브와 식용 꽃으로 장식합니다.
8. 김 퍼프 위에 레몬 커드를 파이핑합니다.
9. 스페츌러를 이용해 7을 위에 올려줍니다.

7. Garnish with fresh herbs and edible flowers.
8. Pipe the lemon curd onto the seaweed puff.
9. Using a spatula, place (7) on top of the seaweed puff.

Brussels sprouts with Cherry Cola Gastrique

가정식
HOME COOKING

미니 양배추와 체리 콜라 게스트릭

이 요리는 제가 좋아하는 체리 콜라에서 영감을 받아 만들어진 요리로, 세스타에서 많은 고객들이 찾는 시그니처메뉴입니다. 차콜(숯의 열을 이용해 조리하는 방식) 레스토랑 콘셉트에 맞춰 미니 양배추의 안쪽 부분은 숯에서 굽고, 겉껍질은 바삭하게 튀겨 한 접시 안에서 두 가지 식감을 느낄 수 있게 한 요리인데요. 여기에서는 가정식 버전으로 팬에서 굽는 방식으로 만들어 보았습니다.

여기에 채소와 중국식 소시지에서 오는 진한 감칠맛, 마카다미아의 고소함, 페타치즈의 산뜻한 산미, 그리고 체리 콜라를 활용해 만든 새콤달콤한 게스트릭 소스가 조화를 이루며 완성됩니다. 메인 요리 전 에피타이저로도, 스테이크 같은 고기 요리와 곁들여도 잘 어울리는 요리입니다.

Inspired by my favorite drink, cherry cola, this dish has become Cesta's signature, beloved by many guests. True to our charcoal-grill concept, the inner parts of Brussels sprouts are grilled over charcoal, while the outer leaves are fried to crispy, bringing together two contrasting textures on a single plate. This version is adapted for home cooking, using pan-frying in place of charcoal grilling.

A rich, savory flavor drawn from vegetables and Chinese sausage, the nutty note of macadamia nuts, the refreshing tang of feta, and a sweet-and-sour cherry cola gastrique come together in harmony to complete the dish. It is perfect as an appetizer before the main course or as a side dish alongside meats like steak.

Ingredients

1접시 분량
Makes 1 plate

체리 콜라 게스트릭*

콜라	3900g
적체리 (통조림)	210g
팔각	1개
통후추	3g
설탕	500g
물	100g
셰리와인 비네거	500g

미니 양배추

천수 소시지	20g
미니 양배추	85g
소금	적당량
후춧가루	적당량
엑스트라버진 올리브오일	적당량
닭육수 또는 물	적당량
체리콜라 게스트릭*	40g

플레이팅

구운 마카다미아 분태	5g
페타치즈	10g
체리콜라 게스트릭*	적당량

CHERRY COLA GASTRIQUE*

3900 g	cola
210 g	canned red cherries
1	star anise
3 g	black peppercorns
500 g	sugar
100 g	water
500 g	sherry wine vinegar

BRUSSELS SPROUTS

20 g	Cheonsu sausage (泉水香肠)
85 g	Brussels sprouts
Q.S.	salt
Q.S.	ground black pepper
Q.S.	extra virgin olive oil
Q.S.	chicken stock or water
40 g	cherry cola gastrique*

PLATING

5 g	roasted chopped macadamia nuts
10 g	feta
Q.S.	cherry cola gastrique*

How to make

체리 콜라 게스트릭

1. 냄비에 콜라, 직체리, 팔각, 통후추를 넣고 600g이 될 때까지 졸여줍니다.
2. 다른 냄비에 설탕과 물을 넣고 가열합니다.

CHERRY COLA GASTRIQUE

1. In a pot, combine the cola, red cherries, star anise, and black peppercorns. Simmer the mixture until reduced to 600 g.
2. In a separate pot, heat the sugar and water.

3. 진한 갈색으로 캐러멜화가 되면 셰리와인 비네거를 조금씩 흘려가며 가열합니다.
4. 3에 1을 넣고 걸쭉한 소스 농도가 될 때까지 가열한 후(약 1320g) 체에 걸러줍니다.

3. Once caramelized to a dark brown, simmer while gradually stirring in the sherry wine vinegar.
4. Add (1) to (3), and continue simmering until it thickens to a sauce consistency (yielding approximately 1320 g), then strain through a sieve.

미니 양배추

1. 친수 소시지는 작은 큐브 모양으로 잘라 준비합니다.
2. 미니 양배추는 겉껍질을 분리한 후 반으로 잘라 준비합니다.
3. 미니 양배추 겉껍질은 180℃로 예열된 식용유에 넣고 바삭하게 튀겨줍니다.

BRUSSELS SPROUTS

1. Dice the Cheonsu sausage into small cubes.
2. Separate the outer leaves of the Brussels sprouts and halve the trimmed sprouts.
3. Deep-fry the outer leaves in cooking oil preheated to 356°F (180°C) until crispy.

4. 소금으로 간을 한 후 식품 건조기에서 보관해 바삭한 상태를 유지합니다.
5. 올리브오일을 두른 팬에 반으로 자른 미니 양배추를 넣고 익혀줍니다.
6. 익히는 동안 수분이 너무 없어져 건조해진다면 닭육수나 물을 추가해가며 익혀줍니다.

4. Season with salt and store in a dehydrator to keep them crispy.
5. Sauté the halved Brussels sprouts in olive oil.
6. If the moisture evaporates too much and the pan becomes dry, add chicken stock or water as needed while cooking.

7. 자른 단면이 노릇하게 익으면 소금과 후춧가루로 간을 합니다.
8. 천수 소시지를 넣고 익혀줍니다.
9. 체리콜라 게스트릭을 넣고 팬 바닥이 타지 않도록 닭육수를 추가해가며 조려줍니다.

7. Once the cut sides turn golden brown, season with salt and black pepper.
8. Add the sausage and stir-fry.
9. Drizzle in the cherry cola gastrique and cook down, adding chicken stock as needed to prevent scorching.

플레이팅

1. 접시에 익힌 미니 양배추와 천수 소시지를 담습니다.
2. 구운 마카다미아 분태와 페타 치즈를 뿌려 마무리합니다.

PLATING

1. Plate the Brussels sprouts and Cheonsu sausage.
2. Sprinkle with the roasted chopped macadamia nuts and feta.

3. 튀긴 미니 양배추 겉껍질을 올려줍니다.
4. 체리 콜라 게스트릭을 뿌려 마무리합니다.

3. Top with the fried Brussels sprout leaves.
4. Finish with a drizzle of cherry cola gastrique.

NAM JEONGSEOK
남정석

처음엔 관광영어를 공부했다. 하지만 언어보다 더 강렬하게 마음을 사로잡은 것이 있었다. 바로 요리였다. 방향을 바꿔 외식조리학을 전공했고, 양식조리기능장 자격을 얻으며 실력을 다져갔다.

2019년, 옥수동에 '로컬릿'을 열었다. 로컬릿은 이름처럼 지역에서 자란 제철 채소로 음식을 만든다. 화려하지 않지만 묵직한 맛. 채소 한 입에도 계절과 땅의 이야기를 담는다. 요리 외의 시간엔 텃밭을 가꾸며 땀으로 길러낸 채소를 다시 요리로 돌려보낸다. 흙에서 식탁까지, 모든 과정을 손끝으로 경험하는 셰프다.

2024년에는 넷플릭스 <흑백요리사: 요리 계급 전쟁>에 출연해 '채소 요리 1인자'라는 별칭을 얻었다. 그는 말한다. 고기는 빠져도, 풍미는 빠지지 않는다고.

강릉에 연 '그린볼'에서도 같은 철학이 이어진다. 채소 식재료 브랜드와 협업하고, 지역의 행사에 적극 참여하며 채소 요리를 더 많은 이들에게 알리고 있다. 요리를 통해 건강한 식탁, 지속 가능한 맛을 만들어 나가는 것이 그의 목표다.

He initially studied tourism English, but found himself captivated by something else—cooking. He went on to major in culinary arts, honing his skills and ultimately earning the title of Master Craftsman Cook in Western Cuisine.

In 2019, he opened his restaurant Local EAT in Oksu-dong. True to its name, Local EAT showcases seasonal vegetables sourced from local farms, crafting dishes that are humble in appearance yet bold in flavor. Each bite embodies the story of the land and the changing seasons. When not in the kitchen, he is in the garden, growing vegetables with his own sweat, only to bring them back to the plate. From farm to table, every step is guided by his hands.

In 2024, he was featured on Netflix's *Culinary Class Wars*, sarning the nickname "Korea's Top Vegetarian Cuisine Chef." As he puts it, *meat may be left out, but never the flavor*.

The same philosophy continues at Green Bowl, his second restaurant in Gangneung City. There, he collaborates with plant-based ingredient brands and actively participates in local events to share his vegetable-forward cuisine with a wider audience. Through his cooking, he aims to create a healthy table and deliver sustainable flavors.

그린볼
green_bowl21

로컬릿
the_local_eater

ncharisma7

Yellow Soybean Hummus with Roasted Vegetables

이야기
STORY

구운 채소를 곁들인 백태콩 후무스

로컬릿의 시그니처메뉴인 '채소 테린'을 플레이트 형식으로 재해석한 요리입니다. 채소 테린은 구운 채소를 백태콩 후무스로 겹겹이 쌓아 만든 비건 채소 요리인데요. 일반적으로 후무스에는 병아리콩(이집트콩)을 사용하지만, 로컬릿은 지역의 제철 식재료를 중요하게 생각하기 때문에 우리나라에서 익숙한 백태콩을 활용했습니다.

저는 어린 시절 가마솥이 있고 소도 키우는 시골에서 살았습니다. 어머니가 메주를 만들기 위해 큰 가마솥에 백태콩을 삶으실 때면, 그 고소한 냄새와 함께 주걱으로 퍼낸 따뜻한 콩을 퍼먹던 기억이 아직도 선명하게 남아 있죠. 그때의 진하고 고소했던 콩 맛을 떠올리며 이 메뉴를 만들어보았습니다.

백태콩 후무스는 병아리콩에 비해 조금 더 가볍고 담백한 맛을 냅니다. 구운 채소와 머스터드 비네그렛과 함께 곁들이면 산뜻하면서도 조화로운 한 끼 채소 요리로 완성되지요. 한 접시에 고소함, 향긋함, 담백함이 어우러진 이 요리는 건강하면서도 포만감 있는 한 끼로 손색이 없습니다.

This dish is a plated take on Local EAT's signature dish, "Vegetable Terrine," a vegan dish made by layering roasted vegetables with yellow soybean hummus. While traditional hummus is typically made with chickpeas (Egyptian peas), this version features yellow soybeans, which are more familiar in Korea, in line with our focus on seasonal and locally sourced ingredients.

In my childhood, I lived in the countryside, where an iron pot sat in the kitchen and cattle roamed the yard. I still remember the days my mother cooked yellow soybeans in that large iron pot to make *meju* (fermented soybean bricks). The moment I scooped the warm beans into my mouth with a rice paddle still remains vivid in my memory, along with their nutty aroma. The rich, savory soybean flavors that linger in my memory inspired me to create this dish.

Lighter and cleaner than traditional chickpea hummus, this yellow soybean hummus pairs perfectly with roasted vegetables and a mustard vinaigrette, coming together as a refreshing, harmonious dish. With its savory, fragrant, and clean flavors beautifully balanced on one plate, it offers more than enough to serve as a wholesome, satisfying meal.

Ingredients

2인 분량
Serves 2

백태콩 후무스

백태콩	150g
타히니	30g
엑스트라버진 올리브오일	30g
레몬즙	15g
차가운 물	200g
얼음	86g
소금	6g
큐민 파우더	적당량

머스터드 비네그렛

소금	1작은술
설탕	1큰술
디종 머스터드	1작은술
레몬즙	1큰술
꿀	1큰술
화이트와인 비네거	1큰술
건조 오레가노	적당량
포도씨유	1큰술
엑스트라버진 올리브오일	2큰술

구운 채소

로마네스코 브로콜리	1/2개
아스파라거스	3개
소금	적당량
흑후추	적당량
엑스트라버진 올리브오일	적당량

가니쉬

허브	적당량
통들깨	적당량
엑스트라버진 올리브오일	적당량
파프리카 파우더	적당량

YELLOW SOYBEAN HUMMUS

150 g	yellow soybeans
30 g	tahini
30 g	extra virgin olive oil
15 g	lemon juice
200 g	cold water
86 g	ice
6 g	salt
Q.S.	cumin powder

MUSTARD VINAIGRETTE

1 tsp	salt
1 tbsp	sugar
1 tsp	Dijon mustard
1 tbsp	lemon juice
1 tbsp	honey
1 tbsp	white wine vinegar
Q.S.	dried oregano
1 tbsp	grapeseed oil
2 tbsp	extra virgin olive oil

ROASTED VEGETABLES

1/2	Romanesco broccoli
3	asparagus spears
Q.S.	salt
Q.S.	black peppercorns
Q.S.	extra virgin olive oil

GARNISHES

Q.S.	fresh herbs
Q.S.	whole perilla seeds
Q.S.	extra virgin olive oil
Q.S.	paprika powder

How to make

백태콩 후무스

1. 백태콩은 사용하기 하루 전날 미리 불려둡니다.
- 껍질을 벗기지 않고 그대로 불려 사용합니다. (삶기 전 백태콩 → 150g, 삶은 후 백태콩 → 340g)
2. 냄비에 불린 백태콩과 백태콩이 잠길 정도의 물을 넣고 중불에서 약 40분간 삶아줍니다.
- 블렌더에서 부드럽게 갈릴 정도로 삶아줍니다. 통조림 콩을 사용하는 경우 삶는 시간은 단축됩니다.
3. 백태콩이 부드럽게 삶아지면 블렌더에 백태콩 후무스 재료를 모두 넣고 곱게 갈아줍니다.
- 얼음을 넣는 이유는 블렌더에서 갈리면서 공기층을 만들어 더 가볍고 부드러운 질감이 되고, 얼음의 차가운 온도가 재료의 유화를 도와 광택이 도는 크리미한 질감의 후무스를 만들어주기 때문입니다. 블렌더에서 간 직후에는 농도가 묽어 플레이팅하기 어려울 수 있으니 냉장고에 잠시 둔 후 사용하는 것이 좋습니다.
- 타히니가 없다면 참기름과 참깨를 섞어 갈아 사용해도 좋습니다.

YELLOW SOYBEAN HUMMUS

1. Soak the yellow soybeans the day before use.
- Soak them with the skins on. (150 g yellow soybeans before cooking; 340 g after cooking)
2. Place the soaked yellow soybeans in a pot and add enough water to cover. Cook over medium heat for about 40 minutes.
- Cook until soft enough to blend smoothly in a blender. Using canned yellow soybeans will reduce the cooking time.
3. Once the yellow soybeans are soft, combine all the yellow soybean hummus ingredients in a blender, then blend until smooth.
- Ice helps trap air during blending, creating a light, soft texture. The cold temperature also promotes emulsification of the mixture, resulting in a glossy, creamy hummus. The mixture may be slightly thin right after blending. Refrigerate until it thickens enough for plating.
- If tahini is unavailable, blend sesame seeds with sesame oil into a paste, then use as a substitute.

머스터드 비네그렛

1. 볼에 포도씨유와 올리브오일을 제외한 모든 재료를 넣고 휘퍼로 섞어줍니다.
2. 설탕과 소금이 녹으면 포도씨유와 올리브오일을 넣고 섞어줍니다.

- 두 가지 오일을 사용하는 이유는 업장의 경우 원가 절감의 이유도 있겠지만, 엑스트라버진 올리브오일을 단독으로 사용하면 톡 쏘는 풀 향기가 너무 강하게 느껴질 수 있기 때문입니다. 그래서 포도씨유와 함께 사용해 향을 중화시켜 올리브오일의 향이 은은하게 퍼지도록 하는 것이 좋습니다.

MUSTARD VINAIGRETTE

1. In a mixing bowl, combine all the ingredients except the grapeseed oil and olive oil, then whisk.
2. Once the sugar and salt have dissolved, whisk in the grapeseed oil and olive oil until well incorporated.

- While partly for cost-saving, blending these two oils also helps balance the flavor. Extra virgin olive oil alone can be overwhelming due to its pungent, grassy notes. Combining it with grapeseed oil tempers those strong notes, allowing its subtle aroma to gently come through.

구운 채소

1. 로마네스코 브로콜리는 반으로 자른 후 한입 크기로 잘라줍니다.
2. 아스파라거스는 작게 어슷썰어줍니다.

ROASTED VEGETABLES

1. Halve the Romanesco broccoli and cut into bite-sized pieces.
2. Cut the asparagus on a bias into pieces.

3. 손질한 로마네스코 브로콜리와 아스파라거스를 팬에 펼친 후 소금, 흑후추, 올리브오일, 강황 가루, 파프리카 파우더를 뿌립니다.
4. 180°C로 예열된 오븐에서 5~6분간 구워줍니다.
- 그릴에 올려 직화로 구워도 좋습니다.

3. Spread the Romanesco broccoli and asparagus on a sheet pan, then season with salt, black pepper, olive oil, cumin powder, and paprika powder.
4. Roast in an oven preheated to 356°F (180°C) for 5-6 minutes.
- Alternatively, you can grill them over an open flame.

플레이팅

1. 큰 스푼이나 주걱을 이용해 접시 중앙에 백태콩 후무스를 넉넉하게 담고 중앙에 홈을 만들어줍니다.
2. 구운 채소를 올려줍니다.
3. 허브로 장식합니다.

PLATING

1. Using a large spoon or spatula, place a generous amount of the yellow bean hummus in the center of a plate, then gently create an indentation in the middle.
2. Arrange the roasted vegetables in the indentation.
3. Garnish with fresh herbs.

4. 백태콩 후무스 위에 통들깨를 뿌리고 구운 채소 위에 머스터드 비네그렛을 뿌려줍니다.
5. 올리브오일을 한 바퀴 둘러줍니다.
6. 파프리카 파우더를 뿌려 마무리합니다.

4. Sprinkle the whole perilla seeds over the hummus, and drizzle the mustard vinaigrette over the roasted vegetables.
5. Swirl a dash of olive oil over the dish.
6. Finish with a sprinkle of paprika powder.

Cabbage Schnitzel with Romesco

로메스코를 곁들인 양배추 슈니첼

가정식
HOME COOKING

매콤한 파프리카 소스인 로메스코를 곁들인 양배추 슈니첼입니다. 원래 슈니첼은 독일이나 오스트리아 등지에서 돼지고기나 송아지고기를 얇게 펴서 튀겨내는 요리로 알려져 있는데요. 저는 이 전통적인 슈니첼을 채소 요리로 재해석해 보았습니다. 고기 대신 두툼하게 자른 양배추를 바삭하게 튀기듯 구워낸 슈니첼은 충분한 포만감을 주면서 동시에 가벼운 맛과 식감을 선사합니다.

양배추 슈니첼에 곁들인 로메스코 소스는 파프리카와 견과류 등을 곱게 갈아 만든 스페인식 매콤한 소스로, 구운 양배추의 고소한 풍미를 한층 더 풍부하게 끌어올려줍니다. 고기 없이도 이렇게 깊은 맛을 낼 수 있다는 점에서 많은 분들이 놀라워하시고, 실제로도 다이어트나 건강을 생각하시는 분들, 혹은 채식을 실천하시는 분들께 큰 호응을 얻고 있는 메뉴입니다. 간단하면서도 새로운 방식으로 채소를 즐기고 싶은 분들께 꼭 추천하는 요리입니다.

This is Cabbage *Schnitzel*, served with romesco—a spicy bell pepper sauce. *Schnitzel* is traditionally known as a breaded and fried cutlet of thinly pounded meat, most commonly pork or veal, in Germany or Austria. This plant-based version reimagines the classic by replacing the meat with thick-cut cabbage. Roasted until crispy, almost as if fried, the cabbage delivers a satisfying sense of fullness with a light flavor and texture.

Romesco, made by blending bell peppers, nuts, and other ingredients into a smooth sauce, enriches the savory flavors of the roasted cabbage. Many are surprised by the depth of flavor achieved without any meat. This dish has also gained popularity among those seeking healthier meals, watching their weight, or adopting a plant-based diet. It is recommended for anyone looking to enjoy vegetables in a simple yet refreshing way.

Ingredients

2인 분량
Serves 2

로메스코

구운 파프리카	2개
선드라이 토마토	15g
아몬드	6개
파프리카 파우더	5g
할라페뇨	15g
엑스트라버진 올리브오일	20g
소금	5g

양배추 슈니첼

양배추	1/2통
소금	적당량
후춧가루	적당량
디종 머스터드	30g
중력분	60g
달걀	2개
빵가루	150g
식용유	300g

가니쉬

파르미자노 레자노 치즈	적당량
이태리 파슬리	적당량
통후추	적당량
엑스트라버진 올리브오일	적당량

ROMESCO

2	roasted bell peppers
15 g	sundried tomatoes
6	almonds
5 g	paprika powder
15 g	jalapeño
20 g	extra virgin olive oil
5 g	salt

CABBAGE SCHNITZEL

1/2	cabbage
Q.S.	salt
Q.S.	ground black pepper
30 g	Dijon mustard
60 g	all-purpose flour
2	eggs
150 g	breadcrumbs
300 g	cooking oil

GARNISHES

Q.S.	Parmigiano-Reggiano
Q.S.	fresh Italian parsley
Q.S.	black peppercorns
Q.S.	extra virgin olive oil

How to make

로메스코

1. 파프리카는 반으로 자르고 씨를 제거한 후 180℃로 예열된 오븐에서 약 8분간 구워줍니다.
2. 구워져 나온 파프리카는 한 김 식힌 후 나머지 재료와 함께 블렌더로 곱게 갈아줍니다.

ROMESCO

1. Halve the bell peppers, remove the seeds, and roast them in an oven preheated to 356°F (180°C) for about 8 minutes.
2. Let the roasted bell peppers cool slightly, then blend them with the remaining ingredients until smooth.

양배추 슈니첼

1. 양배추는 두께 4cm로 가르고 반으로 잘라줍니다.
2. 자른 양배추 위에 소금, 후춧가루를 뿌려줍니다.

CABBAGE SCHNITZEL

1. Cut the cabbage into 4 cm-thick pieces, then halve each piece.
2. Sprinkle the salt and black pepper over the cabbage.

3. 양배추 사방에 디종 머스터드를 골고루 발라줍니다.
4. 중력분 – 달걀 – 빵가루 순서로 골고루 묻혀줍니다.
- 밀가루 대신 튀김가루를 사용해도 좋습니다.

3. Thoroughly coat all sides of the cabbage with the Dijon mustard.
4. Apply all-purpose flour evenly, dip in beaten eggs, then coat with breadcrumbs.
- Frying powder can be used as a substitute for flour.

5. 식용유를 두른 팬에 슈니첼을 넣고 사방이 노릇해지도록 튀기듯 구워줍니다.

5. Pan-fry the cabbage *schnitzel* in cooking oil until golden brown on all sides.

플레이팅

1. 큰 스푼이나 주걱을 이용해 접시 중앙에 로메스코를 넉넉하게 담고 중앙에 홈을 만들어줍니다.
2. 슈니첼을 올린 후 파르미자노 레자노 치즈를 뿌려줍니다.
3. 이태리 파슬리와 후춧가루를 뿌린 후 올리브오일을 한 바퀴 둘러줍니다.

PLATING

1. Using a large spoon or spatula, place a generous amount of the romesco in the center of a plate, then gently create an indentation in the middle.
2. Arrange the *schnitzel* in the indentation and sprinkle with grated Parmigiano-Reggiano.
3. Sprinkle with chopped Italian parsley and black pepper, then finish with a swirl of olive oil.

DAVID LEE

데이비드 리

요리사는 되지 않겠다고 생각했다. 부모님이 고깃집을 운영하셨는데 정작 가족과 함께 식사할 수 있는 시간은 없었기 때문이다. 농구선수가 되고 싶었지만 부족한 신체 조건으로 진로를 변경하고 대학에서 미술을 공부하다 군대에 갔다. 그곳에서 우연히 취사병이 되었고, 하루에 반나절이 넘는 고된 작업 속에서도 동료들이 한 끼를 맛있게 먹는 모습을 보며 요리의 기쁨을 알게 되었다. 그때 처음, '이 일을 평생 해도 좋겠다'라는 마음이 들었다.

제대 후 미술을 접고, 요리를 배우기 위해 뉴욕으로 떠났다. FCI(French Culinary Institute)에서 공부하고, '더 스포티드 피그', '피숄린', '마사' 등 미쉐린 레스토랑을 거쳐 '반주'와 '오삼일'을 오픈하며 뉴욕에서 15년을 일했다.

뉴욕의 속도와 불 앞에서 버텨낸 시간은 그에게 기술이 아닌 감각을 남겼다. 2019년, 한 육가공 회사의 제안으로 귀국해 그곳에서 근무하다가 한남동에 '군몽(軍夢)'을 열었다. 이곳은 '구운 꿈'이라는 뜻 그대로, 장작과 숯불을 이용한 우드파이어 그릴 요리를 선보이고 있다. 뉴욕에서 배운 요리 기술과 한국의 신선한 식재료를 결합한 그만의 특색 있는 요리다.

2024년에는 넷플릭스 <흑백요리사: 요리 계급 전쟁>에 출연해 '고기깡패'라는 별명을 얻었다. 그가 선보인 '가르비뇽(프랑스 뵈프 부르기뇽과 한국 갈비찜을 결합한 요리)'은 그만의 요리 철학을 가장 잘 보여주는 메뉴였다. 전통과 기술, 그리고 불. 그 사이 어딘가에서 그는 가장 자신다운 맛을 만들어간다.

Chef Lee thought he would never be a chef. His parents owned a barbecue restaurant, but they didn't really have time to eat together as a family. He initially wanted to be a basketball player but switched to a career due to his poor physique, and then studied art in college before serving in the military. There, he happened to become a cook and discovered the joy of cooking after seeing his fellow soldiers enjoying a good meal despite the hard work of the day. That's when he realized he could do this for the rest of his life.

After being discharged from the service, he quit studying art and moved to New York to learn to cook. He studied at the French Culinary Institute (FCI), worked at Michelin-starred restaurants such as The Spotted Pig, Picholine, and Martha, and opened Barn Joo and Osamil, keeping him working for 15 years in New York.

New York's pace and time of enduring in the kitchen left him with a sense, not a skill. In 2019, he returned to Korea at the suggestion of a meat processing company and worked there until he opened Guunmong in Hannam-dong. As it translates to "grilled dream," it features wood-fired grilled dishes using firewood and charcoal. These are his distinctive dishes, which combine the culinary techniques he learned in New York with fresh ingredients from Korea.

In 2024, he earned the nickname "Meat Master" for his role in Netflix's *Culinary Class Wars*. His dish, "*Garbignon*" (a combination of French beef bourguignon and Korean braised short ribs, *Garbijjim*), epitomized his culinary philosophy. Tradition, technique, and fire: Somewhere in between, he creates flavors that are most like him.

군몽
guunmong.seoul

meatthegangster

Galbi Bourguignon A.K.A. Garlbignon

갈비 부르기뇽 A.K.A 가르비뇽

이야기
STORY

이 레시피는 저의 뿌리인 한국과 한식, 그리고 뉴욕에서 배운 여러 요리들, 그중에서도 프렌치 요리를 접목하여 만든 요리입니다. 개발 당시 계절은 겨울이었고, 따뜻한 느낌을 줄 수 있는 한식 요리를 고민하던 중 갈비찜이 떠올랐습니다. 그리고 아내의 제안으로, 한식 갈비찜과 프렌치 요리인 '부르기뇽'이 만나면 더 깊은 맛과 아름다운 플레이팅이 가능하겠다는 아이디어에서 이 레시피가 탄생하게 되었습니다.

이 요리는 제가 운영하는 레스토랑 '군몽'에서 많은 손님들에게 큰 사랑을 받았는데요. 개인적으로는 요리 경연 프로그램 <흑백요리사>에 출연해 선보이며 더 많은 분들의 관심을 받게 되어, 저에게 더욱 의미 있는 레시피로 남아 있습니다.

This recipe brings together my roots—Korea and Korean cuisine—and the diverse culinary styles I explored in New York, particularly French cuisine. I first created it in winter, and while searching for a warm, comforting Korean dish, *galbi-jjim* came to mind. My wife then suggested blending Korean *galbi-jjim* with French *boeuf bourguignon*, an idea that inspired me to create a dish delivering deeper flavors and a refined presentation.

This dish has become beloved by many guests at my restaurant, Gunmong, and holds even greater meaning for me after gaining wider recognition through its feature on the culinary survival show *Culinary Class Wars*.

Ingredients

2인 분량
Serves 2

당근 퓌레

당근 또는 단호박	300g
엑스트라버진 올리브오일	15g
소금	적당량
후춧가루	적당량
우유	50g
동물성 휘핑크림	50g
버터	50g
트러플 오일	3g

갈비 양념

당근	50g
마늘	30g
양송이버섯	20g
양파	15g
배	10g
생강	5g
물	185g
레드와인	50g
간장	45g
설탕	20g
후춧가루	5g
통계피	5g

구운 채소

물	적당량
소금	적당량
미니양배추	200g
엑스트라버진 올리브오일	적당량
피칸	15g
방울토마토	50g
건포도	6g
마늘	20g
양파	100g
화이트와인	15g
후춧가루	적당량
버터	적당량

갈비찜

갈비찜용 소고기 (뼈 있는 상태)	1kg
소금	10g
후춧가루	10g
포도씨유	20g
레드와인	250g

장식

청포도	적당량
엑스트라버진 올리브오일	적당량
허브	적당량

CARROT PURÉE

300 g	carrot or sweet pumpkin
15 g	extra virgin olive oil
Q.S.	salt
Q.S.	ground black pepper
50 g	milk
50 g	animal-based whipping cream
50 g	butter
3 g	truffle oil

GALBI MARINADE

50 g	carrot
30 g	garlic
20 g	button mushroom
15 g	onion
10 g	pear
5 g	ginger
185 g	water
50 g	red wine
45 g	soy sauce
20 g	sugar
5 g	ground black pepper
5 g	cinnamon stick

SAUTÉED VEGETABLES

Q.S.	water
Q.S.	salt
200 g	Brussels sprouts
Q.S.	extra virgin olive oil
15 g	pecan
50 g	cherry tomatoes
6 g	raisins
20 g	garlic
100 g	onion
15 g	white wine
Q.S.	ground black pepper
Q.S.	butter

GALBI-JJIM
(Braised beef short ribs)

1 kg	bone-in beef short ribs (for braising)
10 g	salt
10 g	ground black pepper
20 g	grapeseed oil
250g	red wine

GARNISHES

Q.S.	green grapes
Q.S.	extra virgin olive oil
Q.S.	fresh herbs

How to make

당근 퓌레 CARROT PURÉE

당근 퓌레

1. 껍질을 벗긴 당근을 큼직하게 썰어줍니다.
2. 올리브오일을 두른 팬에 손질한 당근을 넣고 노릇하게 익힌 후 소금과 후춧가루로 간을 합니다.
3. 믹서에 구운 당근, 우유, 휘핑크림을 넣고 곱게 갈아줍니다.

CARROT PURÉE

1. Roughly chop the peeled carrot into pieces.
2. Pan-fry the chopped carrot in olive oil until golden brown. Season with salt and black pepper.
3. In a blender, combine the cooked carrot, milk, and whipping cream, then blend until smooth.

갈비 양념 GALBI MARINADE

4. 냄비로 옮긴 후 버터를 넣고 가열하다가 버터가 녹고 걸쭉해지면 트러플 오일을 넣어 마무리합니다.

갈비 양념

믹서에 모든 재료를 넣고 곱게 갈아줍니다.
- 모든 재료는 믹서에 갈릴 정도로 잘라 사용합니다.

4. Pour the mixture into a pot, add the butter, and bring to a simmer. When the butter melts and the mixture begins to thicken, stir in the truffle oil.

GALBI MARINADE

Combine all the ingredients in a blender, then blend until smooth.
- Make sure the ingredients are cut into pieces suitable for blending.

구운 채소

1. 냄비에 물과 소금을 넣고 끓기 시작하면 반으로 자른 미니양배추를 넣고 살짝 데쳐줍니다.
2. 데친 미니양배추는 얼음물에 빠르게 식힌 후 물기를 제거합니다.
3. 올리브오일을 두른 팬에 데친 미니양배추를 넣고 익혀줍니다.

SAUTÉED VEGETABLES

1. Bring the water and salt to a boil in a pot. Add the halved Brussels sprouts and blanch gently.
2. Transfer them to ice water to cool immediately, then drain.
3. Sauté the Brussels sprouts in olive oil.

4. 양배추가 노릇해지면 버터를 제외한 나머지 재료를 모두 넣고 익힌 후 소금과 후춧가루로 간을 합니다.
5. 버터를 한 스푼 넣고 녹여 마무리합니다.

4. Once golden brown, add the remaining ingredients except butter and continue sautéing. Season with salt and black pepper.
5. Add a spoonful of butter and let it melt to finish.

갈비찜

1. 갈비찜용 소고기에 소금, 후춧가루, 포도씨유로 밑간을 합니다.
2. 달군 팬에 소고기를 넣고 구워줍니다.
3. 소고기를 구운 팬에 레드와인을 붓고 절반 정도로 졸여줍니다.

GALBI-JJIM (Braised beef short ribs)

1. Season the beef short ribs with salt, black pepper, and grapeseed oil.
2. Sear the short ribs in a preheated pan.
3. Pour in red wine to deglaze the pan, then simmer until reduced by about half.

4. 압력밥솥에 구운 소고기와 소고기가 잠길 만큼의 갈비 양념, 3을 넣고 약 45분간 조리합니다.

4. In a pressure cooker, add the seared short ribs, enough *galbi* marinade to cover, and (**3**), then cook for about 45 minutes.

마무리

1. 청포도에 올리브오일을 뿌린 후 토치로 그을려줍니다.
2. 접시 중앙에 당근 퓌레를 넓게 펴 발라줍니다.
3. 당근 퓌레 위에 갈비찜을 올려줍니다.

FINISH

1. Drizzle the green grapes with olive oil, and gently char them with a blowtorch.
2. Spread the carrot purée generously in the center of a plate.
3. Place the *galbi-jjim* on top of the purée.

4. 갈비찜 위에 구운 채소를 올려 균형을 맞춰준 후 갈비찜 위에 갈비찜 국물을 살짝 뿌려줍니다.
5. 빈 공간에 그을린 청포도를 올려줍니다.
6. 허브를 올려 마무리합니다.

4. Arrange the pan-fried vegetables over the *galbi-jjim* to create balance, then spoon some braising liquid over the top.
5. Serve the gently charred green grapes on the side.
6. Garnish with fresh herbs.

Doenjang Jalapeño Maekjeok

(Doenjang Jalapeño Marinated Pork)

된장 할라페뇨 맥적

가정식
HOME COOKING

제가 개발한 메뉴들은 대부분 뉴욕에서 현지인들과 소통하며 만든 것들입니다. 이 메뉴 또한 한식을 기반으로 하되, 뉴욕 사람들에게도 익숙하고 친근하게 다가갈 수 있는 맛으로 완성해 본 것 중 하나입니다.

돼지고기를 활용한 요리인데, 처음엔 '폭찹(Pork Chop)'이라는 익숙한 형태에서 출발했습니다. 이를 어떻게 한국적인 방식으로 풀어낼 수 있을까 고민하다가, 오래된 한식 조리법 중 하나인 '맥적'에서 영감을 받아, 돼지고기에 된장 소스를 발라 숙성시킨 뒤 구워내는 스타일로 완성했습니다.

된장은 외국인들에게는 블루치즈처럼 다소 낯설고 어려운 재료일 수 있습니다. 그래서 된장 본연의 깊은 맛은 유지하되, 할라페뇨(또는 고추)를 더해 매콤하고 개운한 풍미를 더했습니다. 이로써 된장의 고유한 맛은 살리면서도, 현지인들에게 부담스럽지 않은 방향으로 조화를 이루려 했습니다.

A large part of my cooking was inspired by connections with locals during my time in New York. This dish is one of those rooted in Korean cuisine but reimagined in a way that feels familiar and approachable, even to New Yorkers.

I started by taking a familiar format—the pork chop. While exploring ways to give it a Korean twist, I drew inspiration from *maekjeok*, a traditional method of marinating and grilling meat. That led me to coat the pork in a doenjang-based marinade, allowing it to age before finishing it on the grilling.

Doenjang, like blue cheese, can be strange and challenging for those less familiar with it. To make it easier to enjoy, I added jalapeño (or other chili peppers) to bring a refreshing heat while preserving its rich, savory depth. In doing so, I sought to create a harmonious flavor that highlights its essence without overwhelming local diners.

Ingredients

1인 분량
Serves 1

| 돼지고기 목살 | 200g |
| 식용유 | 적당량 |

된장 소스*
된장	80g
미림	10g
참기름	10g
꿀	30g
할라페뇨 또는 청양고추	50g
마늘	20g
양파	40g

샐러드
사과	적당량
루꼴라	적당량
된장 소스*	적당량

| 200 g | pork shoulder |
| Q.S. | cooking oil |

DOENJANG MARINADE*
80 g	doenjang (Korean soybean paste)
10 g	mirin
10 g	sesame oil
30 g	honey
50 g	jalapeño or cheongyang green chili peppers
20 g	garlic
40 g	onion

SALAD
Q.S.	apple
Q.S.	arugula
Q.S.	doenjang marinade*

How to make

1. 믹서에 된장 소스 재료를 모두 넣고 곱게 갈아줍니다.
- 사용하는 된장의 염도와 고추의 매운 정도에 따라 다른 맛으로 완성되므로, 처음 만드는 경우라면 된장과 고추를 한 번에 다 넣지 말고 조금씩 늘려가며 최종 간을 확인하시기 바랍니다.
- 꿀은 아카시아꿀이나 밤꿀을 사용하는 것을 추천합니다.
2. 볼에 돼지고기 목살과 된장 소스를 넣고 고르게 버무린 후 냉장고에서 최소 2시간 숙성시켜줍니다.
- 하루 전날 숙성하는 것이 풍미를 극대화하는 가장 좋은 방법입니다.

1. In a blender, combine all the doenjang marinade ingredients and blend until smooth.
- The flavor may vary depending on the saltiness of the doenjang and the heat of the green chili peppers. If you're making it for the first time, gradually add doenjang and green chili peppers, adjusting to taste rather than adding the full amount at once.
- For the honey, acacia or chestnut honey is recommended.
2. In a mixing bowl, evenly toss the pork shoulder with the doenjang marinade, then refrigerate for at least 2 hours.
- For maximum flavor, it is best to marinate it a day in advance.

3. 식용유를 두른 팬을 강불로 예열한 후 중불로 줄여 숙성시킨 돼지고기 목살을 넣고 구워줍니다.
- 직화로 구우면 풍미를 더 높일 수 있습니다.
4. 살 겉면은 캐러멜화가 되도록 굽되, 내부는 촉촉함을 유지하도록 불 조절을 하면 구워줍니다.

3. Preheat a pan with cooking oil over high heat, then reduce to medium and sear the marinated pork shoulder.
- For a richer flavor, grill it over an open flame.
4. Carefully control the heat to caramelize the surface, while keeping the inside juicy.

5. 구운 돼지고기 목살을 잠시 두어 2~3분간 레스팅합니다.
- 돼지고기는 바싹 굽는 것보다 미디엄(겉은 익히고 속은 분홍빛이 돌고 촉촉함이 살아 있게)으로 굽는 것이 맛있습니다.
6. 볼에 얇게 썬 사과와 루꼴라, 남은 된장 소스를 넣고 버무려 샐러드를 완성합니다.
7. 레스팅한 돼지고기 목살을 적당한 크기로 잘라줍니다.

5. Let the pork shoulder rest for 2-3 minutes.
- It is best enjoyed medium—seared on the outside with a pink, juicy center—rather than cooking all the way through.
6. In a mixing bowl, toss the thinly sliced apple and arugula with the remaining doenjang marinade to make the salad.
7. Slice the rested pork shoulder into moderately sized pieces.

8. 접시에 샐러드와 돼지고기 목살을 올려 마무리합니다.

8. Place the sliced pork shoulder and salad together on a plate.

RYU TAEHWAN

류태환

어릴 적부터 미각이 남달랐다. 가족과 함께한 식탁에서 요리의 즐거움을 자연스럽게 익혔고, 더 넓은 세계의 맛을 알고 싶어 요리사의 길을 선택했다. 도쿄 핫토리 영양전문학교에서 요리를 익혔고, 이후 시드니, 런던의 미쉐린 레스토랑에서 실력을 갈고닦으며 미식의 언어를 다채롭게 익혀나갔다.

2011년, 서울 신사동에 자신의 이름을 내건 레스토랑 '류니끄'를 열었다. 현재는 도산공원으로 자리를 옮겨, 한국적인 재료와 그만의 감각을 입힌 요리들을 선보이고 있다.

'류니끄(Ryunique)'는 그의 성 '류(Ryu)'와 '유니크(Unique)'의 합성어로, 셰프 자신만의 고유한 요리를 선보이겠다는 철학을 담고 있다. 이 이름처럼, 그의 요리는 하나의 틀에 머물지 않는다. 프렌치와 한식, 전통과 실험 사이의 경계를 넘나들며 새로운 조합을 만들어내고, 그 안에 한국 식재료의 가치와 가능성을 담아낸다. 섬세한 플레이팅 뒤에는 오랜 시간 공들인 기술과 감각이 깃들어 있고, 한 접시에는 늘 질문과 제안이 공존한다.

그는 오늘도 주방에서 질문을 반복하며 요리를 다시 다듬는다. '이게 정말 새로운가?'라는 물음에서부터, '이게 정말 맛있는가?'라는 확인까지. 류니끄의 테이블 위에는 언제나 그 고민의 흔적이 담긴 한 접시가 놓인다.

From an early age, he had a keen sense of taste. He learned the joy of cooking at the dinner table with his family and chose to become a chef to explore the flavors of the wider world. He studied at Hattori Ecole de Cuisine et Nutrition in Tokyo. He later honed his skills at Michelin-starred restaurants in Sydney and London, where he mastered the language of gastronomy.

In 2011, he opened a restaurant, Ryunique, in Sinsa-dong, Seoul. Today, he has relocated to Dosan Park, where he serves dishes that combine Korean ingredients with his own flair.

Ryunique is a combination of his last name, Ryu, and the word 'unique,' and reflects the chef's philosophy of creating dishes that are uniquely his own. As the name indicates, his dishes don't fit into one box. He creates new combinations, blurring the lines between French and Korean, tradition and experimentation, and captures the value and potential of Korean ingredients. Behind each delicate plate is a long process of skill and sensitivity, and each dish is always a question and a suggestion.

Today, he is back in the kitchen, refining the dishes by asking questions, from asking, "Is this really new?" to confirming, "Is this really good?" There's always a plate on his table that bears the marks of his struggle.

류니끄
ryunique_seoul

chef_ryutaehwan

Boyangsik for Chungmugong Yi Sunsin

(Energy-Boosting Dish for Admiral Yi Sunsin)

충무공 이순신을 위한 보양식

이야기
STORY

전라남도는 식재료가 풍부한 지역으로, 산과 바다, 들에서 나는 재료와 지역 고유의 조리법이 어우러져 특색 있는 음식이 발달해왔습니다. 기후와 지형이 만들어낸 재료에 사람의 손과 기술이 더해져 완성되는 음식은, 지역성과 계절감을 잘 반영한 결과물이죠.

저는 셰프로서 오랜 시간 전라남도에서 식재료를 공부해 왔고, 이 지역을 여행하며 역사적 인물인 이순신 장군의 이동 경로와 겹치는 지점을 발견하는 흥미로운 경험도 했습니다. 우연처럼 보이지만 식재료에 대한 탐구와 역사적 관심이 만나 의미 있는 통찰을 얻을 수 있었습니다.

여기에서 소개하는 요리는 가덕도의 반건조 대구, 울돌목의 전복, 완도의 다시마, 남해의 백합 등 전라남도 식재료를 활용한 보양식입니다. 실제 류니끄에서도 선보였던 메뉴로, 재료의 맛이 깊게 배인 국물에 밥을 곁들이면 한 끼 식사로 든든하게 즐길 수 있습니다.

South Jeolla Province is rich in natural ingredients, giving rise to unique local dishes that harmonize the bounty of the mountains, sea, and fields with traditional culinary techniques. With ingredients shaped by the region's climate and topography, and brought to life through human hands and craftsmanship, each dish faithfully reflects both its regional identity and seasonality.

As a chef, I spent an extended period exploring ingredients in South Jeolla Province. While traveling through the region, I had an unexpected encounter retracing the path of Admiral Yi Sunsin, one of Korea's revered historical figures. Though it may have seemed like a coincidence, the experience brought culinary and historical exploration together, offering me meaningful insights.

This dish is a Korean *boyangsik* (energy-boosting food), made with ingredients from South Jeolla Province, including half-dried cod from Gadeokdo Island, abalone from Uldolmok Strait, kelp from Wando County, and white clams from Namhae County. Once showcased at Ryunique, it becomes a satisfying meal when served with rice and enjoyed with a soup richly infused with these local flavors.

Ingredients

2인 분량
Serves 2

전복	2마리	
반건조 대구	2조각	
대구 이리	적당량	

버섯 스톡*
모렐 버섯	1개
포르치니 버섯	1개
표고버섯	1개
물	360ml

백합 스톡*
백합	2개
물	360ml
정종	18ml
다시마	작은 조각 1개

에그 푸딩
우유	100ml
생강 즙	2ml
계란	1개
알부민 파우더	3g
알긴	소량
물에 푼 감자전분	적당량

▸ 알긴은 에그 푸딩 전체 용량의 약 0.3%를 사용합니다.

버섯 백합 스톡
버섯 스톡*과 백합 스톡*	1:1 비율
무	적당량
알배추	5g
전복 내장	전복 2마리 분량
물에 푼 칡전분	적당량
모렐버섯	적당량
포르치니 버섯	적당량
표고버섯	적당량
은행	2알

장식
채 썬 양배추와 쪽파	적당량
참기름	적당량
돼지감자칩	적당량

2	abalones
2	half-dried cod fillets
Q.S.	cod milt

MUSHROOM STOCK*
1	morel mushroom
1	porcini mushroom
1	shiitake mushroom
360 ml	water

WHITE CLAM STOCK*
2	white clams
360 ml	water
18 ml	sake
1 sheet	kelp (small)

EGG PUDDING
100 ml	milk
2 ml	ginger juice
1	egg
3 g	albumin powder
Q.S.	algin
Q.S.	potato starch slurry

▸ Use 0.3% algin relative to the total weight of egg pudding mixture.

MUSHROOM AND WHITE CLAM STOCK
1:1 ratio	mushroom stock* and white claim stock*
Q.S.	Korean radish
5 g	baby napa cabbage
Q.S.	innards (from 2 abalones)
Q.S.	kudzu starch slurry
Q.S.	morel mushroom
Q.S.	porcini mushroom
Q.S.	shiitake mushroom
2	ginkgo nuts

GARNISHES
Q.S.	sliced cabbage and Korean scallions
Q.S.	sesame oil
Q.S.	sunchoke chips

How to make

 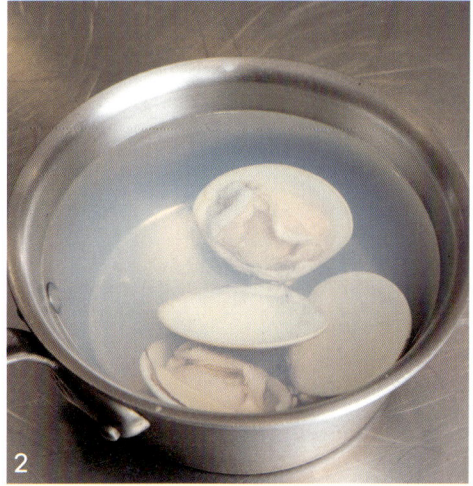 

1. 냄비에 버섯 스톡 재료를 모두 넣고 가열한 후, 끓어오르면 불을 끄고 그대로 두어 버섯의 맛과 향이 우러나도록 합니다.
2. 냄비에 백합 스톡 재료를 모두 넣고 백합이 열릴 때까지 가열합니다.
3. 볼에 물에 푼 감자전분을 제외한 에그 푸딩 재료를 모두 넣고 블렌더로 곱게 갈아준 후 체에 내려줍니다.

1. In a pot, combine all the mushroom stock ingredients and bring to a boil. Once boiling, turn off the heat and let it sit to allow the flavor and aroma of the mushrooms to infuse into the stock.
2. In a separate pot, combine all the white clam stock ingredients and heat until the clams open.
3. In a mixing bowl, combine all the egg pudding ingredients except the potato starch slurry. Blend until smooth and strain through a sieve.

4. 3을 냄비로 옮겨 약불에서 물에 푼 감자전분을 조금씩 넣어가며 농도를 맞춰 부드러운 달걀 푸딩으로 만들어줍니다.
5. 전복은 깨끗이 씻어 껍질과 내장을 분리한 후 적당한 크기로 잘라줍니다. 손질한 전복은 진공백에 담아 90°C에서 20분간 스팀으로 익혀주고, 내장은 다져 버섯 백합 스톡을 만들 때 사용합니다.

4. Pour (3) into a pot and gradually stir in the potato starch slurry over low heat to adjust the consistency, forming a smooth egg pudding.
5. Wash the abalone thoroughly. Separate the abalone meat from the shells and innards, then cut it into bite-sized pieces. Place the meat in a vacuum bag and steam at 194°F (90°C) for 20 minutes. Chop the innards to use in the mushroom and white clam stock.

6. 냄비에 버섯 스톡, 백합 스톡, 작게 깍둑썬 무와 알배추, 다진 전복 내장을 넣고 가열합니다.
- 버섯 스톡과 백합 스톡은 1:1 비율로 사용할 양에 맞춰 준비합니다.
7. 물에 푼 칡전분을 넣어 농도를 맞추고, 슬라이스한 모렐버섯, 포르치니 버섯, 표고버섯, 은행을 넣고 익힌 후 소금으로 간을 합니다.
- 물과 칡전분을 1:1 비율로 섞어, 국물이 걸쭉해지고 약간의 끈적임이 느껴질 정도로 사용합니다.
8. 반건조 대구는 적당한 크기로 잘라 소금을 뿌려 밑간을 한 후 식용유를 두른 팬에서 껍질은 바삭하고 속은 촉촉하게 구워줍니다.

6. In a pot, combine the mushroom stock, white clam stock, diced Korean radish and baby napa cabbage, and chopped abalone innards, then bring to a boil.
- Blend the mushroom and white clam stocks in a 1:1 ratio and prepare as needed.
7. Stir in the kudzu starch slurry to adjust the consistency. Add the sliced morel, porcini, and shiitake mushrooms, along with ginkgo nuts, then season with salt.
- To make the kudzu starch slurry, mix water and kudzu starch in a 1:1 ratio. Stir it into the soup until thickened and slightly viscous.
8. Cut the half-dried cod into moderately sized pieces and season with salt. Pan-fry in cooking oil until the skin is crispy and the inside remains juicy.

9. 접시에 에그 푸딩을 넣고 익힌 대구 이리를 올려줍니다.
- 대구 이리는 끓는 물에서 살짝 데쳐 사용합니다.
10. 익힌 대구를 올려줍니다.

9. Place the egg pudding in a bowl and add the cod milt.
- Gently blanch the cod milt before use.
10. Top with the pan-fried cod.

11. 전복을 담아줍니다.
12. 뜨겁게 데운 **7**을 담아줍니다.
13. 채 썬 양배추와 쪽파를 올려줍니다.

11. Arrange the abalone meat.
12. Gently ladle the hot soup from (**7**) over the dish.
13. Garnish with sliced cabbage and Korean scallions.

14. 참기름을 뿌려줍니다.
15. 돼지감자칩을 뿌려 마무리합니다.
- 얇게 썬 돼지감자를 튀겨 사용합니다. 돼지감자 대신 우엉을 얇게 썰어 튀긴 우엉칩을 사용해도 좋습니다.

14. Drizzle with sesame oil.
15. Finish with sunchoke chips.
- Deep-fry thinly sliced sunchoke before use. Thinly sliced burdock chips can be used as a substitute for sunchoke chips.

Open-Faced Sandwich with Half-Dried Herring

가정식
HOME COOKING

반건조 청어 오픈 샌드위치

청어는 세계적으로 활용도가 높은 생선입니다. 북유럽과 네덜란드에서는 국민 생선이라 불릴 만큼 보편적으로 소비되며, 한때는 경제 성장에 기여한 주요 산업 자원이기도 했습니다. '헤링본(Herringbone)'이라는 직물 패턴 역시 청어의 뼈 모양에서 유래했죠. 일본에서는 청어를 훈연, 건조한 뒤 간장에 졸인 '미가키 니신'을 따뜻한 소바 위에 올려 먹는데, 이는 교토 지역의 대표적인 명물입니다. 한국의 경우 대부분 해풍에 말린 과메기 형태로 소비됩니다. 이처럼 청어는 지역과 문화에 따라 다양한 방식으로 활용되는 재료입니다.

이번에 소개하는 요리는 반건조 청어를 활용한 오픈 샌드위치입니다. 잘 구운 빵 위에 삶은 감자, 달걀, 양파를 섞어 올리고, 청어 껍질을 살짝 그을린 뒤 달콤한 간장 소스를 발라 풍미를 더했습니다. 마지막으로 허브를 올려 마무리하면, 간단하지만 깊은 맛을 느낄 수 있는 한 끼 식사로 완성됩니다.

Herring is a versatile fish, widely enjoyed around the world. Its widespread consumption has earned it the nickname "the national fish" in Northern Europe and the Netherlands. At one time, it was a major industrial resource that played a key role in economic development in these countries. The textile pattern known as "herringbone" also takes its name from the shape of a herring's bones. In Japan, *migaki nishin*—smoked, dried, and then simmered in soy sauce—is a specialty of Kyoto City, often served atop warm soba. In Korea, herring is mostly consumed as *gwamegi*, naturally dried in the sea breeze. As such, herring is enjoyed in a variety of ways, shaped by local traditions and cultural contexts.

This dish is an open-faced sandwich featuring half-dried herring. A mixture of mashed potatoes, eggs, and onions is served on perfectly toasted bread. The herring skin is gently roasted and glazed with a sweet soy sauce to deepen its flavor. A final touch of fresh herbs completes the dish, making it a simple yet substantial meal with deeply layered flavors.

Ingredients

2인 분량
Serves 2

반건조 청어	1마리
핫도그 번	2개
버터	적당량
과일잼	적당량

청어 데리야끼 소스

청어 뼈와 머리	청어 2마리 분량
물	100ml
미림	100ml
설탕	100ml
생강	3g
다시마	3g

달걀 샐러드

삶은 달걀	2개
삶아 으깬 감자	70g
마요네즈	50g
꿀	10g
다진 샬롯	4g
다진 파슬리	2g
소금	적당량
디종 머스터드	적당량

토핑

허브	적당량
건조한 청어알	적당량
엑스트라버진 올리브오일	적당량
카옌페퍼	적당량

1	half-dried herring
2	hot dog buns
Q.S.	butter
Q.S.	fruit jam

HERRING TERIYAKI SAUCE

Q.S.	herring bones and heads (from 2 herrings)
100 ml	water
100 ml	mirin
100 ml	sugar
3 g	ginger
3 g	kelp

EGG SALAD

2	boiled eggs
70 g	mashed potatoes
50 g	mayonnaise
10 g	honey
4 g	chopped shallot
2 g	chopped parsley
Q.S.	salt
Q.S.	Dijon mustard

TOPPINGS

Q.S.	fresh herbs
Q.S.	dried herring roe
Q.S.	extra virgin olive oil
Q.S.	cayenne pepper

How to make

1. 청어는 머리와 꼬리를 자르고, 비늘과 내장을 깨끗이 제거하고 뼈를 바른 후 냉장고에서 이틀간 말려줍니다.
- 청어의 머리와 뼈는 버리지 않고 청어 데리야끼 소스를 만들 때 사용합니다.
2. 말린 청어를 오븐에서 껍질이 노릇하고 바삭해질 때까지 익혀줍니다.

1. Cut off the heads and tails of the herrings, and remove the scales, innards, and bones. Dry the filleted herrings in the refrigerator for 2 days.
- Reserve the heads and tails for making the herring teriyaki sauce.
2. Roast the dried herring fillets in the oven until the skins turn golden brown and crispy.

3. 냄비에 청어 데리야끼 소스 재료를 모두 넣고 소스 농도가 될 때까지 졸인 후 걸러줍니다.
4. 볼에 달걀 샐러드 재료를 모두 넣고 섞어줍니다.

3. In a pot, combine the herring teriyaki sauce ingredients and simmer until reduced to a sauce consistency. Strain through a sieve.
4. In a mixing bowl, combine the egg salad ingredients and mix well.

5. 핫도그 번을 반으로 자른 후 버터를 발라 오븐에서 노릇하게 굽고 살짝 식혀줍니다.
6. 익힌 청어 껍질에 청어 데리야끼 소스를 발라줍니다.
7. 구운 핫도그 번에 과일잼을 얇게 펴 발라줍니다.

5. Cut the hot dog buns in half, butter the cut sides, and toast in the oven until golden. Let cool slightly.
6. Brush the herring skin with the herring teriyaki sauce.
7. Spread the fruit jam onto the toasted buns.

8. 달걀 샐러드를 넉넉하게 올려줍니다.
9. 구운 청어를 올려줍니다.
10. 허브를 올리고 건조한 청어알, 올리브오일, 카옌페퍼를 뿌려 마무리합니다.

8. Top with a generous amount of egg salad.
9. Place the roasted herring fillets on top.
10. Garnish with fresh herbs, dried herring roe, a sprinkle of cayenne pepper, and a drizzle of olive oil.

PARK JOONWOO

박준우

어릴 적부터 언어와 문학에 관심이 많았고, 한때는 시인을 꿈꾸기도 했다. 하지만 2001년, 부모님의 해외 발령으로 인해 벨기에로 떠나게 되면서 삶의 방향이 바뀌었다. 가족과 함께 장을 보고, 유럽의 다양한 식재료와 음식을 접하는 경험이 쌓이면서 자연스럽게 요리에 대한 관심이 깊어졌다.

이후 프랑스로 건너가 파리의 '에콜 페랑디(École Ferrandi)'에서 프랑스 요리와 와인을 정식으로 배웠고, 귀국 후에는 <마스터셰프 코리아 시즌1> 준우승자로 대중에게 이름을 알렸다. 이후 <냉장고를 부탁해>, <수요미식회>, <흑백요리사: 요리 계급 전쟁> 등 다양한 방송에 출연하며 음식에 대한 폭넓은 지식과 감각적인 언어로 주목을 받았다.

현재는 서울 종로구 서촌에서 '카페 오쁘띠베르'를 운영하며, 자신이 가장 사랑하는 디저트와 와인, 요리를 선보이고 있다. 그 공간에서 그는 프랑스와 벨기에의 클래식한 레시피를 대중의 취향에 맞춰 섬세하게 풀어내며, 일상 속에서 편안하게 즐길 수 있는 미식의 형태를 제안하고 있다.

그는 주방에서 요리를 하며 동시에 글을 쓰는, 흔치 않은 이력을 지닌 셰프다. 요리를 언어로 설명할 줄 알고, 맛을 문장으로 풀어낼 줄 아는 그만의 강점은, 셰프로서의 실력뿐 아니라 콘텐츠를 통해 사람들과 연결되는 방식에서도 돋보인다. 그는 오늘도 자신만의 감각으로 요리와 문장, 맛과 언어를 함께 다루고 있다.

From a young age, he was interested in languages and literature and, at one point even dreamed of becoming a poet. However, in 2001, his life changed when his parents were posted overseas and moved to Belgium. As he grew up grocery shopping with his family and gaining experience with the different ingredients and cuisines of Europe, his interest in cooking naturally deepened.

He then moved to France to study French cuisine and wine at École Ferrandi in Paris. After returning home, he became known as the second-place of *MasterChef Korea: Season 1*. Since then, he has appeared on various programs such as *Chef & My Fridge*, *Wednesday Food Talk*, and *Culinary Class Wars*, gaining attention for his extensive knowledge of food and sensuous language.

He currently runs café Aux Petits Verres in Seochon, Jongno-gu, Seoul, where he serves his favorite desserts, wines, and dishes. Here, he delicately translates classic French and Belgian recipes to suit the public's taste, proposing a form of gastronomy that can be enjoyed in the comfort of everyday life.

He has the rare career of being a chef who writes while cooking in the kitchen. His ability to translate food into words and flavors into sentences is what makes him stand out not only as a chef but also in the way he connects with people through his content. Today, he continues to combine food and words, flavor and language in his own unique way.

카페 오쁘띠베르
auxpetitsverres

seoul_1983

Monkfish Médaillon with Whole Wheat Risotto and Champagne Sauce

이야기
STORY

통밀 리소토와 샴페인 소스를 곁들인
아귀 메다이용

저는 2009년 프랑스 파리의 페랑디(Ferrandi)라는 학교에서 요리를 배웠는데요. 이 레시피는 그곳에서 배운 여러 레시피의 구성 요소들을 제 취향껏 추려 모아 발전시켜 본 결과물입니다. 이 요리의 기본 틀은 페랑디의 본과 수업 외 트레퇴르(Traiteur) 과정을 담당하던 교수 앙투완 셰페르(Antoine Schaefers) 셰프의 레시피 'Des ronds dans l'eau et dans l'air en l'envolée Kandinsky'에서 시작한 것입니다. 원래는 아귀 꼬리를 메달 모양으로 고정해 익히고, 쌀 대신 통밀로 만든 리소토를 그릇에 담은 뒤, 다양한 색의 채소를 퓌레와 소스로 만들어 그가 좋아하던 바실리 칸딘스키(Wassily Kandinsky) 그림의 색과 도형을 오마주하여 플레이팅하는 요리였습니다. 저는 그 레시피에서 '칸딘스키적 플레이팅'을 위해 사용한 다양한 색감의 채소들의 수를 줄여 좀 더 심플하게 그릇에 담기로 하고, 셰프가 당시 즐겨 사용하던 아시아의 향신료들 대신, 샴페인의 산미를 살린 소스와 아귀의 간으로 만든 퓌레를 추가했습니다. 이 레시피는 2017년 열었던 파인다이닝 레스토랑 '알테르에고(Alter ego)'의 겨울 메뉴로 처음 선보였고, 이후 명품 브랜드와 호텔, 리조트 등의 VIP 행사의 객원 셰프로 초청받을 때마다 준비하는 제 시그니처메뉴 중 하나가 되었습니다.

In 2009, I studied culinary arts at Ferrandi in Paris, France. This recipe is the result of my personal interpretation, drawing on elements from various recipes I learned there. Its foundation originates from *Des ronds dans l'eau et dans l'air en l'envolée Kandinsky*, a dish created by Professor Antoine Schaefers, who headed the Traiteur course offered outside the regular curriculum at Ferrandi. The original dish features monkfish tail shaped into medallions, served with risotto made with whole wheat instead of rice. It is plated with colorful vegetable purées and sauces, paying homage to the colors and geometric forms often found in the works of Wassily Kandinsky. For my version, I simplified the variety of colorful vegetables used in the "Kandinsky-style plating" to create a cleaner presentation, and replaced the Asian spices he favored at the time with a sauce that highlights Champagne's acidity along with a monkfish liver purée. This dish was first showcased on the winter menu at Alter ego, a fine-dining restaurant I opened in 2017. It has since become one of my signature dishes, which I often prepare whenever I am invited as a guest chef for luxury brands, hotels, and resorts.

Ingredients

2인 분량
Serves 2

아귀 스테이크

아귀 꼬리 살	140g
소금	적당량
후춧가루	적당량
엑스트라버진 올리브오일	적당량
마늘	1알
타임	2줄기
버터	적당량
펜넬 줄기	적당량

생선 육수*

데친 생선 뼈	50g
물	500ml
양파	60g
당근	20g
셀러리	15g
파	5g
파슬리 줄기	적당량
타임	3줄기

통밀 리소토

통밀	50g
엑스트라버진 올리브오일	10ml
양파	40g
샬롯	20g
셀러리	10g
샴페인	20ml
생선 육수*	50ml
사프란	0.5g
소금	적당량
백후추	적당량
주키니	5g
버터	10g
이탈리안 파슬리	1g
처빌	2g

샴페인 소스

카놀라유	5ml
버터	5g
양파	40g
샬롯	20g
처빌 줄기	1.5g
샴페인	125ml
생선 육수*	140ml
생크림	110ml
소금	적당량
코리앤더 시드 파우더	적당량

아귀 간 퓌레

아귀 간	30g
우유	50ml
타임	1g
버터	10g
생크림	10ml
코냑	5ml
소금	적당량
흑후추	적당량

가니시

펜넬	50g
버터	적당량
레몬즙	적당량
화이트 아스파라거스	30g
레드 파프리카	10g
엑스트라버진 올리브오일	적당량

장식

허브	적당량

MONKFISH STEAK

140 g	monkfish tail meat
Q.S.	salt
Q.S.	ground black pepper
Q.S.	extra virgin olive oil
1	garlic clove
2	fresh thyme sprigs
Q.S.	butter
Q.S.	fennel stalks

FISH STOCK*

50 g	blanched fish bones
500 ml	water
60 g	onion
20 g	carrot
15 g	celery
5 g	green onion
Q.S.	fresh parsley stems
3	fresh thyme sprigs

WHOLE WHEAT RISOTTO

50 g	whole wheat
10 ml	extra virgin olive oil
40 g	onion
20 g	shallot
10 g	celery
20 ml	Champagne
50 ml	fish stock*
0.5 g	saffron
Q.S.	salt
Q.S.	ground white pepper
5 g	zucchini
10 g	butter
1 g	fresh Italian parsley
2 g	fresh chervil

CHAMPAGNE SAUCE

5 ml	canola oil (rapeseed oil)
5 g	butter
40 g	onion
20 g	shallot
1.5 g	fresh chervil stems
125 ml	Champagne
140 ml	fish stock*
110 ml	fresh cream
Q.S.	salt
Q.S.	coriander seed powder

MONKFISH LIVER PURÉE

30 g	monkfish liver
50 ml	milk
1 g	fresh thyme
10 g	butter
10 ml	fresh cream
5 ml	Cognac
Q.S.	salt
Q.S.	ground black pepper

GARNISHES

50 g	fennel bulb
Q.S.	butter
Q.S.	lemon juice
30 g	white asparagus
10 g	red bell pepper
Q.S.	extra virgin olive oil

PLATING DECORATION

Q.S.	fresh herbs

How to make

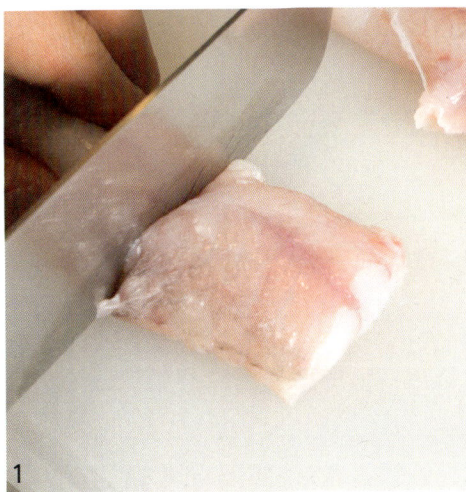  

아귀 스테이크

1. 아귀를 발라 꼬리 살을 적당한 크기로 자른 후 소금과 후춧가루로 밑간을 합니다.
- 손질된 아귀 꼬리 살을 구입해 사용해도 좋습니다.
2. 올리브오일을 두른 팬에 마늘과 타임을 넣고 향을 냅니다.
3. 손질한 아귀 꼬리 살을 넣고 익혀줍니다.

MONKFISH STEAK

1. Fillet the monkfish tails and cut the tail meat into moderately sized pieces. Season with salt and black pepper.
- Pre-filleted monkfish tail meat can also be used.
2. In a pan with olive oil, add the garlic and thyme to infuse their aromas.
3. Place the tail meat into the pan and pan-fry.

4. 아귀 꼬리 살이 익기 시작하면, 큼직하게 썬 버터와 펜넬 줄기를 넣습니다.
5. 버터를 아귀 꼬리 살에 끼얹어가며 고르게 익힌 후 후춧가루를 뿌리고 건져냅니다.

4. Once the tail meat begins to cook, add the roughly sliced fennel stalks along with the butter.
5. Baste the tail meat with the pan liquid until evenly cooked. Sprinkle with black pepper and remove from the pan.

생선 육수

1. 냄비에 모든 재료를 넣고 강불로 가열하다가 거품이 올라오면 중불로 줄이고 거품을 제거합니다.
- 아귀를 발라내고 남은 뼈를 사용하면 좋습니다.
2. 약 45분간 끓인 후 체에 걸러줍니다.
3. 키친타월을 이용해 생선 육수 표면에 뜬 기름을 제거합니다.

FISH STOCK

1. In a pot, combine all the fish stock ingredients and bring to a boil over high heat. Once the scum rises to the surface, reduce the heat to medium and skim it off.
- Add the monkfish bones left after filleting to the stock.
2. Continue cooking for about 45 minutes, then strain through a sieve.
3. Remove any grease from the surface of the stock using a kitchen towel.

통밀 리소토

1. 통밀은 전날 미리 불려 물기를 제거해 준비합니다.
2. 올리브오일을 두른 팬에 작게 깍둑썬 양파, 샬롯, 셀러리를 넣고 볶아줍니다.
3. 채소가 익기 시작하면 불려둔 통밀을 넣고 볶아줍니다.

WHOLE WHEAT RISOTTO

1. Soak the whole wheat a day in advance, then drain and set aside.
2. In a pan with olive oil, stir-fry the finely diced onion, shallot, and celery.
3. When the vegetables begin to soften, add the soaked whole wheat and stir-fry.

4. 통밀이 익기 시작하면 샴페인을 넣고 수분을 날려줍니다.
5. 샴페인이 졸아들면 생선 육수와 샤프란을 넣고 소금과 백후추로 간을 합니다.
6. 생선 육수가 졸아들고 통밀이 적당하게 익으면 불을 끄고 작게 깍둑썬 주키니를 넣고 잔열로 익혀줍니다.

4. When the whole wheat starts to cook, pour in the Champagne and allow the moisture to evaporate.
5. Once the Champagne has reduced, add the fish stock and saffron. Season with salt and white pepper.
6. Once the fish stock has reduced and the whole wheat is partially cooked, turn off the heat. Stir in the finely diced zucchini, and let it cook in the residual heat.

7. 주키니가 익으면 버터, 다진 이탈리안 파슬리와 처빌을 넣고 섞어 마무리합니다.

7. Once the zucchini is cooked, add the chopped Italian parsley and chervil, then mix well.

샴페인 소스

1. 카놀라유와 버터를 두른 팬에 작게 자른 양파, 샬롯, 처빌 줄기를 넣고 볶아줍니다.
2. 채소가 익기 시작하면 샴페인을 넣고 가열하다가 생선 육수를 부어 졸여줍니다.
- 샴페인 대신 스파클링 와인 또는 화이트와인을 사용해도 좋습니다.
3. 체에 걸러 국물만 남긴 후 생크림을 넣고 가열해 농도를 맞추고, 소금과 코리앤더 시드 파우더로 간을 합니다.

CHAMPAGNE SAUCE

1. Heat the canola oil and butter in a pan, then stir-fry the chopped onion, shallot, and chervil stems.
2. Once the vegetables begin to soften, add the Champagne and heat. Pour in the fish stock and simmer until reduced.
- Other sparkling or white wines can be used as substitutes for Champagne.
3. Strain through a sieve to obtain the sauce base. Add the fresh cream and simmer to adjust the consistency. Season with salt and coriander seed powder.

아귀 간 퓌레

1. 아귀 간에 우유를 붓고 약 40분간 잠시 담가둡니다.
2. 아귀 간에 묻은 우유를 닦아낸 후, 찜기에서 익혀 큼직하게 잘라줍니다.
3. 냄비에 **2**와 타임, 버터, 생크림을 넣고 데워줍니다.

MONKFISH LIVER PURÉE

1. Pour the milk over the monkfish liver and let it soak for about 40 minutes.
2. Gently remove the milk from the monkfish liver, then steam and cut into large pieces.
3. In a pot, combine the thyme, butter, fresh cream, and (**2**), then heat gently.

4. 아귀 간이 익으면 타임을 건져내고 체에 내린 후, 코냑을 섞고 소금과 흑후추로 간을 합니다.
5. 냄비로 옮겨 한 번 더 가열합니다.

4. Once the monkfish liver is cooked, remove the thyme and strain through a sieve. Add the cognac, then season with salt and black pepper.
5. Return to the pot and reheat.

가니시

1. 펜넬은 줄기를 제거한 후 밑동을 4등분으로 잘라줍니다.
2. 버터를 두른 팬에 펜넬 밑동을 넣고 익힌 후 레몬즙을 뿌려줍니다.

GARNISHES

1. Remove the stalk from the fennel and cut the bulb into quarters.
2. Heat butter in a pan, add the fennel, and drizzle with lemon juice.

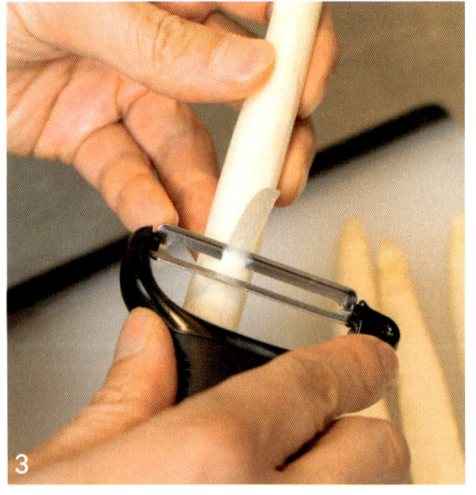  

3. 화이트 아스파라거스는 겉껍질을 제거한 후 큼직하게 잘라줍니다.
4. 버터를 두른 팬에 화이트 아스파라거스를 넣고 익혀줍니다.
5. 레드 파프리카는 직화로 겉면을 태우고 얼음물에 담가 탄 부분을 긁어낸 후 꼭지와 씨, 껍질 안쪽의 흰 막을 제거합니다.

3. Peel the white asparagus and cut into large pieces.
4. Heat the butter in a pan and stir-fry the white asparagus.
5. Char the skin of the red bell pepper over an open flame, then soak it in ice water. Scrape off the blackened skin, then remove the stem, seeds, and white inner membranes.

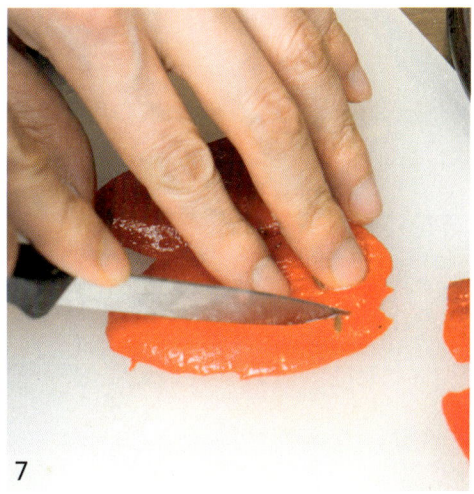

6. 냄비에 파프리카가 잠길 정도의 올리브오일과 **5**를 넣고 끓지 않을 정도로 약하게 불을 조절해 파프리카를 천천히 부드럽게 익혀줍니다.
7. 콩피한 파프리카를 적당한 크기로 잘라줍니다.

6. In a pot, place (**5**) and add enough olive oil to cover. Gently heat, keeping it below boiling, and slowly until tender.
7. Cut the bell pepper confit into bite-sized pieces.

플레이팅

1. 접시에 통밀 리소토를 담고 그 위에 아귀 꼬리 살을 올려줍니다.
2. 가니시로 만든 펜넬, 화이트 아스파라거스, 레드 파프리카 콩피를 올려줍니다.
3. 한 쪽에는 아귀 간 퓌레를, 다른 한 쪽에는 샴페인 소스를 놓고, 허브를 장식해 마무리합니다.

PLATING

1. Place the whole wheat risotto on a plate and top with the monkfish tail meat.
2. Garnish with the fennel bulb, white asparagus, and red bell pepper confit.
3. Serve with monkfish liver purée on one side and the Champagne sauce on the other. Finish with herbs.

Shiitake Mushroom Trilogy: Cream, Rillettes and Sablé

가정식
HOME COOKING

표고버섯 사블레와 표고버섯 리에트를 곁들인 표고버섯 크림

2023년 겨울, 넷플릭스에서 셰프 100명을 모아 서바이벌 프로그램을 제작한다며 섭외 요청이 왔습니다. 넷플릭스에서 미리 공개한 심사위원이 마음에 안 들기도 했지만, 한참을 <마스터셰프 코리아 시즌 1>에서 준우승한 것으로 먹고 살았는데, 굳이 똑같은 콘셉트의 프로그램에 나가 리스크를 짊어져야 하나 싶어 한참을 고민했습니다. 그러다 결국 '나가면 출연료도 나오는 일인데, 밑져야 본전'이라는 마음으로 출연을 결정했습니다.(하지만 결국 본선 1차전에서 탈락하여 분량도 챙기지 못했으니, 본전을 건지지 못한 것이 사실입니다.)

흑셰프와 백셰프 1:1 대결 미션에서 말린 표고버섯이 주제로 선정되어 2주간의 고민 끝에 제작진에게 '수란과 볶은 근대를 올린 표고버섯 통밀 리소토와 표고버섯 리에트와 프로마주 블랑을 올린 표고버섯 사블레 그리고 표고버섯 육수로 만든 크렘'이라는 이름의 레시피를 전달하였으나, 레시피와 이름 모두 너무 복잡하다며 반려되었는데요. 레시피만 제가 고집을 부려 유지하고, 단지 이름만 '표고버섯 크림과 리소토, 사블레' 정도의 이름으로 바꾸게 되었습니다.

여기에서는 그때의 레시피를 이름뿐 아니라, 재료와 조리 과정까지 훨씬 간단하게 바꿔 실었습니다. 실제로 방송 이후, 간편하게 바꾼 이 레시피의 사블레는 카페 오쁘띠베르에서 술안주 메뉴로 만들어 판매하게 되었고, 리에트와 크림은 외부 행사나 이벤트용 메뉴로 활용하고 있습니다.

In the winter of 2023, Netflix reached out with an offer to join a culinary survival show featuring 100 chefs. The judges' lineup, which was pre-released by Netflix was intriguing—but one name did give me pause. Having long lived off the honor of my second-place finish on Season 1 of *MasterChef Korea*, I hesitated for quite some time, wondering whether it was worth risking another competition with a similar concept. Eventually, I decided to give it a try, thinking to myself, *They're even paying me to show up—nothing to lose.* (Well, I was eliminated in the first round of the main competition and ended up with just a few brief scenes, so there was something to lose after all.)

In the one-on-one round of the show, dried shiitake mushrooms were selected as a theme. After two weeks of deliberation, I submitted to the staff my recipe titled *Shiitake Mushroom and Whole Wheat Risotto with Poached Egg and Stir-Fried Swiss Chards, Shiitake Sablé with Shiitake Rillettes and Fromage Blanc, and Shiitake Stock Crème*. However, it was turned down for being overly complicated, both in name and recipe. But I stuck to the recipe, changing only its name to *Shiitake Mushroom Cream, Risotto and Sablé*.

This version is made much simpler than the original—not only in name, but also in ingredients and preparation. After being featured on the show, the *sablé* from this recipe has been served as a snack with drinks at café Aux Petits Verres, while the rillettes and cream have been used for off-site occasions or other events.

Ingredients

2인 분량
Serves 2

표고버섯 리에트

타임	3줄기
마늘	1/2알
양파	20g
샬롯	10g
표고버섯	80g
양송이버섯	80g
이탈리안 파슬리	5g
처빌	3g
소금	적당량
후춧가루	적당량
버터	10g
프로마주 블랑	30g
디종 머스터드	15g
엑스트라버진 올리브오일	5ml
헤이즐넛	적당량
레몬 제스트	적당량

표고버섯 크림

엑스트라버진 올리브오일	10ml
판체타	15g
표고버섯	250g
양송이버섯	250g
양파	40g
샬롯	20g
마늘	5g
타임	적당량
이탈리안 파슬리	적당량
마데이라	적당량
닭육수	300ml
생크림	450ml
버터	10g
소금	적당량
후춧가루	적당량

표고버섯 사블레

박력분	90g
표고 분말	20g
그라나파다노 치즈	15g
버터	40g
엑스트라버진 올리브오일	20g
달걀	50g
소금	적당량
후춧가루	적당량
우유	적당량

가니시

버터	적당량
근대	적당량
소금	적당량

장식

볶은 헤이즐넛 분태	적당량
레몬 제스트	적당량
처빌	적당량

SHIITAKE RILLETTES

3	fresh thyme sprigs
1/2	garlic clove
20 g	onion
10 g	shallot
80 g	shiitake mushrooms
80 g	button mushrooms
5 g	fresh Italian parsley
3 g	fresh chervil
Q.S.	salt
Q.S.	ground black pepper
10 g	butter
30 g	fromage blanc
15 g	Dijon mustard
5 ml	extra virgin olive oil
Q.S.	hazelnuts
Q.S.	lemon zest

SHIITAKE CREAM

10 ml	extra virgin olive oil
15 g	pancetta
250 g	shiitake mushrooms
250 g	button mushrooms
40 g	onion
20 g	shallot
5 g	garlic
Q.S.	fresh thyme
Q.S.	fresh Italian parsley
Q.S.	Madeira
300 ml	chicken stock
450 ml	fresh cream
10 g	butter
Q.S.	salt
Q.S.	ground black pepper

SHIITAKE SABLÉ

90 g	cake flour
20 g	shiitake mushroom powder
15 g	Grana Padano
40 g	butter
20 g	extra virgin olive oil
50 g	whole egg
Q.S.	salt
Q.S.	ground black pepper
Q.S.	milk

GARNISH

Q.S.	butter
Q.S.	Swiss chards
Q.S.	salt

PLATING DECORATIONS

Q.S.	roasted chopped hazelnuts
Q.S.	lemon zest
Q.S.	fresh chervil

How to make

표고버섯 리에트

1. 올리브오일(분량 외)을 두른 팬에 잘게 다진 타임, 슬라이스한 마늘, 양파, 샬롯을 넣고 볶아줍니다.
2. 슬라이스한 표고버섯과 양송이버섯, 버터(분량 외)를 넣고 볶아줍니다.
3. 버섯이 익으면 잘게 다진 이탈리안 파슬리와 처빌을 넣고 섞은 후, 소금과 후춧가루로 간을 합니다.

SHIITAKE RILLETTES

1. In a pan with olive oil, stir-fry the chopped thyme, sliced garlic, onion, and shallot.
1. Add the sliced shiitake and button mushrooms, along with butter, then continue stir-frying.
3. Once the mushrooms are cooked, stir in the chopped Italian parsley and chervil, then season with salt and pepper.

4. 믹서로 옮겨 원하는 질감으로 갈아줍니다.
5. 볼에 옮긴 후 버터, 프로마주 블랑, 디종 머스터드, 올리브오일을 넣고 섞어줍니다.
6. 고르게 섞이면 다진 헤이즐넛과 레몬 제스트를 넣고 섞어 마무리합니다.

4. Place into a blender and blend to the desired consistency.
5. Transfer to a mixing bowl, add the butter (10 g), fromage blanc, Dijon mustard, and olive oil (5 ml), then mix well.
6. Once evenly incorporated, mix in the chopped hazelnuts and lemon zest.

표고버섯 크림

1. 올리브오일을 두른 팬에 작게 썬 판체타를 넣고 볶아줍니다. 판체타에서 기름이 나오기 시작하면 슬라이스한 표고버섯, 양송이버섯, 양파, 샬롯, 다진 마늘, 타임, 이탈리안 파슬리를 넣고 중불에서 볶아줍니다.
2. 채소가 절반 정도 익으면 마데이라를 넣고 플람베합니다.
- 마데이라 대신 다른 주정강화와인이나 화이트와인을 사용해도 좋습니다.
- 플람베(flambé)는 술을 넣고 불을 붙여 알코올을 태우는 조리법입니다.
3. 닭육수를 넣고 절반 정도로 졸여줍니다.

SHIITAKE CREAM

1. In a pan with olive oil, stir-fry the chopped pancetta. When the pancetta begins to render its fat, add the sliced shiitake and button mushrooms, onion, shallot, minced garlic, thyme, and Italian parsley. Continue stir-frying over medium heat.
2. When the vegetables are halfway cooked, add the Madeira and *flambé*.
- Other fortified or white wines can be used as substitutes for Madeira.
- *Flambé* is a cooking technique in which alcohol is added and ignited to burn off the alcohol content.
3. Pour in the chicken stock and simmer until reduced by about half.

4. 생크림과 버터를 넣고 가열합니다.
5. 버섯이 완전히 익으면 블렌더로 갈아준 후, 체에 걸러줍니다.
6. 소금과 후춧가루로 간을 합니다.

4. Add the fresh cream and butter, then continue simmering.
5. Once the mushrooms are fully cooked, blend and strain through a sieve.
6. Season with salt and black pepper.

표고버섯 사블레

1. 볼에 체 친 박력분과 표고 분말, 강판에 간 그라나파다노 치즈를 넣고 고르게 섞어줍니다.
2. 차가운 상태의 버터를 넣고 손으로 비비듯 부슬부슬한 모래알 상태로 만들어줍니다.
3. 올리브오일, 달걀, 소금, 후춧가루를 넣고 고르게 섞어줍니다.

SHIITAKE SABLÉ

1. In a mixing bowl, combine the sifted cake flour, shiitake mushroom powder, and grated Grana Padano, then mix thoroughly.
2. Add the cold butter and gently rub the mixture between your hands until it resembles coarse crumbs.
3. Add the olive oil, egg, salt, and black pepper, then mix thoroughly.

4. 반죽을 한 덩어리로 만들어줍니다.
5. 바닥에서 반죽을 밀어 펴는 작업을 해 재료가 고르게 섞이도록 한 후 냉장고에서 잠시 숙성시켜 밀어 펴기 좋은 상태로 만듭니다.

4. Bring the mixture together into a single dough.
5. Knead and press the dough on the work surface until evenly combined. Chill in the refrigerator for a while to make rolling easier.

6. 숙성한 반죽을 약 3mm 두께로 밀어 폅니다.
7. 원하는 크기로 자른 후 반죽 표면에 우유를 발라줍니다.

6. Roll out the dough to 3 mm thick.
7. Cut the dough into the desired size, and brush the surface with milk.

8. 표고 분말, 그라나파다노 치즈, 후춧가루 순서로 뿌려줍니다. (분량 외)
9. 타공팬에 반죽을 올린 후 철판을 덮어 180℃로 예열된 오븐에서 약 12분간 구워줍니다.

8. Sprinkle with additional shiitake mushroom powder, Grana Padano, and black pepper, in that order.
9. Place the dough on a perforated pan and press with a iron baking tray. Bake in an oven preheated to 356°F (180°C) for about 12 minutes.

가니시

1. 버터를 두른 팬에 근대를 볶고 소금으로 간을 합니다.
2. 익힌 근대를 키친타월에 받쳐 기름기를 제거합니다.

GARNISH

1. Heat butter in a pan, stir-fry the Swiss chard and season with salt.
2. Drain on a kitchen towel to remove excess oil.

플레이팅

1. 숟가락 두 개를 이용해 표고버섯 리에트의 모양을 잡아준 후, 표고버섯 크림과 표고버섯 사블레가 놓인 접시에 올려줍니다.
2. 표고버섯 리에트 위에 볶은 헤이즐넛 분태와 레몬 제스트를 뿌려줍니다.
3. 처빌을 올려 마무리합니다.

PLATING

1. Shape a quenelle of the shiitake rillettes using two spoons, and place it on the plate alongside the shiitake mushroom cream and *sablé*.
2. Sprinkle roasted chopped hazelnuts and lemon zest over the rillettes.
3. Garnish with chervil.

PARK JIYOUNG

박지영

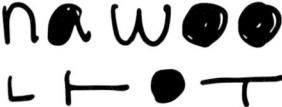

어릴 적부터 요리에 흥미가 많았고, 학창 시절 문학과 예술에도 관심이 깊었다. 하지만 다양한 창의력을 가장 잘 펼칠 수 있는 공간이 주방이라는 걸 깨닫고, 자연스럽게 요리사의 길을 걷게 되었다.

요리학교 졸업 후 미국 뉴욕에서 커리어를 시작한 그녀는, 미쉐린 2스타 이탈리아 씨푸드 레스토랑 '마레아'에서 근무하며 해산물 요리에 대한 깊은 이해를 쌓았다. 이후 스페인으로 건너가 유럽의 다양한 요리 문화를 익히며, 자신만의 감각을 넓혀갔다. 한국으로 돌아온 뒤에는 한식과 세계 각국의 요리를 접목한 새로운 스타일을 구상했고, 현재는 서울 남영동에 위치한 비스트로이자 와인바 콘셉트 공간인 '나우남영'을 운영하고 있다.

2024년에는 넷플릭스 요리 서바이벌 프로그램 <흑백요리사: 요리 계급 전쟁>에 출연해 '키친 갱스터'라는 이름으로 존재감을 드러냈다. 특히 심사위원인 안성재 셰프에게는 '손맛이 좋다'는 극찬을 통해, 그녀의 섬세하면서도 강렬한 조리 감각을 인정받았다.

그녀는 지속 가능한 식재료 사용과 로컬 푸드에 꾸준한 관심을 가지고 있으며, 이를 실제 요리에 반영하고 있다. 정기적으로 팝업 레스토랑과 협업 프로젝트에 참여하며 다양한 방식의 요리 실험을 이어가고 있으며, 계절과 재료에 맞춘 메뉴를 직접 개발해 선보이고 있다.

Chef Park Jiyoung has been interested in cooking since she was a child, and she also enjoyed literature and art during her school days. However, she realized that the kitchen was the best place to express her creativity, so she naturally chose to become a chef.

After culinary school, she began her career in New York City, where she worked at the two-Michelin-starred Italian seafood restaurant Marea, developing a deep understanding of seafood cuisine. She then moved to Spain, where she immersed herself in the diverse culinary cultures of Europe, expanding her own sensibilities. Upon returning to Korea, she envisioned a new style of cooking that combines Korean cuisine with global influences. She is currently the owner of Nawoo Namyeong, a bistro and wine bar concept space in Namyeong-dong, Seoul.

In 2024, she made a name for herself as the "kitchen gangster" on Netflix's culinary survival show *Culinary Class Wars*. Notably, she was recognized for her delicate yet intense sensibility by Judge Chef Ahn Sungjae, who praised her for having "good sense in taste."

She has an ongoing interest in sustainable ingredients and local food, which is reflected in her cooking. She regularly participates in pop-up restaurants and collaborative projects to experiment with different cooking methods, and she creates her own menus tailored to the season and available ingredients.

나우 남영
nawoo_more.better

jyp_jijipark

Abalone in Herb and Seaweed Butter

이야기
STORY

허브 김 버터 전복 구이

이 요리는 작년에 제가 참여했던 요리 경연 프로그램 <흑백요리사> 2차전 1:1 흑백 대결에서 선보였던 메뉴의 새로운 버전입니다. 당시에는 매생이를 주제로, 매생이 관자 리조또를 만들어 큰 호응을 얻었는데, 그 이후로 '좀 더 완성도 높고 사계절 내내 즐길 수 있는 메뉴로 발전시켜보자'는 생각에서 이 요리를 구상하게 되었습니다.

겨울 한정 재료인 매생이 대신 사계절 내내 활용 가능한 김을 사용했고, 여기에 허브를 더해 푸릇한 색감과 향긋한 맛을 살렸습니다. 또한 주재료였던 쌀 대신 쌀 모양의 작은 파스타를 활용해 더욱 부드럽고 색다른 식감을 구현했고, 전복은 허브 향의 버터로 익혀 깊은 감칠맛을 더했습니다.

처음 이 요리를 구상하며 고민했던, 계절을 넘어 맛을 이어가는 법에 대한 저만의 해답이기도 합니다.

This dish is an upgraded take on the Seaweed Fulvescens Scallop Risotto, which was featured in the one-on-one round of the culinary survival show's second stage and received significant attention. From there, it grew from the idea of refining the original into a more complete and seasonless offering.

In this version, dried seaweed takes the place of the winter-limited seaweed fulvescens, while fresh herbs deliver a vibrant green hue and a refreshing note. Traditional rice is substituted with rice-shaped small pasta to create a more delicate, unexpected texture. The abalone is gently cooked while being basted with herb-infused butter to enhance its savory depth.

The dish also represents the answer I have been exploring since its conception: how to carry the flavor beyond the seasons.

Ingredients

2인 분량
Serves 2

허브 퓌레*

샬롯	40g
마늘	40g
식용유	적당량
조개 파우더	1/2작은술
닭육수 또는 물	4oz
바질	30g
파슬리	30g
김	3장

전복

전복	1kg × 4마리
식용유	적당량
허브 퓌레*	10g
버터	30g

파스타

엑스트라버진 올리브오일	적당량
쌀 모양 파스타 (젠틸레 리조 디 세몰라)	30g
닭육수 또는 물	60g

마무리 (1접시 기준)

골뱅이 육수 (371p)	2oz
바지락살	20g
허브 퓌레*	15g
버터	20g
레몬즙	적당량

장식

처빌	적당량
엑스트라버진 올리브오일	적당량

HERB PURÉE*

40 g	shallots
40 g	garlic cloves
Q.S.	cooking oil
1/2 tsp	clam powder
4 oz	chicken stock or water
30 g	fresh basil
30 g	fresh parsley
3 sheets	dried seaweed (gim)

ABALONE

4	whole abalones (1 kg each)
Q.S.	cooking oil
10 g	herb purée*
30 g	butter

PASTA

Q.S.	extra virgin olive oil
30 g	rice-shaped pasta (Gentile, riso di semola)
60 g	chicken stock or water

FINISH (for 1 bowl)

2 oz	whelk broth (p.371)
20 g	Manila clam meat
15 g	herb purée*
20 g	butter
Q.S.	lemon juice

GARNISH

Q.S.	fresh chervil
Q.S.	extra virgin olive oil

How to make

허브 퓌레

1. 샬롯과 마늘을 얇게 슬라이스합니다.
2. 식용유를 두른 팬에 **1**을 넣고 볶아줍니다.
3. 샬롯과 마늘이 노릇하게 익으면 조개 파우더와 닭육수를 넣고 살짝 졸인 후 완전히 식혀줍니다.

HERB PURÉE

1. Thinly slice the shallots and garlic cloves.
2. Pan-fry (**1**) in cooking oil.
3. Once golden brown, add the clam powder and chicken stock. Simmer gently to reduce, then let the mixture cool completely.

4. 끓는 물에 바질과 파슬리를 넣고 약 10초간 빠르게 데치고 찬물에서 식힌 후 물기를 꼭 짜내 큼직하게 잘라줍니다.
5. 볼에 **3**과 **4**, 김을 넣고 블렌더로 곱게 갈아줍니다.

4. Blanch the basil and parsley in boiling water for about 10 seconds, then transfer to ice water to cool. Squeeze out any excess water and roughly chop.
5. In a bowl, combine (**3**), (**4**), and the dried seaweed, then blend the mixture until smooth.

전복

1. 전복을 진공팩에 넣고 압축한 후 82°C로 맞춘 수비드 기계에서 5시간 조리합니다.
- 전복은 브러시를 이용해 흐르는 물에서 깨끗이 씻은 후 껍질과 내장을 제거해 사용합니다.
  (초보자의 경우 손질된 전복을 사용해도 좋습니다.)
- 수비드가 끝나면 포장된 상태로 얼음물에 담가 완벽하게 식혀줍니다.
2. 식용유를 두른 팬에 수비드한 전복을 넣고 앞뒤로 익혀줍니다.
3. 허브 퓌레와 버터를 넣고 전복에 끼얹어가며 노릇하게 익혀줍니다.
- 남은 허브 줄기가 있다면 추가해주세요.

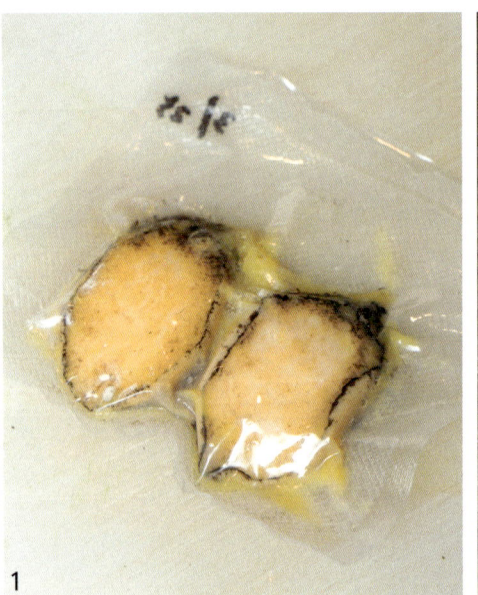

ABALONE

1. Seal the abalone in a vacuum bag and cook in a sous-vide machine at 180°F (82°C) for 5 hours.
- Scrub the abalone thoroughly under running water with a brush. Separate the abalone meat from the shells and innards before use. (Pre-cleaned abalone is recommended for beginners.)
- Once cooked, transfer the vacuum bag directly to ice water and let it cool completely.
2. Pan-fry the sous-vide abalone meat in cooking oil on both sides.
3. Add the herb purée and butter to the pan, and baste the abalone with the pan liquid until golden.
- If available, add any leftover herb stems to the pan.

파스타

1. 올리브오일을 두른 팬에 쌀 모양 파스타를 넣고 중불에서 볶아줍니다.
2. 파스타의 색이 노릇하게 변하기 시작하면 닭육수를 넣고 4~5분간 볶아줍니다.
3. 파스타가 80% 정도로 익으면 트레이에 넓게 펼쳐 식혀줍니다.
- 잔열이 있어 식히는 동안에도 파스타가 익기 때문입니다.

PASTA

1. In a pan with olive oil, stir-fry the rice-shaped pasta over medium heat.
2. Once it turns golden brown, pour in the chicken stock and continue stir-frying for 4 to 5 minutes.
3. When the pasta is about 80% cooked, spread it out on a tray to cool.
- The pasta will finish cooking in the residual heat as it cools.

마무리

1. 소스용 작은 냄비에 골뱅이 육수를 넣고 가열합니다.
2. 끓어오르기 시작하면 익힌 쌀 모양 파스타와 바지락 살을 넣고 가열합니다.
3. 바지락 살이 익기 시작하면 허브 퓨레를 넣고 잘 섞어가며 가열합니다.

FINISH

1. In a saucepan, pour the whelk broth and bring to a boil.
2. Once it comes to a boil, add the rice-shaped pasta and Manila clam meat.
3. When the clam meat begins to cook, stir in the herb purée.

4. 버터를 넣고 녹여줍니다.
5. 레몬즙을 살짝 뿌려 마무리합니다.

4. Add the butter and stir until melted.
5. Add a splash of lemon juice.

6. 그릇에 **5**를 담고 반으로 자른 전복을 올려줍니다.
7. 전복 위에 처빌을 올려줍니다.
8. 올리브오일을 부려 마무리합니다.

6. Transfer (**5**) to a bowl and top with the halved abalone.
7. Garnish the abalone with chervil.
8. Finish with a drizzle of olive oil.

White Whelk al Ajillo

가정식
HOME COOKING

백골뱅이 알 아히오

가정에서 손님을 초대했을 때, 손쉽게 만들 수 있으면서도 꽤 근사해 보이는 메뉴를 소개합니다. 스페인의 대표적인 타파스 요리인 '감바스 알 아히요'를 변형한 요리로, 새우 대신 백골뱅이를 사용하고 버터를 더한 점이 가장 큰 차이점입니다. 감바스 특유의 마늘과 올리브오일 향은 살리고, 여기에 버터의 고소함을 더해 깊은 풍미를 느낄 수 있는 요리로 완성했습니다.

이 메뉴는 제가 을지로 '보틀러'에서 근무할 당시 시그니처 메뉴로 선보였던 요리이기도 합니다. 을지로는 '골뱅이 골목'이 있을 정도로 골뱅이로 유명한 동네인데, 그 지역적 특색을 살려 한식에서 주로 사용되던 재료인 골뱅이를 양식으로 재해석해보자는 마음으로 만들었습니다. 익숙한 재료를 새로운 방식으로 표현한 이 요리가, 일상 속 특별한 순간을 만들어줄 수 있기를 바랍니다.

This dish is easy to prepare, yet elegant enough to serve when hosting guests at home. A twist on *Gambas al Ajillo*, the classic Spanish tapas, this version replaces shrimp with white whelk and adds butter—that's the key difference. While it retains the original aromas of garlic and olive oil, the addition of savory butter creates a deeper, richer flavor.

This was also a signature dish during my time at Bottler in Euljiro, a neighborhood so famous for whelk that it even has a "Whelk Alley." Reflecting the local character, whelk—an ingredient widely used in Korean cuisine—was reimagined with a Western touch. I hope this fresh take on familiar ingredients brings a special moment to your everyday life.

Ingredients

2인 분량

Serves 2

골뱅이 육수*	
생골뱅이	1kg
채소	적당량
골뱅이 육수*	2oz
마늘	40g
식용유	3oz
페페론치노	적당량
소금	적당량
방울토마토	2개
버터	20g
파슬리	4g
바게트	적당량

WHELK BROTH*	
1 kg	fresh white whelk
Q.S.	vegetables
2 oz	whelk broth*
40 g	garlic
3 oz	cooking oil
Q.S.	peperoncino
Q.S.	salt
2	cherry tomatoes
20 g	butter
4 g	fresh parsley leaves
Q.S.	baguette

How to make

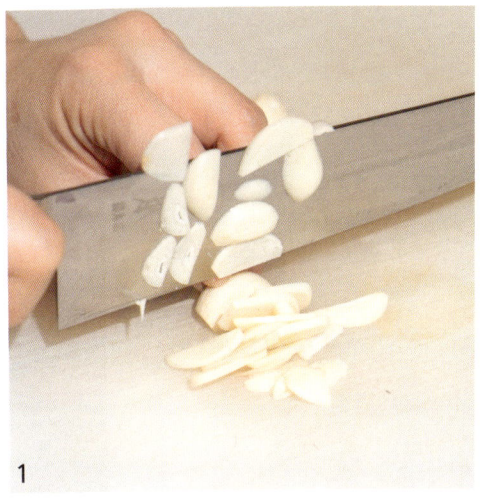 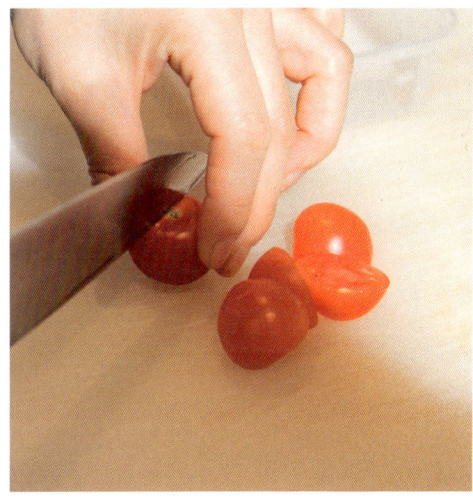 

1. 마늘은 얇게 슬라이스하고, 방울토마토는 반으로 잘라 준비합니다.
2. 파슬리는 잎 부분만 잘게 다져 준비합니다.

1. Thinly slice the garlic and halve the cherry tomatoes.
2. Finely chop the parsley leaves.

 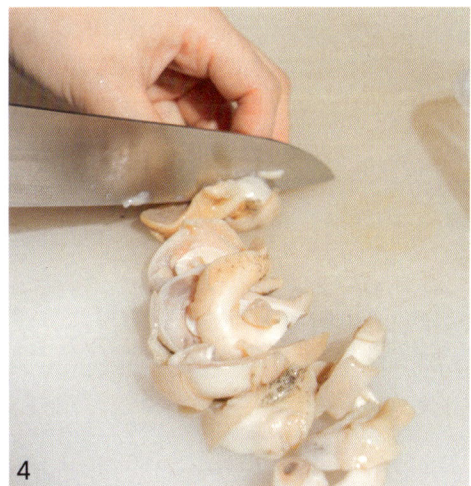 

3. 냄비에 깨끗이 씻은 생골뱅이와 골뱅이가 잠길 정도의 물, 채소를 담고 15~20분간 중불로 삶아 골뱅이 육수를 완성합니다.
- 당근, 양파 등 사용하고 남은 채소가 있다면 큼직하게 썰어 함께 삶아주세요.
4. 골뱅이가 익으면 건져내 껍질과 내장을 제거한 후 한입 크기로 잘라줍니다.
5. 냄비에 골뱅이 육수, 마늘, 식용유, 페페론치노, 소금을 넣고 중약불로 가열합니다.

3. Wash the fresh whelks thoroughly and place them in a pot. Add enough water to cover, along with vegetables. Simmer over medium heat for about 15 to 20 minutes to make the whelk broth.
- If available, roughly chop any leftover vegetables such as carrots and onions, then add them to the pot and simmer together.
4. Once the whelks are cooked, separate the whelk meat from the shells and innards, then cut it into bite-sized pieces.
5. In a pot, combine the whelk broth, garlic, cooking oil, peperoncino, and salt. Heat over medium-low heat.

6. 마늘이 투명하게 변하기 시작하면 익힌 골뱅이, 반으로 자른 방울토마토, 버터를 넣고 3~5분 더 가열합니다.

7. 버터가 녹으면 다진 파슬리를 넣어 마무리합니다.

8. 바게트 빵을 구워 함께 곁들여도 좋습니다.

6. When the garlic begins to turn translucent, add the whelk pieces, halved cherry tomatoes, and butter. Stir-fry for 3 to 5 more minutes.

7. Once the butter melts, stir in the chopped parsley leaves.

8. Serve with toasted baguette on the side, if desired.

PARK CHANIL

박 찬 일

서울에서 태어나 문예창작을 전공했다. 처음엔 기자로 사회생활을 시작했지만, 글을 쓰다 보니 요리에 대한 관심이 점점 커졌고, 결국 방향을 틀어 요리사의 길을 걷게 됐다. 어린 시절 어머니를 도와 음식을 만들던 기억이 떠올랐고, 그 기억이 삶의 흐름을 바꿨다.

서른을 넘긴 나이에 안정적인 삶을 뒤로하고 이탈리아로 떠났다. ICIF에서 본격적으로 요리를 배우면서, 단순한 조리 기술을 넘어 요리를 삶과 이야기로 바라보게 되었다. 그 경험은 이후 그의 요리 철학을 형성하는 데 중요한 바탕이 되었다.

셰프이자 작가인 그는 「노포의 장사법」, 「추억의 절반은 맛이다」, 「밥 먹다가, 울컥」 등의 책을 통해 음식에 깃든 사람, 기억, 삶의 이야기를 풀어내고 있다. 요리는 그에게 기술이 아닌, 인간과 문화, 그리고 역사가 담긴 그릇이다.

그에게 요리는 생계의 일이면서도, 동시에 가장 사랑하는 일이기도 하다. 그가 꿈꾸는 요리는 '미식을 위한 요리'가 아니라, 누구나 편하게 즐길 수 있는 '진짜 음식'이다.

He was born in Seoul and majored in creative writing. He began his career as a journalist, but as he continued to write, his interest in cooking grew, and he eventually took a different path of becoming a chef. He recalled helping his mother cook, and that memory changed the course of his life.

In his thirties, he left his secure life behind and moved to Italy. At ICIF (International Culinary Institute for Foreigners), he learned to cook in a full-fledged manner, which led him to understand cooking as a way of life and the story it tells beyond simple cooking techniques. Such experience has become an essential foundation for shaping his culinary philosophy.

As a chef and writer, he has unraveled the stories of people, memories, and life embedded in food through his books, such as *"Shack Diners: Living Legends," "Half of Memory is Taste,"* and *"While Eating, I Cried."* For him, cooking is not a technique; it's a bowl containing people, culture, and history.

For Chef Park, cooking is not only his livelihood but also his greatest passion. His dream is not to cook 'gourmet food' but rather 'real food' that anyone can enjoy comfortably.

chanilchef

Kalguksu with Jjajang Sauce and Green Onion

(Korean Knife-Cut Noodles with Black Bean Sauce and Green Onion)

이야기
STORY

대파와 칼국수 짜장면

중국에서 들어와 한반도의 사람들이 가장 좋아하는 음식이 된 짜장면. 저는 어렸을 때부터 동네마다 있던 화교 요리사들의 수타 소리를 들으며 자란 세대입니다. 그 쿵쿵, 내리치는 반죽 소리는 이국의 두려움, 호기심, 나아가 식욕을 불러오는 강렬한 타격음이었습니다. 이제 수타 짜장면은 일부러 찾아가지 않으면 먹을 수도 없습니다. 지금의 한국 짜장면은 거의 무너져가고 있습니다. 소다를 너무 넣어 질긴 고무줄 같습니다. 옛 화교의 수타 짜장면(화교들은 수타면 대신 '라면拉麵'이라고 부릅니다)을 먹고 싶으면 손수 해 먹습니다. 옛날 수타면은 아니지만 부드럽고 희고 졸깃한 면은 우리의 칼국수가 얼마든지 대신할 수 있습니다. 전분을 많이 풀어서 걸쭉하고 양 많은 소스 대신 짭짤하고 다부진 짜장을 만들어 비벼 먹습니다. 그게 저의 기쁨입니다.

Jjajangmyeon, originally brought over from China, has grown into one of South Korea's most beloved dishes. Since childhood, my generation grew up hearing the thuds of dough being pounded by the hands of Chinese immigrant chefs. That striking sound of dough hitting the table stirred a strange mix of emotions—fear of the unfamiliar, curiosity, and even appetite. These days, hand-pulled *jjajangmyeon* is rarely found unless sought out deliberately. Korean *jjajangmyeon* is on the verge of decline. The excessive use of baking soda has made the noodles overly tough, almost rubbery. So when I crave the old-style hand-pulled *jjajangmyeon* once made by Chinese immigrant chefs—what they called *lamian* (拉麵)—I make it myself. Even without traditional hand-pulled noodles, their white, tender, and pleasantly chewy texture can be readily replicated with Korean *kalguksu* noodles. I enjoy pairing them with a savory, substantial jjajang sauce, rather than drowning them in something overly starchy and heavy. That's one of my pleasures.

Ingredients

2인 분량
Serves 2

부드러운 칼국수 면 (시판)	2인 분량

짜장 소스

돼지고기 (앞다리살)	200g
양파	50g
대파	30g
식용유	적당량
맛술	20g
짜장 분말	50g
두반장	10g
황장	30g
물	적당량
후춧가루	적당량

▶ 황장은 된장으로 대체 가능합니다.

장식

다진 마늘	20g
채 썬 오이	50g

2 servings	tender *kalguksu* noodles (store-bought)

JJAJANG SAUCE (Black bean sauce)

200 g	pork (picnic shoulder)
50 g	onion
30 g	green onion
Q.S.	cooking oil
20 g	matsul (Korean cooking wine)
50 g	jjajang powder (black bean sauce powder)
10 g	doubanjiang (Chinese broad bean paste)
30 g	yellow bean sauce
Q.S.	water
Q.S.	ground black pepper

▶ Doenjang can be used as a substitute for yellow bean sauce.

GARNISHES

20 g	minced garlic
50 g	sliced cucumber

How to make

1. 돼지고기, 양파, 대파를 먹기 좋은 크기로 자릅니다.
   - 돼지고기는 살코기와 비계를 분리합니다. 분리한 비계는 재료를 볶을 때 기름을 내어 사용하면 좋습니다.

1. Chop the pork, onion, and green onion into bite-sized pieces.
   - Separate the lean meat from the fat. Render the fat to obtain oil for stir-frying.

2. 팬에 식용유와 돼지고기 비계를 넣고 볶다가, 돼지고기 비계의 기름이 나오면 다진 양파와 대파를 넣고 볶습니다.
3. 양파와 대파가 거의 익을 때쯤 돼지고기를 넣고 볶습니다.

2. In a pan, combine the pork fat with cooking oil. Once rendered into oil, add the chopped onion and green onion, then stir-fry.
3. When almost cooked, add the lean meat and continue stir-frying.

4. 맛술을 부려 잡내를 없앱니다.
5. 짜장 분말, 두반장, 황장을 넣고 장이 타지 않도록 천천히 볶습니다.
6. 물을 넣어 소스의 농도를 맞춥니다.

4. Add the matsul to eliminate any unpleasant odor.
5. Add the jjajang powder, doubanjiang, and yellow bean sauce, then stir-fry slowly to prevent scorching.
6. Add water to adjust the consistency.

7. 후춧가루를 부려 소스를 완성합니다.
- 완성된 소스는 삶은 칼국수 면 위에 뿌립니다. 다진 마늘과 채 썬 오이를 얹어 마무리합니다.

7. Sprinkle with black pepper to complete the sauce.
- Pour the sauce over the cooked kalguksu noodles. Top with the minced garlic and sliced cucumber.

Tomato-Braised Trippa

가정식
HOME COOKING

토마토 내장찜

옛날 엄마들은 비싼 고기 대신 정육점에서 소나 돼지 내장을 사서 식구들의 단백질을 보충했습니다. 늘 먹던 것이 소의 양과 곱창이었습니다. 그때는 그게 참 쌌습니다. 국도 끓이고, 볶아서도 먹었습니다. 이탈리아에 갔더니 소 내장 요리를 즐기는 게 아닙니까. 깜짝 놀랐습니다. 이 메뉴는 제가 서울에서 장사하면서 늘 인기가 높았습니다. 아마도 한국에서 가장 먼저 소 내장 요리를 이탈리아 식당에서 팔았던 게 제가 아닌가 싶습니다. 그 기억을 되살려 간편하게 가정에서 즐길 수 있는 조리법을 소개합니다.

Back in the day, mothers often bought beef or pork offal from the butcher instead of more expensive cuts, as a cost-effective way to provide the family with enough protein. Beef tripe and intestines were common on the table. They were inexpensive at that time and enjoyed as everyday dishes, simmered in soup or stir-fried. I still remember how surprised I was to see people enjoying *trippa* in Italy. What began as a discovery has since become a steady favorite at my restaurant in Seoul. Perhaps I was one of the first to showcase *trippa* in an Italian restaurant in Korea. Recalling that memory, I am sharing a recipe you can easily prepare and enjoy at home.

Ingredients

2인 분량

Serves 2

토마토 내장찜

산 마르자노종의 토마토 캔 (필드 토마토 홀)	300g
소금	3g
설탕	2g
소고기 육수	200g
소 깐 양 삶은 것	300g
쪽파	15g
미나리	적당량
엑스트라버진 올리브오일	적당량
으깬 마늘	10g
양파	40g
고추장	8g
화이트와인 (또는 청주나 맛술)	20g

장식

그라나파다노 치즈 가루	50g
엑스트라버진 올리브오일	적당량
후춧가루	적당량
허브	적당량

TOMATO-BRAISED TRIPPA

300 g	canned San Marzano tomatoes (whole peeled tomatoes)
3 g	salt
2 g	sugar
200 g	beef stock
300 g	boiled beef tripe
15 g	Korean scallions
Q.S.	water parsley
Q.S.	extra virgin olive oil
10 g	crushed garlic
40 g	onion
8 g	gochujang (Korean red chili paste)
20 g	white wine (or Korean cooking wine, or refined rice wine)

GARNISHES

50 g	Grana Padano cheese powder
Q.S.	extra virgin olive oil
Q.S.	ground black pepper
Q.S.	fresh herbs

How to make

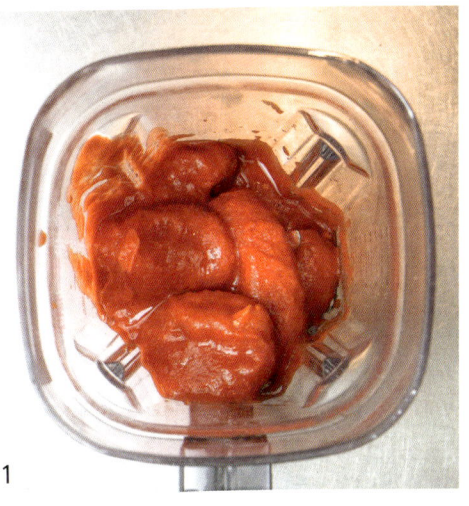

1. 홀 토마토는 블렌더에서 곱게 갑니다.
2. 냄비로 옮겨 부피가 1/3이 되도록 조린 후 소금, 설탕을 넣어 간을 합니다.

1. Blend the whole peeled tomatoes until smooth in a blender.
2. Transfer the blended tomatoes to a pot, reduce by one-third, then season with salt and sugar.

3. 소고기 육수는 냄비에 소고기와 소고기가 잠길 정도의 물을 넣고 60분 내외로 끓여 사용합니다.
4. 소 깐 양은 쪽파, 미나리와 함께 냄비에서 데친 후 찬물에 헹굽니다.
5. 소 깐 양을 먹기 좋은 크기로 자릅니다.

3. To make the beef stock, place beef in a pot, add enough water to cover, and cook for about 60 minutes.
4. In a separate pot, blanch the beef tripe with Korean scallions and water parsley in boiling water. Remove and rinse under cold water.
5. Cut the beef tripe into bite-sized pieces for easier eating.

6. 올리브오일을 두른 팬에 으깬 마늘, 큼직하게 썬 양파를 넣고 볶습니다.
7. 양파가 거의 익으면 깐 양을 넣고 가볍게 볶습니다.
8. 고추장을 넣고 볶습니다.

6. In a pan with olive oil, stir-fry the crushed garlic and roughly chopped onion.
7. When the onion is nearly cooked, add the beef tripe and stir-fry gently.
8. Stir in the gochujang.

9. 화이트와인, 소고기 육수 순서로 넣고 천천히 뭉근하게 조립니다.
10. 2를 넣고 졸여 농도를 조절한 후, 2cm 정도로 썬 미나리를 넣고 불을 끕니다.
- 접시에 옮겨 그라나파다노 치즈 가루, 올리브오일, 후춧가루를 뿌리고 허브를 올려 마무리합니다.

9. Add the white wine and pour in the beef stock, then simmer slowly until reduced.
10. Stir in (2) and continue simmering to adjust the consistency. Add the water parsley, cut into about 2 cm lengths. Turn off the heat.
- Arrange the trippa on a plate. Garnish with grated Grana Padano, black pepper, olive oil and herbs.

SUNG SIWOO

성시우

한식을 재해석하는 이노베이티브 레스토랑 '스와니예'의 창립 멤버이자 헤드셰프로서 9년간 근무하며, 레스토랑이 미쉐린 2스타에 오르기 까지 핵심적인 역할을 했다. 2023년 4월, 자신의 요리 철학을 온전히 담은 100% 식물성 기반 파인 다이닝 레스토랑 '레귬 Légume'을 신사동에 오픈했다.

프랑스어로 '채소'를 뜻하는 레귬은, 이름 그대로 모든 요리를 식물성 재료로만 구성하며 비건 다이닝의 새로운 가능성을 열었다. 오픈한 지 1년 10개월 만에 미쉐린 1스타를 획득하며, 한국 최초이자 아시아 유일, 세계 여섯 번째 미쉐린 스타 비건 레스토랑이라는 이례적인 기록을 세웠다.

레귬에서는 대체육이나 비건 치즈 같은 가공 식품 없이, 자연에서 온 식재료만을 활용해 창의적이고 세련된 비건 요리를 선보인다. 감각적인 플레이팅과 절제된 조리법, 제철 재료를 중심으로 구성된 코스 요리에서 레귬만의 정체성이 고스란히 드러난다. 나아가 재료 낭비를 최소화하는 조리법과 친환경 아이템을 적극 활용하여 지속 가능한 외식 문화를 만들어 가기 위해 노력하고 있다.

As an original member of SOIGNÉ—an innovative restaurant showcasing contemporary Korean cuisine—he served as head chef for nine years and played a key role in earning two Michelin stars. In April 2023, he opened LÉGUME, a 100% plant-based fine dining restaurant in Sinsa-dong, fully embodying his culinary philosophy.

True to its name—*légume*, meaning "vegetable" in French—the restaurant offers a tasting menu composed entirely of plant-based ingredients, redefining the possibilities of vegan fine dining. Within just one year and ten months, it earned a Michelin star—an exceptional milestone as the first vegan restaurant in Korea, the only one in Asia, and the sixth in the world.

Without relying on artificial products such as meat substitutes or vegan cheese, LÉGUME delivers innovative and refined vegan cuisine made exclusively with natural ingredients. Its tasting course, featuring sensory plating, understated techniques, and seasonal produce, faithfully reflects its distinctive culinary identity. Furthermore, it is committed to promoting sustainable dining practices by adopting waste-minimizing cooking methods and eco-friendly kitchenware.

레귬
legume.seoul

sung_choux

Steamed Eggplant Skewer with Sesame Sauce

이야기
STORY

참깨 소스를 발라 구운 가지찜 꼬치

레귐의 팀원들이 머리를 맞대어 함께 만들어 낸 가지찜 꼬치입니다. 10대 때 처음 만나 갓 요리를 시작했던 친구들이 한동안 각자의 길을 걷다가 인연이 닿아 다시 한 곳에 모여 서로의 색깔을 더했습니다.

부드러운 가지찜과 진한 참깨 소스, 퀴노아 크럼블, 팀원들이 각자 만든 요소를 조합해 꼬치 형태로 완성한 한입 거리 음식입니다. 상반되는 식감 덕분에 오히려 조화로움이 돋보이는 이 요리는, 강한 개성의 팀원들이 서로 균형을 맞춰 가며 더욱 빛을 발하는 레귐의 모습과도 닮아 있습니다.

This steamed eggplant skewer was collaboratively created by our team members, who began their culinary journey with me in their teens at SOIGNÉ. Though each of them pursued their own path for a while, fate brought us back together.

Now, each one adds their own distinct touch to this bite: tender steamed eggplant, rich sesame sauce, and crisp quinoa crumbles. Crafted individually by different team members, these components come together on a single skewer. Their contrasting textures make the harmony stand out even more. This single bite is also a reflection of LÉGUME itself, where uniquely talented individuals come together to find balance that makes the whole shine even brighter.

Ingredients

6피스 분량

Makes 6 pieces

가지	1개		1	eggplant
소금	적당량		Q.S.	salt

깨 소스

깨 페이스트	50g		50 g	sesame paste
올리브 오일	20g		20 g	olive oil
구운 마늘	4알		4	roasted garlic cloves
미소된장	10g		10 g	miso
설탕	20g		20 g	sugar
물	20g		20 g	water
소금	적당량		Q.S.	salt

장식

GARNISHES

튀긴 퀴노아	적당량		Q.S.	fried quinoa
처빌 꽃	적당량		Q.S.	fresh chervil flower

How to make

1. 볼에 깨 소스 재료를 모두 넣고 블렌더로 곱게 갈아줍니다.
2. 가지는 통째로 찜기에서 약 20분간 찝니다.

1. Combine all the sesame sauce ingredients in a mixing bowl and blend until smooth.
2. Steam the whole eggplant for about 20 minutes.

3. 찐 가지는 식힌 후 2~2.5cm 두께로 자르고 껍질 부분을 도려냅니다.
4. 키친타월을 이용해 가지의 물기를 최대한 제거합니다.

3. Let it cool, cut into 2 to 2.5 cm-thick rounds, then pare off the skin.
4. Pat them dry with a kitchen towel to remove as much moisture as possible.

5. 물기를 제거한 가지 앞면과 뒷면에 소금을 뿌려 밑간을 합니다.
6. 가지 윗면에 깨 소스를 바른 후 180°C로 예열된 오븐에서 1분 정도 따듯하게 데워줍니다.
7. 퀴노아를 끓는 물에 부드럽게 익힌 후 물기를 완전히 제거합니다.

5. Season both sides of the eggplant with salt.
6. Coat the top of the eggplant with sesame sauce and warm in a preheated oven at 356°F (180°C) for about 1 minute.
7. Cook the quinoa in boiling water until tender, then drain thoroughly.

8. 퀴노아를 180°C로 예열된 식용유에 넣고 바삭해질 때까지 튀긴 후 소금으로 간을 합니다.

8. Deep-fry the quinoa in cooking oil preheated to 356°F (180°C) until crispy, then season with salt.

9. 오븐에서 꺼낸 가지의 소스 부분을 토치로 그을려 캐러멜화시켜줍니다.
10. 튀긴 퀴노아와 처빌 꽃을 올린 후 꼬치를 꽂아 마무리합니다.

9. Remove the eggplant from the oven, and use a blowtorch to gently char the top, caramelizing the sauce.
10. Garnish with fried quinoa and chervil flowers, then skewer to finish.

Cham-Dureup Cutlets

(Angelica Tree Shoot Cutlets)

참두릅 커틀릿

가정식
HOME COOKING

봄철이 되면 잠깐 모습을 드러내는 귀한 제철 식재료인 참두릅을 활용한 요리입니다. 튀김옷을 얇게 입힌 후 가볍게 튀겨내 두릅 본연의 형태와 향긋한 맛, 아삭한 식감을 최대한 살려보았습니다.

봄이 너무 짧아 아쉬운 마음에 만들어 본 이 요리에는 따뜻한 온기와 산나물의 향긋한 봄내음이 고스란히 담겨 있습니다. 고소한 튀김과 은은한 참기름 향기가 달콤쌉쌀한 두릅을 부드럽게 감싸 안으며, 잠시 머물다 가는 봄의 순간을 우리의 기억 속에서 더욱 오래도록 빛나게 해줄 것입니다.

The dish features Cham-dureup, a rare seasonal ingredient that makes a brief appearance in springtime. Lightly fried in a thin coating, it is prepared to retain its natural shape, refreshing aroma, and delicate crunch at their finest.

Crafted with a sense of wistfulness for this ephemeral season, the dish carries the comforting warmth and fragrant breath of spring. A savory batter coating and a delicate hint of sesame oil gently embrace the bittersweet dureup, allowing this fleeting moment of spring to shine a bit longer in our memory.

Ingredients

한 접시 분량
Makes 1 plate

참두릅	4개
건식 빵가루	적당량
소금	적당량
히말라야 블랙솔트◆	적당량

◆ 히말라야 블랙솔트는 유황 특유의 독특한 향미가 남아있어 인도, 파키스탄 등의 남아시아 채소 요리에 많이 사용됩니다. 비건 커틀릿 반죽에는 달걀이 들어가지 않기 때문에 히말라야 블랙솔트를 곁들여 삶은 달걀 같은 풍미를 더해보았습니다.

튀김 반죽

박력분	500g
정수물	600g
소금	7g

참기름 디핑 소스

두유	190g
마늘	15g
카놀라유	200g
참기름	50g
셰리와인 비네거	30g
디종 머스터드	30g
메이플 시럽	20g
소금	7g

4	cham-dureup shoots
Q.S.	dry breadcrumbs
Q.S.	salt
Q.S.	Himalayan black salt ◆

◆ With its distinct sulfur-derived aroma and flavor, Himalayan black salt is widely used in vegetable-based dishes across South Asian countries such as India and Pakistan. Since the vegan batter for this cutlet contains no eggs, the black salt is served alongside to add a flavor reminiscent of boiled eggs.

BATTER

500 g	cake flour
600 g	filtered water
7 g	salt

SESAME OIL DIPPING SAUCE

190 g	soymilk
15 g	garlic
200 g	canola oil (rapeseed oil)
50 g	sesame oil
30 g	sherry wine vinegar
30 g	Dijon mustard
20 g	maple syrup
7 g	salt

How to make

1. 참두릅은 질긴 겉껍질을 제거한 후 밑동을 칼로 도려냅니다.
2. 볼에 튀김 반죽 재료를 모두 넣고 휘퍼로 고르게 섞은 후 체로 걸러줍니다.

1. Remove the tough outer skin of cham-dureup and cut off the base.
2. In a mixing bowl, combine all the batter ingredientsr and whisk thoroughly, then strain through a sieve.

3. 손질한 참두릅은 두 개씩 겹쳐 줄기 부분만 튀김 반죽에 담근 후 빵가루를 묻혀줍니다.

3. Pair two cham-dureup shoots together, dip only the stems into the batter, then coat them with breadcrumbs.

4. 믹서에 참기름 디핑 소스 재료를 모두 담고 곱게 갈아 유화시켜줍니다.
5. 180°C로 예열된 식용유에 약 1분간 바삭하게 튀겨줍니다.
6. 튀긴 참두릅에 소금으로 간을 합니다.

4. In a blender, combine all the sesame oil dipping sauce ingredients, then blend until emulsified.
5. Deep-fry in canola oil preheated to 356°F (180°C) for about 1 minute, until crisp.
6. Season the fried cham-dureup with salt.

7. 접시에 참기름 비건 디핑 소스와 히말라야 블랙솔트를 담아줍니다.
8. 참두릅 커틀릿 2조각을 올려 마무리합니다.

7. Arrange the sesame oil-based vegan dipping sauce and a pinch of Himalayan black salt on a plate.
8. Place two pieces of cham-dureup cutlet beside them.

LEE DAEGEON

이 대 건

MARIPOSA

이대건 셰프는 현재 페어몬트 앰배서더 서울 호텔의 총주방장으로, 호텔의 시그니처 레스토랑 '마리포사'에서 모던 유러피안 다이닝을 선보이고 있다. 그는 국내외에서 쌓은 폭넓은 경험을 바탕으로 자신만의 요리 철학을 정립해왔으며, 이를 통해 마리포사를 서울의 수준 높은 파인 다이닝 중 하나로 자리매김시켰다.

호텔 총주방장으로서 그는 단일 고객층이 아닌, 다양한 취향과 기대를 가진 고객 모두를 만족시켜야 하는 책임을 안고 있다. '누구에게나 매력적으로 다가갈 수 있는 메뉴'를 만들면서도, 호텔에 걸맞은 높은 퀄리티를 유지하는 것이 가장 중요한 과제라고 말하는 이대건 셰프는 '페어몬트 호텔 안에 있는 레스토랑'이 아닌, '마리포사'라는 이름 그 자체로 기억되는 공간을 만들기 위해 노력하고 있다.

그는 식재료 본연의 맛을 살리는 단순하고 정직한 조리법을 추구한다. 한 가지 재료를 다양한 방식으로 조리해 다채롭게 표현하는 것을 좋아하며, 신선한 재료가 가진 결을 해치지 않으면서도 마리포사만의 개성과 깊이를 더하기 위해 직접 만든 페이스트와 소스 등을 곁들이는 방식을 즐겨 사용한다. 재료의 맛은 섬세하게 다듬고, 맛의 구조는 입체적으로 설계해내는 것이다.

그는 앞으로도 신선한 재료의 본질을 살리고, 재료에 맞춘 정확한 조리법으로 깊이 있는 맛을 전하는 요리를 통해 마리포사만의 정체성을 더욱 선명하게 만들어갈 계획이다.

Chef Lee Daegeon is currently the executive chef at Fairmont Ambassador Seoul Hotel, where he is responsible for modern European dining at the hotel's signature restaurant, Mariposa. His extensive experience in Korea and abroad has shaped his culinary philosophy, which has established Mariposa as one of Seoul's premier fine dining destinations.

As the hotel's executive chef, he is responsible for catering to not only a single customer base but also guests with diverse tastes and expectations. Hence, he says his main challenge is to create a "menu that appeals to everyone" while maintaining the high quality that befits the hotel. He strives to create a space that is not just a restaurant inside the Fairmont Hotel but a place that is remembered for the Mariposa itself.

He believes in honest and straightforward recipes that bring out the natural flavors of the ingredients. He enjoys experimenting with a single ingredient by cooking it in various ways, often adding his own pastes and sauces to give it character and depth without compromising the texture of the fresh ingredients. The flavors of the ingredients are delicately refined, and the structure of the flavor is designed to be multi-dimensional.

He plans to continue fine-tuning Mariposa's identity further through dishes that capture the essence of fresh ingredients and deliver profound flavors with precise recipes tailored to each ingredient.

마리포사
mariposa_m29

daegeonl

Smoked Scallops and Cauliflower Emulsion

이야기
STORY

훈연한 관자와 콜리플라워 에멀전

이 레시피는 최근 이사를 하면서 우연히 찾게 된, 15년 전 마카오에서 일할 때 항상 들고 다니던 수첩에서 시작되었습니다. 새로운 메뉴를 구상하던 시기였고, 문득 발견한 오래된 수첩을 한 장씩 넘기다 보니 어린 시절 요리를 배우며 메모했던 손글씨와 함께, 그 시절 내가 품고 있던 열정과 새로운 것에 대한 갈망이 고스란히 떠올랐습니다.

콜리플라워 에멀전이라고 적힌, 철자도 틀린 영어 레시피 한 줄을 보며 웃음도 났습니다. 지금 보면 아주 간단한 조리법이고 특별한 재료가 들어가는 것도 아닌데, 그땐 왜 그렇게 간절하게 배우고 싶었는지 모르겠습니다. 그 시절 다양한 국적의 친구들과 나눴던 소중한 기억들도 함께 떠오르며, 문득 그 시절의 요리를 다시 꺼내어 보고 싶은 마음이 들었습니다.

그래서 제가 좋아하는 관자와 그때의 레시피를 합쳐 새로운 요리를 만들어보았습니다. 추억과 현재가 한 접시에 담긴, 개인적으로도 의미가 깊은 메뉴입니다. 여러분께도 그런 따뜻한 한 입이 되기를 바랍니다.

This dish began with a notebook I stumbled upon while moving house recently. It was the small pocket notebook I always carried with me during my time working in Macao 15 years ago, when I was exploring ideas for new menu items. As I flipped through its pages, I came across my handwritten notes from those early days of learning to cook, reminding me of the hunger for something new and the passion I had back then.

I even chuckled when I saw my old misspelling of "Cauliflower Emulsion." Looking back now, I wonder why I was so eager to learn this recipe, simple as it was and with no special ingredients. The cherished memories I shared with my colleagues from around the world flooded back, compelling me to revisit the dishes I once made.

So I created this new dish, reimagining the original recipe with my favorite ingredient—scallop. This single dish holds both memory and the present, making it deeply meaningful to me. I hope you can feel the heartfelt warmth in every bite.

Ingredients

2인 분량
Serves 2

콜리플라워 에멀전

콜리플라워	200g
우유	150g
생크림	150g
통마늘	1.5개
화이트와인 비네거	15g
엑스트라버진 올리브 오일	50g

훈연 관자

관자	4알
훈연용 사과나무 껍질	적당량
소금	적당량
후춧가루	적당량
식용유	적당량
버터	10g
타임	적당량

장식

캐비어	10g
허브 또는 식용꽃	적당량
라임제스트	적당량

CAULIFLOWER EMULSION

200 g	cauliflower
150 g	milk
150 g	fresh cream
1.5	garlic cloves
15 g	white wine vinegar
50 g	extra virgin olive oil

SMOKED SCALLOPS

4	scallops
Q.S.	apple wood chips
Q.S.	salt
Q.S.	ground black pepper
Q.S.	cooking oil
10 g	butter
Q.S.	fresh thyme

GARNISHES

10 g	caviar
Q.S.	fresh herbs or edible flowers
Q.S.	lime zest

How to make

콜리플라워 에멀전

1. 콜리플라워를 2cm 크기로 잘라줍니다.
2. 콜리플라워 일부(약 6대)를 끓는 물에서 2분 정도 삶은 후 건져내 식혀줍니다.
- 걸러진 국물을 버리지 말고 에멀전의 농도를 맞추는 데 사용합니다.
3. 냄비에 우유, 생크림, 통마늘, 남은 콜리플라워를 넣고 콜리플라워가 익을 때까지 약 15분간 가열합니다.

CAULIFLOWER EMULSION

1. Cut the cauliflower into 2 cm pieces.
2. Cook some of the cauliflower (about 6 pieces) in boiling water for about 2 minutes. Remove and let cool.
- Reserve the cooking liquid to adjust the consistency of the emulsion.
3. In a pot, combine the milk, fresh cream, garlic cloves, and the remaining cauliflower. Simmer for about 15 minutes until the cauliflower is cooked.

4. 콜리플라워가 푹 익으면 믹서로 옮겨 화이트와인 비네거와 함께 곱게 갈아줍니다.
5. 가는 중간 올리브오일을 넣어가며 유화시켜줍니다.

4. Once fully cooked, transfer the mixture to a blender and blend with the white wine vinegar until smooth.
5. While blending, drizzle in the olive oil to emulsify.

훈연 관자

1. 훈연용 사과나무 껍질에 불을 붙여줍니다.
2. **1** 위에 손질한 관자가 담긴 타공 팬을 올린 후 랩핑해 관자에 훈연향이 스며들도록 15~20분간 둡니다.
3. 훈연한 관자에 소금과 후춧가루를 뿌려 간을 합니다.

SMOKED SCALLOPS

1. Ignite the apple wood chips.
2. Place a perforated pan with the cleaned scallops over (**1**). Cover with plastic wrap and let sit for 15 to 20 minutes, allowing the scallops to absorb the smoky aroma.
3. Season the smoked scallops with salt and black pepper.

4. 식용유를 두른 팬에 훈연한 관자를 넣고 익혀줍니다.
5. 관자의 한쪽 면이 익으면 뒤집어 다른 쪽 면이 1/3 정도 익으면 버터와 타임을 넣고 관자에 부려가며 익혀줍니다.
- 팬의 온도가 너무 높으면 버터가 탈 수 있으니 주의합니다.
6. 관자가 반 정도 익으면 건져냅니다.
- 반 정도 익었을 때 건져내도 잔열로 충분히 익습니다.

4. Pan-fry the scallops in cooking oil.
5. Once one side is done, flip the scallops and cook the other side until about one-third done. Add the butter and thyme, then baste the scallops with the pan liquid.
- Avoid overheating the pan to prevent the butter from burning.
6. When the scallops are halfway cooked, remove from the pan.
- The scallops will finish cooking with the residual heat.

마무리

1. 접시에 콜리플라워 에멀젼을 담고 평평하게 정리합니다.
2. 콜리플라워 에멀젼 위에 익힌 관자 두 개와 삶은 콜리플라워를 올려줍니다.
3. 반구형으로 만든 캐비어를 올려줍니다.
- 캐비어는 계량스푼 등의 도구를 이용해 모양을 만들어 사용합니다.

FINISH

1. Spoon the cauliflower emulsion onto a plate and spread it out evenly.
2. Place two smoked scallops and the cooked cauliflower on top of the emulsion.
3. Top with dome-shaped caviar.
- Use a tool such as a measuring spoon to shape the caviar.

4. 허브 또는 식용꽃을 올린 후 라임제스트를 뿌려 마무리합니다.

4. Garnish with fresh herbs or edible flowers, and a sprinkle of lime zest.

LEE DAEGEON

Zucchini Royale with Shrimp Parmesan Sauce

애호박 로얄, 새우 파르메산 소스

가정식
HOME COOKING

개인적으로 달걀을 참 좋아합니다. 다양한 방식으로 조리할 수 있는 데다 어떤 재료와도 잘 어울리는, 무한한 가능성을 가진 식재료라고 생각하거든요. '로얄'이라는 말이 낯선 분들도 계실 텐데요. 프랑스식 달걀찜 정도로 이해하면 좋을 것 같습니다. 저는 달걀을 애호박으로 만든 퓌레와 섞은 후 부드럽게 익혀 완성해 보았습니다.

냉동 새우, 생크림, 달걀처럼 마트에서 쉽게 구할 수 있는 익숙한 재료를 가지고도 의외로 근사한 한 접시를 만들 수 있습니다. 이 요리가 바로 그렇습니다. 누구나 집에서도 손쉽게 따라 할 수 있으면서도 식탁 위에서는 특별한 느낌을 주는 메뉴가 되어줄 거예요.

I am especially fond of eggs, as I believe they offer infinite potential. Eggs are versatile across a variety of techniques and pair well with any other ingredient. The word *royale* may sound unfamiliar to some; it can be considered the French equivalent of steamed eggs. In this version, eggs are blended with zucchini purée before steaming.

With nothing more than everyday ingredients easily found at any store—such as frozen shrimp, fresh cream, and eggs—it is possible to create an unexpectedly elegant dish. This dish serves as a perfect example. Simple enough for anyone to try at home, it brings a special charm to the table.

Ingredients

2인 분량
Serves 2

파르메산 소스

양파	20g
버터	10g
마늘	10g
화이트 와인	5g
생크림	100g
후춧가루	적당량
타임	적당량
파르메산 치즈	14g
페페론치노	적당량

애호박 로얄

애호박	150g
우유	25g
생크림	50g
달걀	50g
노른자	9g
소금	2g
후춧가루	1g

가니시

식용유	적당량
새우	6개
피클무	1줄
구운 견과류	적당량

장식

식용꽃	적당량
이탈리안 파슬리	적당량

PARMESAN SAUCE

20 g	onion
10 g	butter
10 g	garlic
5 g	white wine
100 g	fresh cream
Q.S.	ground black pepper
Q.S.	fresh thyme
14 g	Parmesan
Q.S.	peperoncino

ZUCCHINI ROYALE

150 g	zucchini
25 g	milk
50 g	fresh cream
50 g	whole egg
9 g	egg yolk
2 g	salt
1 g	ground black pepper

GARNISHES

Q.S.	cooking oil
6	shrimps
1 piece	pickled radish
Q.S.	roasted nuts

PLATING DECORATIONS

Q.S.	fresh edible flowers
Q.S.	fresh Italian parsley

How to make

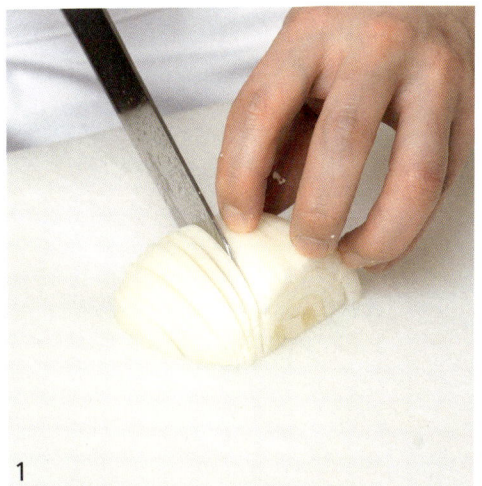  

파르메산 소스

1. 양파를 적당한 크기로 채 썰어줍니다.
2. 냄비에 버터, 채 썬 양파, 마늘을 넣고 아린 맛과 향이 없어질 때까지 볶아줍니다.
- 마늘은 칼등으로 가볍게 찧어 사용합니다.
- 너무 진한 색이 나지 않도록 주의하며 중불로 볶아줍니다.
3. 양파가 익으면 화이트와인을 넣고 볶아줍니다.

PARMESAN SAUCE

1. Slice the onion into moderately sized pieces.
2. In a pot, combine the butter, sliced onion, and garlic, then stir-fry until the sharp flavor and aroma have softened.
- Gently crush the garlic with the back of a knife before use.
- Be sure to cook over medium heat to avoid browning it too much.
3. Once the onion is cooked, add the white wine and stir-fry.

4. 화이트와인이 졸아들면 생크림, 후춧가루, 타임을 넣고 가열합니다.
5. 타임의 향이 우러나면 건져낸 후 강판에 간 파르메산 치즈, 페페론치노를 넣고 약불에서 소스 농도가 될 때까지 졸여줍니다.
6. 블렌더로 옮겨 곱게 갈아줍니다.

4. When the white wine has reduced, add the fresh cream, black pepper, and thyme, then heat.
5. Once the thyme has released its aroma, add the grated Parmesan and peperoncino. Simmer over low heat until reduced to a sauce consistency.
6. Transfer the mixture to a blender and blend until smooth.

애호박 로얄

1. 애호박을 반으로 잘라 씨 부분을 제거한 후 0.5cm 두께로 잘라줍니다.
2. 냄비에 물과 소금(분량 외)을 넣고, 끓어오르면 애호박을 넣고 익힌 후 건져냅니다.
3. 익힌 애호박을 믹서에 넣고 곱게 간 후 식혀줍니다.

ZUCCHINI ROYALE

1. Halve the zucchini, remove the seeds, and slice into 0.5 cm-thick pieces.
2. Combine water and salt in a pot and bring to a boil. Once boiling, cook the zucchini and remove from the pot.
3. Blend the cooked zucchini until smooth, then let cool.

4. 볼에 3과 우유, 생크림, 달걀, 노른자, 소금, 후춧가루를 넣고 섞어줍니다.
5. 전자레인지용 용기에 담아줍니다.
6. 용기 입구를 랩핑하고 구멍을 낸 후 전자레인지 또는 찜기에서 익혀줍니다.
- 전자레인지를 사용할 경우 40초씩 끊어가며 총 두 번 익히고, 찜기를 사용할 경우 80℃ 온도에서 약 20분간 익혀줍니다.

4. In a mixing bowl, combine the milk, fresh cream, whole egg, egg yolk, salt (2 g), and black pepper, then mix well.
5. Pour the mixture into a microwave-safe container.
6. Cover with plastic wrap, pierce small holes, and cook in a microwave or steamer.
- If using a microwave, cook for 40 seconds twice. If using a steamer, cook at 176°F (80°C) for about 20 minutes.

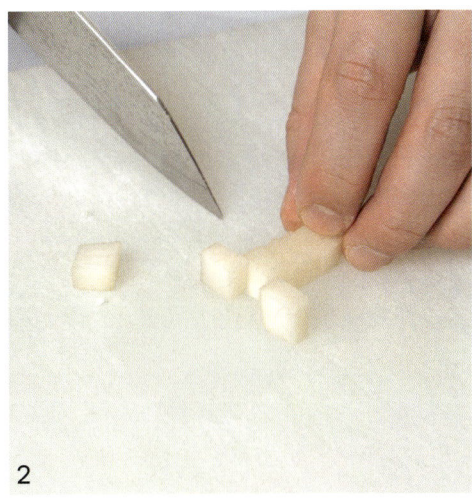

가니시

1. 식용유를 두른 팬에 새우를 넣고 노릇하게 익혀줍니다.
- 새우는 소금과 후춧가루로 간을 한 후 사용합니다.
2. 피클무는 큐브 모양으로 작게 잘라줍니다.

플레이팅

1. 애호박 로얄 위에 익힌 새우를 올려줍니다.

GARNISHES

1. Pan-fry the shrimp in cooking oil until golden.
- Season the shrimp with salt and black pepper before use.
2. Dice the pickled radish into small cubes.

PLATING

1. Place the shrimp on top of the zucchini *royale*.

2. 무 피클과 구운 견과류를 군데군데 올려줍니다.
3. 파르메산 소스를 뿌려줍니다.
4. 식용꽃과 다진 이탈리안 파슬리를 뿌려 마무리합니다.

2. Scatter the pickled radish and nuts on top.
3. Drizzle the Parmesan sauce over the dish.
4. Garnish with edible flowers and chopped Italian parsley.

JANG JISOO
장지수

어린 시절부터 요리에 남다른 관심을 보였다. 초등학교 때부터 어머니 곁에서 재료를 만지며 요리를 놀이처럼 즐겼고, 중학생 때 요리학원에 다니며 본격적인 꿈을 키우기 시작했다. 성인이 되어 양식 요리에 매료된 그는 더 넓은 세계로 나아가고자 미국 샌프란시스코로 떠났다. 현지에서 미슐랭 스타 셰프 마이클 미나의 레스토랑에 몸담으며 체계적인 양식 조리법을 익혔다.

귀국 후 다양한 레스토랑에서 경험을 쌓던 중, 2020년 2월 청와대 양식 담당 셰프로 발탁되며 새로운 전환점을 맞았다. 문재인 대통령의 첫 식사로 준비한 샐러드는 잊을 수 없는 기억으로 남아 있고, 김정숙 여사가 극찬한 '오리 콩피'는 외빈 접대 자리에서 특히 깊은 인상을 남겼다.

이후 SPC 삼립의 식품 R&D 파트에서 잠시 연구직을 경험했지만, 주방에 대한 그리움은 커져갔다. 결국 2024년, 강릉 안목해변 인근의 레스토랑 '미트 컬쳐(Meat Culture)'로 돌아왔고, 이곳에서 그는 정제된 기술을 바탕으로, 자신만의 요리를 펼쳐 보이고 있다.

미트컬쳐
meat_culture

jangjisoo1

He showed a keen interest in cooking from an early age. From elementary school, he played with food ingredients by his mother's side, and in middle school, he began to pursue his dream in earnest by attending a local cooking academy. As an adult fascinated by Western cuisine, he traveled to San Francisco to explore the world beyond. There, he worked at Michelin-starred chef Michael Mina's restaurant, where he learned to master systematic Western cooking methods.

After returning to Korea, he gained experience in various restaurants. However, his career took a new turn in February 2020 when he was selected as the chef in charge of western cuisine at the Blue House. The salad he prepared for President Moon Jae-in's first meal remains unforgettable, and his duck confit, which First Lady Kim Jung-sook praised, made a particular impression at state dinners.

He then worked briefly as a researcher at SPC Samlip's food R&D department, but his longing for the kitchen grew stronger. In 2024, he returned to Meat Culture, a restaurant located near Anmok Beach in Gangneung, where he presents his own dishes based in his refined skills.

East Sea Cod Steak with Mashed Potatoes & Chorizo Sausage

이야기
STORY

동해안 대구 스테이크와 매시드 포테이토 & 초리소 소시지

강릉을 대표하는 식재료 중 하나인 '대구'를 활용해 만든 요리입니다. 대구는 부드럽고 담백한 살을 가진 생선으로, 다양한 조리법에 잘 어울리는 재료인데요. 저는 이 대구에 제가 개인적으로 좋아하는 프랑스식 생선 스튜인 부야베스(Bouillabaisse)를 응용한 소스를 곁들여 보았습니다. 일반적인 부야베스는 국물 형태지만, 이 메뉴에서는 그 풍부한 맛을 응축해 농축된 소스 형태로 재해석했습니다.

메인인 대구 스테이크와 함께 부드러운 매시드 포테이토, 촉촉하게 구운 관자, 볶은 케일과 튀긴 명이나물을 함께 플레이팅했습니다. 각각의 재료가 가진 맛과 식감, 향이 조화롭게 어우러져 바다와 땅의 기운을 함께 느낄 수 있는 이 메뉴는 강릉의 지역성과 개인적인 취향, 그리고 클래식한 유럽 요리에 대한 애정이 자연스럽게 녹아든 한 접시입니다.

This dish features cod, one of the representative ingredients of Gangneung City, known for its tender, clean flesh, and versatile across a variety of cooking techniques. It is paired with a sauce inspired by *bouillabaisse*, the classic French fish stew that I personally love. While *bouillabaisse* is traditionally served as a soup, this version has been reimagined as a reduced sauce that concentrates its original flavors.

The cod is plated as the main feature, complemented by smooth mashed potatoes, pan-fried juicy scallops, stir-fried kale, and fried wild garlic leaves. The interplay of flavors, aromas, and textures from each ingredient creates a harmonious expression of land and sea. This creation reflects the regional identity of Gangneung City, naturally infused with my personal culinary taste and a fondness for classic European cuisine.

Ingredients

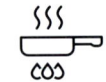

3접시 분량
Makes 3 plates

대구 스톡*

양파	1/2개
대파	1줄기
셀러리	1줄기
대구머리와 뼈 (대구 1마리 분량)	7kg
월계수잎	1장
마늘	2알
화이트와인	250ml
물	4L

소스

양파	1/2개
대파	1줄기
셀러리	1줄기
식용유	적당량
화이트와인	250ml
토마토 페이스트	100g
대구 스톡*	2L
펜넬씨드	1작은술
오렌지 껍질	오렌지 1/2개 분량
브라운 루	적당량
소금	적당량
후춧가루	적당량
레드와인 비네거	적당량

매시드 포테이토

우유	100ml
생크림	200ml
두백감자	400g
소금	적당량
후춧가루	적당량
버터	200g

대구 스테이크

대구	180g × 3개
소금	적당량
식용유	적당량
버터	적당량
타임	1줄기
마늘	2알

곁들임

버터	적당량
가리비	12알
식용유	적당량
초리소 소시지	3줄
마늘	1알
페페론치노	2개
케일	50g
소금	적당량
후춧가루	적당량
레드와인 비네거	적당량

가니시

튀긴 명이나물	적당량
엑스트라버진 올리브오일	적당량

COD STOCK*

1/2	onion
1	green onion stalk
1	celery stalk
7 kg	cod head and bones (from 1 cod)
1	bay leaf
2	garlic cloves
250 ml	white wine
4 L	water

SAUCE

1/2	onion
1	green onion stalk
1	celery stalk
Q.S.	cooking oil
250 ml	white wine
100 g	tomato paste
2 L	cod stock*
1 tsp	fennel seeds
Q.S.	orange peel (from 1/2 orange)
Q.S.	brown roux
Q.S.	salt
Q.S.	ground black pepper
Q.S.	red wine vinegar

MASHED POTATOES

100 ml	milk
200 ml	fresh cream
400 g	Dubaek potatoes
Q.S.	salt
Q.S.	ground black pepper
200 g	butter

COD STEAK

3	cod fillets (180 g each)
Q.S.	salt
Q.S.	cooking oil
Q.S.	butter
1	fresh thyme sprig
2	garlic cloves

SIDES

Q.S.	butter
12	scallops
Q.S.	cooking oil
3	chorizo sausages
1	garlic clove
2	peperoncino peppers
50 g	kale
Q.S.	salt
Q.S.	ground black pepper
Q.S.	red wine vinegar

GARNISHES

Q.S.	fried wild garlic leaves
Q.S.	extra virgin olive oil

How to make

대구 스톡

1. 양파, 대파, 셀러리를 큼직하게 잘라줍니다.
2. 냄비에 대구 스톡 재료를 모두 넣고 약불에서 40분간 가열한 후 체에 걸러줍니다.
- 대구 머리와 뼈는 핏물이 빠질 때까지 찬물에 담근 후 건져 사용합니다.

COD STOCK

1. Roughly slice the onion, green onion, and celery.
2. Combine all the cod stock ingredients in a pot and simmer over low heat for 40 minutes. Strain through a sieve.
- Before use, soak the head and bones of the cod in cold water to remove any blood.

소스

1. 양파, 대파, 셀러리를 큼직하게 썰어줍니다.
2. 식용유를 두른 팬에 채소를 넣고 색이 나지 않게 볶아준 후 화이트와인을 넣어 수분을 날립니다.
3. 토마토 페이스트를 넣고 약불에서 약 3분간 볶아줍니다.

SAUCE

1. Roughly slice the onion, green onion, and celery.
2. In a pan with cooking oil, stir-fry the vegetables in olive oil, preserving their color. Pour in the white wine and cook until the moisture evaporates.
3. Add the tomato paste and continue cooking over low heat for about 3 minutes.

4. 대구 스톡, 팬넬씨드, 오렌지 껍질을 넣고 약 20분간 가열합니다.
5. 체에 거른 후 다시 불에 올려줍니다.
6. 브라운 루를 넣어 농도를 맞춘 후 소금, 후춧가루, 레드와인 비네거를 넣고 섞어줍니다.
- 브라운 루(brown roux)는 밀가루와 버터를 1:1 비율로 갈색이 될 때까지 볶아 만듭니다. 만들어둔 브라운 루는 냉장 또는 냉동 보관하며 필요한 만큼 사용할 수 있습니다.

4. Pour in the cod stock, add the fennel seeds and orange peel, then simmer for about 20 minutes.
5. Strain through a sieve and return the liquid to the heat.
6. Stir in the brown roux to adjust the consistency. Season with salt, black pepper, and red wine vinegar, then mix well.
- To make the brown roux, cook flour and butter in a 1:1 ratio, stirring constantly until browned. Store in the refrigerator or freezer, and use as needed.

매시드 포테이토

1. 팬에 우유와 생크림을 넣고 약불에서 살짝 데워줍니다.
2. 익힌 두백감자를 넣고 가열한 후 소금과 후춧가루로 간을 맞춘 후 버터를 넣고 녹여 체에 걸러줍니다.
- 두백감자는 220℃로 예열된 오븐에서 50분간 구운 후 껍질을 제거하고 체에 내려 사용합니다.

MASHED POTATOES

1. In a pan, gently warm the milk and fresh cream over low heat.
2. Add the Dubaek potatoes, season with salt and black pepper, then melt in the butter. Pass through a sieve.
- Before use, roast the Dubaek potatoes in an oven preheated to 428°F (220°C) for 50 minutes. Peel and pass through a sieve.

대구 스테이크

1. 손질한 대구는 소금으로 간을 합니다.
2. 식용유를 두른 팬에 손질한 대구, 버터, 타임, 마늘을 넣고 약불에서 천천히 색을 내며 익혀줍니다.
- 대구 윗면에 버터를 끼얹어가며 익혀줍니다.
3. 대구 중심부의 온도가 54℃ 정도가 되면 마무리합니다.

COD STEAK

1. Season the cod fillets with salt.
2. In a pan with cooking oil, place the fillets along with butter, thyme, and garlic. Gently cook over low heat until lightly browned.
- Baste the top of the fillets with the pan liquid while cooking.
3. Cook until the center reaches approximately 129°F (54°C).

곁들임

1. 버터를 두른 팬에 가리비를 넣고 익혀줍니다.
- 가리비는 힘줄을 제거해 사용합니다.
2. 식용유를 두른 팬에 초리소 소시지를 넣고 익혀줍니다.
- 초리소 소시지는 안쪽까지 고르게 익도록 뾰족한 도구로 중간중간 찌른 후 사용합니다.

SIDES

1. Heat the butter in a pan and cook the scallops.
- Remove the side muscles from the scallops before use.
2. Pan-fry the chorizo sausages in cooking oil.
- Poke the sausages in several places to ensure even cooking.

3. 익힌 초리소 소시지를 한입 크기로 잘라줍니다.
4. 식용유를 두른 팬에 마늘, 페페론치노를 넣고 볶다가 케일을 넣고 숨이 죽을 때까지 살짝만 익힌 후 소금, 후춧가루, 레드와인 비네거를 넣고 섞어줍니다.
- 케일은 적당한 크기로 잘라 사용합니다.

3. Cut the sausages into bite-sized pieces.
4. In a pan with cooking oil, stir-fry the garlic and peperoncino. Add the kale and cook until slightly wilted. Season with salt, black pepper, and red wine vinegar, then toss well.
- Cut the kale into moderately sized pieces before use.

플레이팅

1. 접시에 매쉬드 포테이토를 담아줍니다.
- 파이핑백을 이용해 봉긋하게 짜주거나 큰 숟가락으로 떠줍니다.
2. 매쉬드 포테이토 위에 익힌 초리소 소시지와 관자를 올려줍니다.
3. 중앙에 볶은 케일을 올려줍니다.

PLATING

1. Place the mashed potatoes on a plate.
- Pipe the mashed potatoes into a mound using a piping bag, or spoon them onto the plate.
2. Arrange the chorizo sausages and scallops on the mashed potatoes.
3. Top with the kale in the center.

4. 대구 스테이크와 채 썰어 튀긴 명이나물을 올려줍니다.
5. 소스를 담아줍니다.
6. 올리브오일을 뿌려 마무리합니다.

4. Set the cod steak on top, and garnish with fried wild garlic leaf slices.
5. Spoon the sauce around the plate.
6. Finish with a drizzle of olive oil.

Octopus Plate

가정식
HOME COOKING

참문어 플레이트

강릉 주문진 앞바다에서 잡은 참문어를 주재료로 한 요리입니다. 이곳의 참문어는 서해안에서 잡히는 문어에 비해 살결이 더 부드럽고, 맛 또한 깊고 진한 것이 특징입니다. 참문어는 강릉의 다양한 해산물 중에서도 특히 그 신선도와 식감 때문에 많은 셰프들이 선호하는 재료이기도 하죠.

참문어를 메인으로, 참문어와 잘 어울리는 또 하나의 강릉 대표 식재료인 감자를 매칭했습니다. 그리고 토치로 그을린 오렌지, 바삭한 비트칩, 산뜻하고 상큼한 토마틸로 소스와 부드럽고 고소한 아이올리 소스를 함께 플레이팅하고, 향긋한 라벤더 버터로 향을 입혀 완성했습니다. 강릉의 바다와 땅에서 온 재료들, 그리고 자연의 향이 조화롭게 담긴 요리로, 플레이팅과 맛, 향의 균형이 인상적인 메뉴입니다.

This dish features octopus caught in the waters off Jumunjin, Gangneung City, prized for its tender texture and deeper, richer flavor compared to that of the West Sea. Among the region's diverse seafood, octopus stands out for its freshness and distinctive texture, making it a favorite among many chefs.

The octopus takes center stage, paired perfectly with potatoes, another specialty of Gangneung City. It is served with blow-torched orange, crispy beetroot chips, smooth, nutty aioli, and refreshing tomatillo sauce, then finished with a touch of aromatic lavender butter. This dish presents a bounty from the region's sea and land, delicately infused with the fragrance of nature. Every element comes together in perfect harmony, offering a remarkable balance of presentation, flavor, and aroma.

Ingredients

3접시 분량
Makes 3 plates

참문어

물	4L
소금	1/2컵
식초	1/4컵
참문어	1kg

곁들임

두백감자	1개
식용유	적당량
비트	200g
오렌지	1개

라벤더 버터

버터	200g
라벤더 티백	2개

오렌지 딜 아이올리 소스

마요네즈	500g
다진 딜	2g
오렌지제스트	오렌지 2개 분량
간 마늘	마늘1개 분량

토마틸로 소스

으깬 토마틸로	900g
설탕	200g
환만식초	200g
소금	10g

장식

딜	적당량

OCTOPUS

4 L	water
1/2 cup	salt
1/4 cup	vinegar
1 kg	octopus

SIDES

1	Dubaek potato
Q.S.	cooking oil
200 g	beetroot
1	orange

LAVENDER BUTTER

200 g	butter
2	lavender tea bags

ORANGE AND DILL AIOLI

500 g	mayonnaise
2 g	chopped dill
Q.S.	orange zest (from 2 oranges)
Q.S.	grated garlic (from 1 clove)

TOMATILLO SAUCE

900 g	crushed tomatillo
200 g	sugar
200 g	Hwanman vinegar
10 g	salt

GARNISH

Q.S.	fresh dill

How to make

참문어

1. 끓는 물(4L)에 소금 1/2컵, 식초 1/4컵, 참문어를 넣고 약불에서 30분간 익혀줍니다.
- 참문어는 내장을 제거한 후 소금 한 큰술 정도를 뿌리고 손으로 비비듯 씻어 점액질을 제거해 사용합니다.
2. 익힌 참문어는 얼음물에 넣어 식힌 후 1.5cm 길이로 잘라줍니다.
3. 자른 참문어는 220℃로 예열된 오븐에서 약 3분간 익혀줍니다.

OCTOPUS

1. In a pot, combine 4 L of boiling water, 1/2 cup of salt, 1/4 cup of vinegar, and the octopus. Cook over low heat for 30 minutes.
- Before use, remove the octopus innards, add 1 tablespoon of salt, and rub the octopus between your hands to remove any mucus.
2. Soak the octopus in ice water, let cool, and cut into 1.5 cm lengths.
3. Roast the octopus in an oven preheated to 428°F (220°C) for about 3 minutes.

곁들임

1. 두백감자는 2cm 두께로 썰어 끓는 물에 넣고 익힌 후, 175℃로 예열된 식용유에서 약 3분간 튀기고 소금으로 간을 합니다.
2. 비트는 껍질을 제거하고 얇게 썰어 150℃로 예열된 식용유에서 약 3분간 튀겨줍니다.
- 만돌린을 사용하면 더 쉽고 얇게 슬라이스할 수 있습니다.

SIDES

1. Cut the Dubaek potato into 2 cm-thick pieces and cook in boiling water. Deep-fry in cooking oil preheated to 347°F (175°C) for about 3 minutes, then season with salt.
2. Peel the beetroot, slice thinly, and deep-fry in cooking oil preheated to 302°F (150°C) for about 3 minutes.
- Use a mandolin for easier and thinner slicing.

3. 오렌지는 칼로 돌려가며 껍질을 벗겨 냅니다.
4. 속 껍질 사이사이 알맹이 부분만 칼로 잘라 준비합니다.
5. 토치로 그을려줍니다.

3. Using a knife, rotate the orange to remove all the peel and white pith.
4. Cut between the membranes to separate the segments, extracting only the flesh.
5. Gently char with a blowtorch.

라벤더 버터

냄비에 버터를 넣고 약불에서 녹인 후 라벤더 티백을 넣고 15분간 우려 라벤더 버터를 완성합니다.

오렌지 딜 아이올리 소스

볼에 오렌지 딜 아이올리 소스 재료를 모두 넣고 섞어 오렌지 딜 아이올리 소스를 완성합니다.

토마틸로 소스

냄비에 토마틸로 소스 재료를 모두 넣고 중불에서 졸인 후 곱게 갈아 토마틸로 소스를 완성합니다.

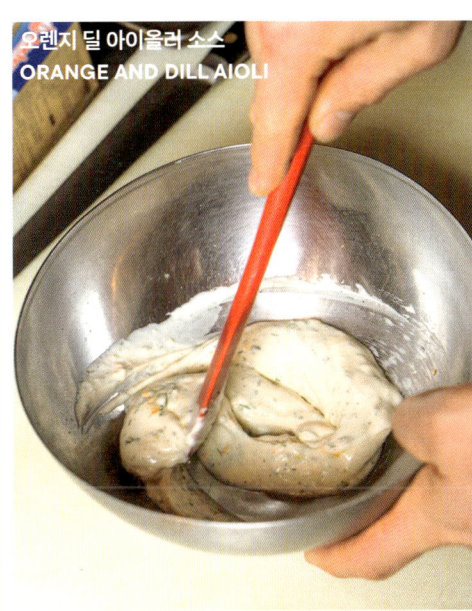

LAVENDER BUTTER

Melt the butter in a pot over low heat, add the lavender tea bags, and infuse for 15 minutes to make the lavender butter.

ORANGE AND DILL AIOLI

In a mixing bowl, combine all the orange and dill aioli ingredients to make the aioli.

TOMATILLO SAUCE

In a pot, combine all the tomatillo sauce ingredients. Simmer over medium heat to reduce, then blend until smooth to make the tomatillo sauce.

플레이팅

1. 접시에 감자와 문어를 담고 토마틸로 소스와 오렌지 딜 아이올리 소스를 군데군데 파이핑합니다.
2. 토치로 그을린 오렌지를 올려줍니다.
3. 비트칩과 딜을 올려줍니다.

PLATING

1. Arrange the potato and octopus on a plate. Pipe small dots of the orange and dill aioli and the tomatillo sauce.
2. Top with the blow-torched orange segments.
3. Garnish with beetroot chips and dill.

4. 라벤더 버터를 뿌려 마무리합니다.

4. Spoon the lavender butter over the dish.

JO WOORAM
조우람

LEE EUNHEE
이은희

프랑스 식료품점 '메종조'는 조우람, 이은희 셰프가 함께 쌓아온 시간과 진심이 고스란히 담긴 공간이다. 서로 다른 출발점에서 요리를 시작한 두 셰프는, 결국 같은 방향을 향해 나란히 걸어가게 되었다.

이은희 셰프는 국내에서 파티시에로 일하며 식사빵을 만들던 중, 발효라는 세계에 매료되었다. 빵에 대한 궁금증이 점점 깊어지던 어느 날, 함께 일하던 조우람 셰프 또한 이탈리안 셰프에서 샤퀴티에로의 전향을 고민하고 있었고, 그렇게 두 사람은 뜻을 모아 프랑스로 유학을 떠나게 된다.

프랑스 유학 시절, 조우람 셰프에게 전환점이 찾아온 건 장날 시장에서 맛본 잠봉과 파테였다. 그날 처음 맛본 루이 오스피탈의 잠봉과 파테 바스크, 그리고 그것을 바게트에 발라 코르니숑과 함께 베어 문 순간, 거칠면서도 섬세하게 다듬어진 풍미에 전율을 느꼈다. 그때 그는 언젠가 꼭 저 샤퀴테리를 만드는 곳에서 일해보리라 결심했다. 결국 그는 바스크 지방의 작은 마을 아스파렌(Hasparren)에 있는 루이 오스피탈로 향했고, 그곳에서의 경험은 셰프로서 그의 방향을 완전히 바꿔놓았다.

두 셰프가 프랑스에서 보낸 5년은 단순한 유학이 아니었다. 취향을 나누고, 감각을 축적하고, 서로의 세계를 확장해가는 시간이었다. 특히 지역 특산물을 중심으로 운영되는 식료품점과 전통 요리를 캐주얼하게 즐길 수 있는 카페와 비스트로를 찾아다니며 맛에 대한 감각과 경험을 쌓았고, 한국에 돌아온 후엔 그 기억을 '메종조'라는 이름 아래 펼치기로 했다.

메종조는 단순히 프랑스풍 베이커리와 샤퀴테리를 파는 곳이 아니다. 누구나 편하게 즐길 수 있는 클래식한 프랑스 빵과 요리, 샤퀴테리를 선보이며, 그 속에는 두 셰프의 취향과 철학, 그리고 삶의 리듬이 녹아 있다. 메종조의 주방에서는 지금 이 순간에도, 두 셰프가 사랑해온 시간과 감각이 조용히 음식으로 이어지고 있다.

The French grocery store Maison Jo is a reflection of the time and sincerity of chefs Jo Wooram and Lee Eunhee. The two chefs started cooking from different starting points, but now they are walking side by side in the same direction.

Chef Lee Eunhee was working as a pastry chef in Korea, making bread for meals, when she became fascinated by the world of fermentation. One day, as her curiosity about bread deepened, her co-worker, chef Jo Wooram, was considering switching from an Italian chef to a charcuterie specialist, and the two decided to study abroad in France.

While studying in France, chef Jo's turning point came when he tasted jambon and pâté at a market. The first time he tasted Louis Ospital's jambon and pâté Basque, and the moment he spread it on a baguette and bit into it with a cornichon, he was struck by the rough yet delicately refined flavors. He decided that one day, he would work at a place that made that particular charcuterie. Eventually, he made his way to Louis Ospital in the small Basque town of Hasparren, and his experience there changed his direction as a chef forever.

The five years the two spent in France were more than just a study-abroad experience. It was a time of sharing tastes, accumulating sensations, and expanding each other's worlds. In particular, they explored grocery stores centered around local specialties, cafes, and bistros serving traditional dishes in a casual setting, gaining a sense of flavor and experience that they decided to bring back to Korea under the name Maison Jo.

Maison Jo is more than just a French-inspired bakery and charcuterie. It serves classic French breads, dishes, and charcuterie that are accessible to all, reflecting the chefs' tastes, philosophies, and rhythms of life. In Maison Jo's kitchen, the time and sensations that the two chefs love are quietly translated into food.

메종조
maison_jo_

Pâté au Piment d'Espelette

(Basque-Style Pâté)

조우람 / JO WOORAM

이야기 / STORY

파테 오 피멍 데스플레트
(바스크 스타일 파테)

파테(Pâté)는 프랑스 샤퀴테리 가운데 잠봉 블랑, 소시송과 함께 가장 널리 사랑받는 메뉴 중 하나로, 식사나 빵과 샐러드에 곁들이거나 레드와인 한 잔과 함께하기에 좋은 음식입니다. 주로 돼지 간과 돼지고기를 주재료로 만들어지며, 담백하지만 깊은 풍미를 지니고 있죠.

프랑스 유학 시절 루이 오스피탈(Louis Ospital)의 잠봉과 파테 바스크를 바게트에 발라 코르니송과 함께 먹었을 때, 거칠어 보이지만 섬세하게 다듬어진 그 맛에 큰 충격을 받았고, 이때의 기억과 경험으로 메종조의 파테를 만들고 있습니다.

처음에는 클래식한 프랑스식 파테가 한국인의 입맛에도 잘 맞을까 고민이 많았습니다. 한국에서 흔히 보이는 파테는 베이컨으로 감싸거나 다양한 재료가 섞여 있는 경우가 많았기 때문입니다. 하지만 제가 프랑스에서 맛본, 군더더기 없는 맛을 제대로 살린 클래식 파테를 한국에서도 제대로 구현해보자는 마음으로 만들기 시작했습니다.

특히 바스크 지방은 한국처럼 고춧가루가 유명한데요. 한국의 고춧가루처럼 곱게 갈린 형태이지만 매운맛은 거의 없고 은은하고 섬세한 풍미가 특징인데, 이 고춧가루가 자칫 느끼할 수 있는 파테의 맛을 부드럽게 잡아주는 역할을 합니다. 메종조에서는 '파테 드 캄파뉴'라는 이름으로 소개하고 있지만, 실제로는 바스크식 파테의 방식에 충실하게 만들어 판매하고 있습니다.

Pâté, one of the beloved French charcuterie items alongside *jambon blanc* and *saucisson*, is an excellent accompaniment to a meal, whether served with bread, salad, or enjoyed with a glass of red wine. Typically made with pork and pork liver, it offers a clean yet deeply rich flavor.

During my time studying in France, I was deeply impressed by the *jambon* and *pâté basque* from Louis Ospital, served on a slice of baguette with a few cornichons. I was struck by their delicately refined flavors, despite their rustic appearance. That memory and experience continue to inspire me to make *pâté* at Maison Jo.

At first, I was unsure whether a classic French *pâté* would appeal to the Korean palate. At that time, variations in Korea often featured versions wrapped in bacon or blended with various ingredients. However, I decided to present the classic *pâté*, bringing the essential flavors I had experienced in France to Korean diners.

Like Korea, the Basque region is well-known for its finely ground chili pepper powder, which offers a mild, delicate heat. This chili pepper powder helps to gently balance the rich flavor of *pâté*, which might otherwise feel overly heavy. At Maison Jo, while this dish is served under the name *Pâté de campagne*, it is prepared faithfully in the Basque style.

Ingredients

4인 분량
Serves 4

삼겹살 (지방이 많은 부위)	600g
돼지 간	200g
월계수 잎	1장
통후추	5알
우유	100ml
양파A	1/2개
마늘	2알
엑스트라버진 올리브오일	적당량
양파B	1/2개
달걀	55g
소금	10g
흑후추	2g
맵지 않은 고춧가루	1/2작은술

토핑

허브	적당량
슬라이스한 마늘	적당량
맵지 않은 고춧가루	적당량
후춧가루	적당량

600 g	pork belly (fatty part)
200 g	pork liver
1	bay leaf
5	black peppercorns
100 ml	milk
1/2	onion (A)
2	garlic cloves
Q.S.	extra virgin olive oil
1/2	onion (B)
55 g	whole egg
10 g	salt
2 g	ground black pepper
1/2 tsp	mild chili pepper powder

TOPPINGS

Q.S.	fresh herbs
Q.S.	sliced garlic
Q.S.	mild chili pepper powder
Q.S.	ground black pepper

How to make

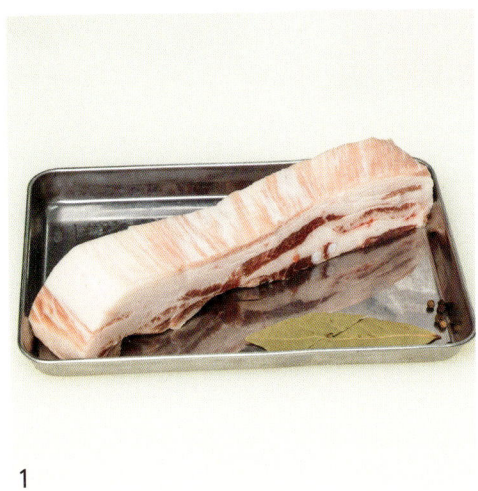 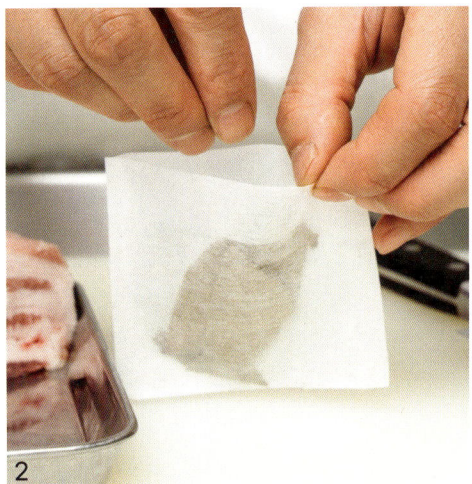 

1. 삼겹살은 지방이 많은 부위로 준비합니다.
2. 다시용 티백에 월계수 잎과 통후추를 넣어 준비합니다.
3. 냄비에 우유, 슬라이스한 양파A와 마늘을 넣고 향이 잘 우러나도록 약불에서 가열합니다.

1. Prepare the fatty parts of the pork belly.
2. Place the bay leaf and black peppercorns in a culinary tea bag.
3. In a pot, combine the milk, sliced onion (A), and garlic, then simmer over low heat to infuse their aromas.

4. 살짝 끓어오르면 불을 끄고 뚜껑을 덮거나 랩을 씌워 천천히 식혀줍니다.
5. 4가 식으면 티백을 제거한 후 체에 걸러줍니다. 걸러진 우유와 채소는 따로 보관합니다.
6. 올리브오일을 두른 팬에 곱게 다진 양파B를 넣고 단맛이 올라오고 진한 갈색 빛이 돌 때까지 충분히 볶은 후 식혀줍니다.

4. Once it comes to a gentle boil, turn off the heat. Cover with a lid or plastic wrap, then let it cool slowly.
5. Once (**4**) has cooled, remove the tea bag and strain through a sieve. Reserve the strained milk and vegetables separately.
6. In a pan with olive oil, add finely diced onion (B). Stir-fry until dark brown and caramelized, then let cool.

  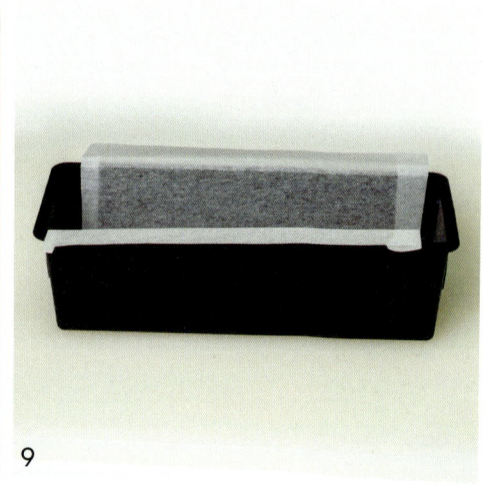

7. 민찌 기계에 삼겹살, 돼지 간, **5**에서 거른 양파와 마늘을 넣고 갈아줍니다.
8. 볼에 **7**과 **5**에서 거른 우유, 달걀, 소금, 흑후추, 고춧가루를 넣고 고기 덩어리들이 잘 연결되도록 충분히 섞어줍니다.
9. 사용할 틀을 준비하고, 틀의 크기에 맞춰 유산지를 깔아줍니다.
- 여기에서는 가로 22cm, 세로 9cm, 높이 9cm 사이즈의 틀을 사용했습니다.

7. Using a meat grinder, mince the pork belly and liver together with the reserved onion and garlic from (**5**).
8. In a mixing bowl, combine (**7**) with the reserved milk from (**5**), egg, salt, black pepper, and chili pepper powder. Mix thoroughly until well incorporated.
9. Prepare a mold and line it with parchment paper cut to fit.
- This recipe uses a mold measuring 22 cm long, 9 cm wide, and 9 cm high.

10. 틀에 **8**을 담고 평평하게 펼쳐줍니다.
11. 허브, 슬라이스한 마늘, 고춧가루, 후춧가루를 뿌려줍니다.
12. 120°C로 예열한 오븐에서 약 90분간 구워줍니다.
- 중심부의 온도가 74°C까지 올라가면 오븐에서 꺼내 실온에서 식힌 후 랩으로 살짝 덮어 냉장고에서 하루 동안 식혀줍니다.

10. Transfer (**8**) to the mold and spread it evenly.
11. Sprinkle the top with herbs, sliced garlic, chili pepper powder, and black pepper.
12. Bake in an oven preheated to 248°F (120°C) for about 90 minutes.
- When the internal temperature at the center reaches 165°F (74°C), remove from the oven and let cool at room temperature. Loosely cover with plastic wrap and refrigerate for one day.

조우람
JO WOORAM

Beef Top Blade Confit

가정식
HOME COOKING

소 부채살 콩피

소고기 부채살을 이용해 만든, 프랑스 가정식 스타일의 클래식한 요리를 소개합니다.

한 번 준비하면 4~6인이 넉넉하게 즐길 수 있어 가족 식사나 손님 초대용 요리로도 제격인데요. 가스불로 오래 조리하는 방식이 아니라, 오븐에서 천천히 익히기 때문에 태울 걱정 없이 안정적으로 만들 수 있습니다. 또한 꼬꼬뜨(무쇠냄비)를 활용하면 테이블 위에서도 멋진 비주얼을 자랑하는 파티 요리로 완성됩니다.

부채살은 중심에 굵은 힘줄이 길게 자리하고 있지만, 저온에서 오랜 시간 조리하면 이 힘줄이 부드럽게 풀어지며 고기와 어우러져 진한 콜라겐 식감을 만들어냅니다. 따뜻할 때 먹으면 소스와 고기가 조화롭게 어우러져 깊은 풍미를 느낄 수 있어, 클래식한 프랑스식 콩피 요리의 매력을 제대로 경험하실 수 있습니다.

This is a classic French home-style dish made with beef top blade.

The generous portion serves 4 to 6 people, making it perfect for a family meal or a special offering when entertaining guests. Slowly cooked in the oven rather than simmered over a gas flame for a long time, it can be prepared safely without the risk of scorching. Served directly in a *cocotte* (cast iron Dutch oven), it becomes a festive centerpiece, creating a striking presentation at the table.

The top blade has a thick tendon at its center, which softens and melds into the meat during long, gentle cooking, creating a rich, collagen-like texture. When served warm, the meat and sauce come together in perfect harmony, allowing you to fully enjoy the pleasures of a classic French confit.

Ingredients

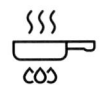

4~6인 분량
Serves 4-6

소고기 부채살	1kg		1 kg	beef top blade
소금	적당량		Q.S.	salt
후춧가루	적당량		Q.S.	ground black pepper
엑스트라버진 올리브오일	적당량		Q.S.	extra virgin olive oil
양파	큰 것 4개		4	large onions
당근	1개		1	carrot
셀러리	1줄기		1	celery stalk
마늘	3알		3	garlic cloves
판체타	적당량		Q.S.	pancetta
버터A	30g		30 g	butter (A)
엑스트라버진 올리브오일	30ml		30 ml	extra virgin olive oil
소금	적당량		Q.S.	salt
후춧가루	적당량		Q.S.	ground black pepper
토마토 페이스트	1큰술		1 tbsp	tomato paste
꿀	2큰술		2 tbsp	honey
발사믹식초	30ml		30 ml	balsamic vinegar
레드와인	200ml		200 ml	red wine
물 또는 닭육수	500ml		500 ml	water or chicken stock
로즈메리	2줄기		2	rosemary sprigs
버터B	20g		20 g	butter (B)

How to make

1. 소고기 부채살은 소금과 후춧가루로 밑간을 합니다.
- 지방이 있는 경우 제거해줍니다.
2. 양파는 4등분으로 잘라 줍니다.

1. Season the beef top blade with salt and black pepper.
- Remove any excess fat.
2. Quarter the onion.

3. 당근과 셀러리는 1cm 크기로 깍둑썰어줍니다. 마늘은 작게 다지고, 판체타는 성냥 크기로 잘라줍니다.
- 판체타 대신 베이컨이나 라르도를 사용해도 좋습니다.
4. 올리브오일을 두른 무쇠냄비에 밑간을 한 소고기 부채살을 넣고 익혀줍니다.
5. 고기 앞뒷면이 갈색이 돌면 소고기를 꺼냅니다.

3. Dice the carrot and celery into 1 cm cubes. Chop the garlic, and cut the pancetta into matchstick-sized pieces.
- Bacon or lardo can be used as substitutes for pancetta.
4. In a cast iron pot (Dutch oven) with olive oil, sear the seasoned beef top blade.
5. Once both sides are browned, remove the meat from the pot.

6. 5의 냄비에 버터A와 올리브오일을 넣고 양파를 익혀줍니다.
7. 양파가 익으면 건져낸 후 판체타, 당근, 셀러리, 마늘 순서로 중불로 볶고 소금과 후춧가루로 간을 합니다.

6. Add butter (A) and olive oil to the pot used in (5), then cook the onion.
7. Once the onion is cooked, remove from the pot. Over medium heat, stir-fry the pancetta, carrot, celery, and garlic, in that order. Season with salt and black pepper.

8. 노릇하게 색이 나면 약불로 줄인 후 토마토 페이스트를 넣고 섞어줍니다.
9. 재료가 80% 정도로 익으면 꿀, 소금, 후춧가루를 넣고 1분 정도 볶아줍니다.

8. Once golden brown, reduce the heat to low and stir in the tomato paste.
9. When about 80 % cooked through, add the honey, salt, and black pepper, then stir-fry for another minute.

10. 익힌 소고기를 넣고 발사믹식초, 레드와인을 넣고 알코올이 날아가도록 2분 정도 가열합니다.
11. 물 또는 닭육수를 추가합니다.
12. 뚜껑을 닫고 160℃로 예열된 오븐에서 약 2시간 익힌 후, 익힌 양파와 로즈메리를 넣고 1시간 더 익혀줍니다.

10. Return the beef to the pot, then pour in the balsamic vinegar and red wine. Simmer for about 2 minutes to evaporate the alcohol.
11. Pour in the water or chicken stock.
12. Cook in an oven preheated to 320°F (160°C) for about 2 hours with a lid on. Add the onion and rosemary, then continue cooking another hour.

13. 소고기를 꺼낸 후 버터B를 넣고 가열해 소스 농도를 맞춰줍니다.
14. 적당한 두께로 자른 고기를 넣고 데워줍니다.
15. 접시에 고기와 소스, 채소를 담아 완성합니다.

13. Remove the beef from the pot. Add butter (B) and simmer to adjust the jus consistency.
14. Slice the beef into moderately thick pieces, return to the pot, then heat through.
15. Arrange the meat, jus, and vegetables on a plate.

Quiche Lorraine

이은희
LEE EUNHEE

이야기
STORY

키슈 로렌

프랑스 유학 시절을 떠올리며 만들어본 키슈를 소개합니다. 키슈는 프랑스의 샤퀴테리 가게나 블랑제리에서 흔히 볼 수 있는 일상적인 메뉴인데요. 그중에서도 가장 잘 알려진 것은 베이컨, 크림, 우유, 달걀로 만드는 로렌 지방의 '키슈 로렌'입니다.

여기에서 소개하는 레시피는 여기에 양파와 그뤼에르 치즈를 더한, 깊은 풍미가 매력적인 알자스 지방 스타일의 키슈입니다. 기본 레시피를 바탕으로 좋아하는 재료를 더해, 여러분만의 풍성한 키슈를 만들어보시길 바랍니다.

This *quiche* was created in memory of my time studying in France. *Quiche* is a familiar dish, commonly found in charcuteries and boulangeries throughout France. Among its many variations, the best known is *Quiche Lorraine*, made with bacon, cream, milk, and eggs.

In this version, the recipe features an Alsatian *quiche*, with onion and Gruyère added to highlight their deeper flavors. Feel free to enrich the *quiche* with your favorite ingredients to make it your own.

Ingredients

지름 24cm, 높이 4cm 타르트틀
1개 분량

For a 24 cm diameter,
4 cm high tart mold

파트 브리제

중력분	200g
깍둑썬 차가운 버터	100g
차가운 물	40g
천일염	3g
비정제 설탕	3g

아파레이유

달걀	3개
천일염	1g
후춧가루	한 꼬집
너트맥가루	한 꼬집
생크림	150g
우유	150g

충전물

엑스트라버진 올리브오일	1큰술
양파	200g
소금	1g
후춧가루	한 꼬집
베이컨	100g
그뤼에르 치즈	80g

PÂTE BRISÉE

200 g	all-purpose flour
100 g	diced cold butter
40 g	cold water
3 g	sea salt
3 g	unrefined sugar

APPAREIL

3	eggs
1 g	sea salt
1 pinch	ground black pepper
1 pinch	nutmeg powder
150 g	fresh cream
150 g	milk

FILLING

1 tbsp	extra virgin olive oil
200 g	onion
1 g	salt
1 pinch	ground black pepper
100 g	bacon
80 g	Gruyère

How to make

1

2

1. 볼에 중력분과 차가운 상태의 버터를 넣고 손으로 비벼가며 부슬부슬한 모래알 상태로 만들어줍니다.
2. 차가운 물에 천일염과 비정제 설탕을 넣고 녹인 후 **1**에 넣고 손으로 꾹꾹 눌러가며 반죽합니다.
- 부서지는 듯한 식감을 주기 위해 반죽을 치대지 않습니다.

1. In a mixing bowl, combine the all-purpose flour and cold butter. Gently rub the mixture between your hands until it resembles coarse crumbs.
2. Dissolve the sea salt and unrefined sugar in the cold water. Add the liquid to (**1**), and press the mixture together with your hands to form a dough.
- Avoid kneading the dough to achieve a crumbly texture.

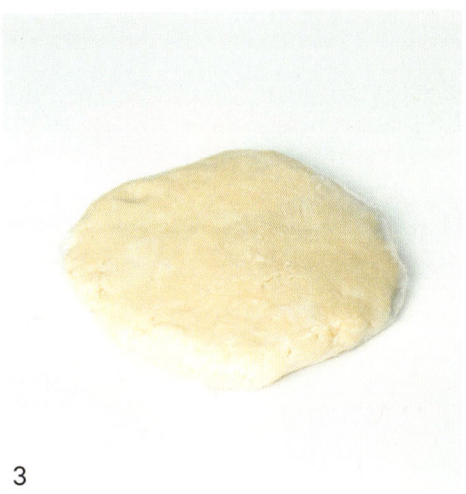
3

4

5

3. 반죽이 한 덩어리로 뭉쳐지면 밀어 펴기 쉽게 약 1cm 두께로 만든 후, 비닐에 싸 냉장고에 잠시 보관합니다.
4. 볼에 달걀, 천일염, 후춧가루, 너트맥가루를 넣고 잘 풀어줍니다.
5. 달걀이 잘 풀리고 재료가 섞이면 생크림과 우유를 넣고 섞어 아파레이유를 완성한 후 냉장고에 잠시 보관합니다.

3. Once it comes together into a single dough, flatten it to about 1 cm thickness for easier rolling. Wrap in plastic wrap and refrigerate for a while.
4. In a mixing bowl, beat the eggs. Add the sea salt, black pepper, and nutmeg powder, then whisk well.
5. Once well combined, stir in the fresh cream and milk to make the *appareil*. Chill in the refrigerator for a while.

  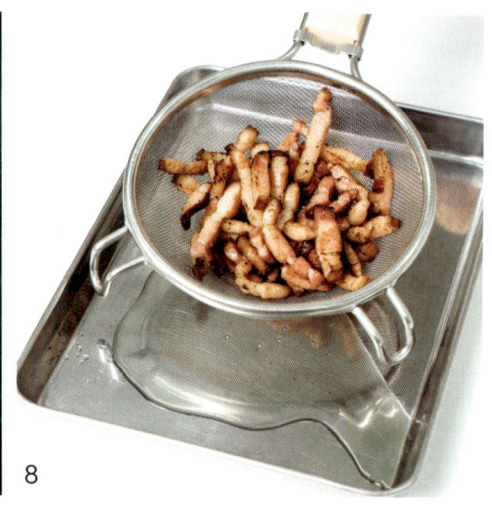

6. 올리브오일을 두른 팬에 약 1cm로 깍둑썬 양파를 넣고 투명해지고 수분이 날아갈 때까지 볶은 후, 소금과 후춧가루로 간을 합니다.
7. 기름을 두르지 않은 팬에 적당한 크기로 자른 베이컨을 넣고 노릇하게 볶아줍니다.
8. 베이컨이 익으면 체에 받쳐 기름을 분리합니다.
- 걸러진 기름은 사용하지 않습니다.

6. In a pan with olive oil, add the onion, diced into about 1 cm pieces, then stir-fry until translucent and the moisture has evaporated. Season with salt and black pepper.
7. In a dry pan, add the bacon, cut into moderately sized pieces, then stir-fry until golden brown.
8. Once cooked, strain the bacon fat through a sieve.
- The strained fat is discarded.

9. 냉장고에서 휴지시킨 반죽을 밀대를 이용해 2~2.5mm 두께로 밀어 펴줍니다.
10. 키슈 틀에 반죽을 올린 후 틀에 맞춰 반죽을 밀착시킵니다.
- 여기에서는 지름 24cm, 높이 4cm 사이즈의 틀을 사용했습니다.

9. Roll out the chilled dough to 2 to 2.5 mm thickness using a rolling pin.
10. Line the *quiche* mold with the dough, pressing gently to fit.
- This recipe uses a mold measuring 24 cm in diameter and 4 cm in height.

11. 반죽 바닥 부분에 포크를 이용해 구멍을 냅니다.
12. 반죽 위에 유산지를 얹고 누름돌을 채워줍니다.
13. 170℃로 예열된 오븐에서 20분간 굽고, 유산지와 누름돌을 제거한 후 5분 더 구운 후 한김 식혀줍니다.

11. Prick small holes in the bottom of the dough.
12. Line the dough with parchment paper and fill with pie weights.
13. Bake in an oven preheated to 338°F (170°C) for 20 minutes. Remove the parchment paper and pie weights. Bake for another 5 minutes and let cool slightly.

14. 식힌 반죽에 볶은 양파와 베이컨, 그뤼에르 치즈 순서로 고르게 펼쳐 넣어줍니다.
- 그뤼에르 치즈는 에멘탈 치즈나 콩테 같은 경성 치즈로 대체해도 좋습니다.
15. 아파레이유를 체에 거른 후 14에 부어줍니다.
16. 170℃로 예열된 오븐에서 20~25분간 구워줍니다.
- 오븐의 사양에 따라 굽는 시간은 달라질 수 있습니다. 표면이 황금색이 나고, 중심부가 푸딩처럼 탱글탱글해지면 꺼내줍니다.

14. Evenly layer the onion, bacon, and Gruyère into the cooled baked crust, in that order.
- Emmental or Comté can be used as substitutes for Gruyère.
15. Strain the *appareil* through a sieve and pour it over (**14**).
16. Bake in an oven preheated to 338°F (170°C) for 20-25 minutes.
- Baking time may vary depending on oven performance. Remove from the oven once the surface is golden and the center is gently set, with a puddling-like bounce.

Chorizo Sablé

이은희 — LEE EUNHEE

가정식 — HOME COOKING

초리소 사블레

발효가 잘 된 건조 초리소 소시지와 파르미자노 레자노 치즈는 그 자체로 훌륭한 아페리티프(Apéritif, 식전에 즐기는 술이나 안주)입니다.

파티가 끝난 뒤 혹은 집에 남아 있는 하몽, 프로슈토, 잠봉 같은 다양한 발효 소시지와 치즈 그라인더에 갈릴 정도로 단단한 경성 치즈들을 활용하면, 여러 가지 맛의 사블레를 만들 수 있는데요. 깊은 풍미를 지닌 발효 식재료가 고소한 버터 반죽과 만나면, 전혀 다른 식감과 향을 가진 사블레로 완성됩니다.

만드는 방법도 간단하고, 반죽을 미리 만들어 냉동해두었다가 필요할 때 꺼내 구워 먹을 수 있어 더욱 실용적인 레시피입니다.

Well-aged dried chorizo sausage and Parmigiano-Reggiano are excellent *apéritifs* (light drinks or small bites served before a meal) on their own.

Various types of *sablé* can be made using leftover aged sausages from a home party, such as *jamón*, *prosciutto*, or *jambon*, along with hard cheeses firm enough to be grated with a cheese grinder. The combination of these deeply flavored aged ingredients and rich butter dough creates a *sablé* with a distinct texture and a unique aroma.

This recipe is not only simple to prepare but also practical, as the *sablés* can be made in advance and baked straight from the freezer whenever needed.

Ingredients

지름 4cm 사블레
약 30개 분량

Yields approximately 30 *sablés*
(each 4 cm in diameter)

중력분	70g
통밀가루	30g
파프리카 파우더◆	3g
베이킹파우더	2g
천일염	2g
비정제 설탕	4g
후춧가루	1g
깍둑썬 차가운 버터	50g
잘게 슬라이스한 초리소 세크 (건조시킨 초리소)	30g
파르미자노 레자노 치즈	30g
차가운 물	20g

◆ 파프리카 파우더는 훈연 또는 시즈닝 제품이 아닌, 파프리카 100% 제품을 사용합니다.

70 g	all-purpose flour
30 g	whole wheat flour
3 g	paprika powder ◆
2 g	baking powder
2 g	sea salt
4 g	unrefined sugar
1 g	ground black pepper
50 g	diced cold butter
30 g	finely sliced *chorizo sec* (dried chorizo)
30 g	Parmigiano-Reggiano
20 g	cold water

◆ For the paprika powder, use 100% pure paprika rather than smoked or seasoned products.

How to make

1

2

1. 볼에 차가운 물을 제외한 모든 재료를 넣고 손으로 비벼가며 부슬부슬한 모래알 상태로 만들어줍니다.
- 가루 재료는 체 쳐 사용합니다.
2. 차가운 물을 넣고 한 덩어리로 뭉쳐줍니다.
- 부서지는 듯한 식감을 주기 위해 반죽을 치대지 않습니다.

1. In a mixing bowl, combine all the ingredients except the cold water. Gently rub the mixture between your hands until it resembles coarse crumbs.
- Sift the dry ingredients before use.
2. Add the cold water, then bring the mixture together into a single dough.
- Avoid kneading the dough to achieve a crumbly texture.

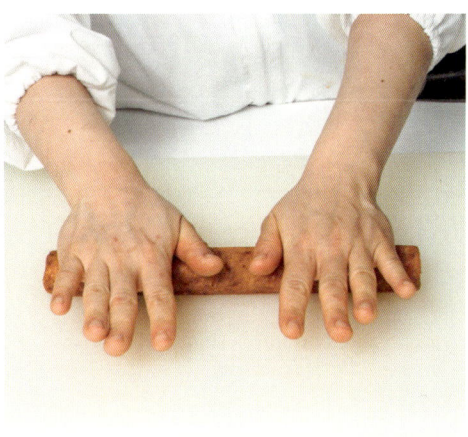

3

3. 반죽을 지름 약 4cm, 길이 약 25cm 원통형으로 만들어줍니다.

3. Shape the dough into a cylinder about 4 cm in diameter and 25 cm in length.

4. 반죽을 비닐로 싸 냉장고에서 30~60분간 굳혀 자르기 좋은 상태로 만들어줍니다.
- 냉동실(약 1달)에 보관하며 필요할 때마다 사용할 수 있습니다.
5. 굳힌 반죽을 약 5mm 두께로 잘라줍니다.
6. 철판에 팬닝한 후 160℃로 예열된 오븐에서 약 15분간 구워줍니다.

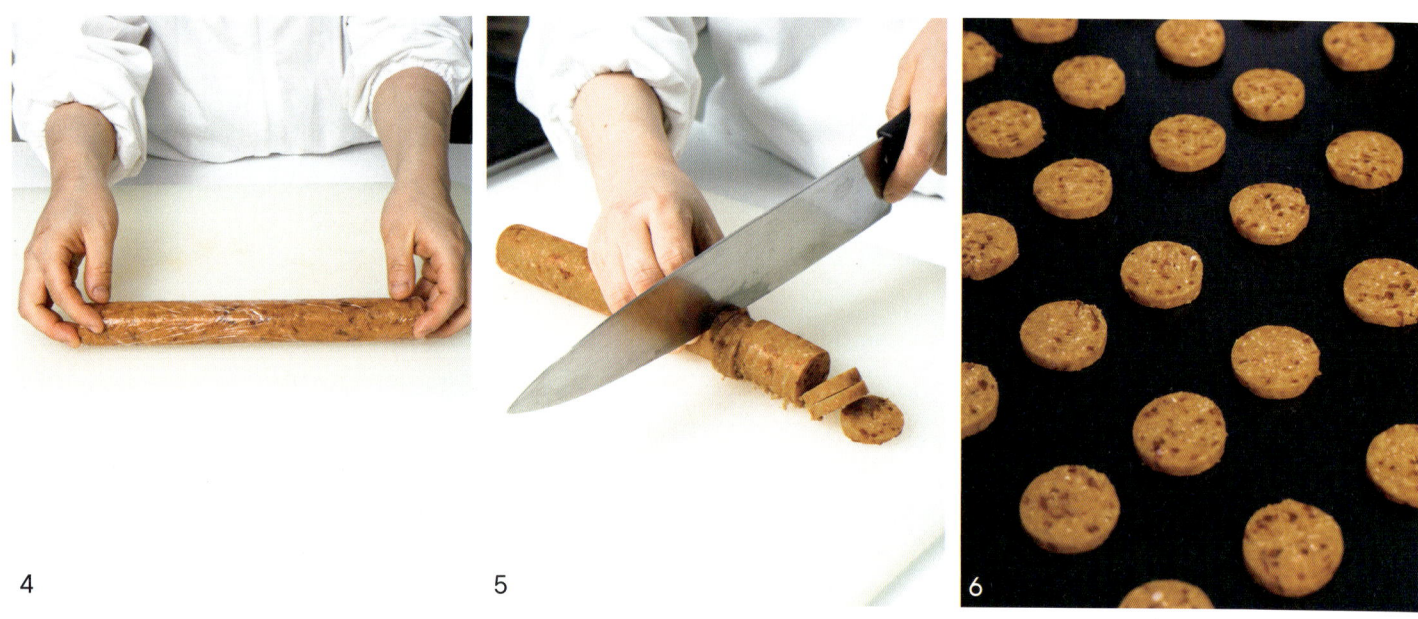

4. Wrap the dough in plastic wrap, refrigerate for 30 to 60 minutes until firm enough to slice easily.
- The dough can be stored in the freezer (for up to one month) and used as needed.
5. Cut the dough into 5 mm thick slices.
6. Arrange on a baking tray and bake in an oven preheated to 320°F (160°C) for about 15 minutes.

CHO EUNJU

조은주

대학에서 전통조리를 전공하며 요리사의 길을 본격적으로 걷기 시작했다. 63빌딩 뷔페 레스토랑에서의 현장 실습은 그녀에게 주방의 치열한 세계를 체감하게 했고, 이 경험은 요리에 대한 열정을 더욱 확고하게 만들었다.

졸업 후 한화호텔앤드리조트에 입사해 63빌딩 내 다양한 레스토랑에서 실력을 쌓아갔다. 특히 '워킹온더클라우드'에서 부책임 셰프로 근무하며 서양 요리에 대한 이해를 넓혔고, 2018년에는 63빌딩 프렌치 레스토랑 '터치더스카이'의 수석 셰프로 발탁되었다. 이는 63빌딩 역사상 첫 여성 수석 셰프 임명으로, 업계의 큰 주목을 받았다. 남성 중심의 주방에서 그녀는 탁월한 감각과 섬세한 리더십으로 팀을 이끌며 '터치더스카이'를 서울의 대표 프렌치 레스토랑으로 성장시키는 데 기여했다.

2016년, 싱가포르에서 열린 세계 3대 요리 대회 'FHA Culinary Challenge'에서는 타파스 & 핑거푸드 부문과 4가지 메인 요리 부문에서 각각 금메달을 수상하며 국제적인 인정을 받았다. 이는 여성 셰프로서는 유례없는 기록으로, 그녀의 창의적인 요리 역량을 입증한 순간이었다.

이러한 경험을 후배들에게 나누고자 현재는 경남정보대학 호텔조리과에서 교육자로서 두 번째 인생을 시작하고 있다.

She began her career as a chef, majoring in traditional cuisine during her college years. Her on-the-job training at the buffet restaurant in the 63 Building exposed her to the fierce world of the kitchen, which further solidified her passion for cooking.

After graduation, she joined Hanwha Hotel & Resorts, where she honed her skills at various restaurants in the 63 building. In particular, she worked as a sous chef at 'Walking on the Cloud' to broaden her understanding of Western cuisine, and in 2018, she was appointed as the executive chef of the 63 Building's French restaurant 'Touch the Sky.' It was the first in the history of the 63 building to appoint a female executive chef, garnering significant attention from the industry. In a male-dominated kitchen, she led her team with great flair and sensitive leadership, helping to grow 'Touch the Sky' into Seoul's leading French restaurant.

In 2016, she received international recognition at the FHA Culinary Challenge in Singapore, one of the world's top three culinary competitions, where she won gold medals in both the Tapas & Finger Food and Four Main Dishes category. This was an unprecedented feat for a female chef, a testament to her creative culinary skills.

To share this experience with the younger generation, she is now starting her second chapter as an educator at the Department of Hotel and Culinary Arts at Kyungnam College of Information & Technology.

cho_eun_ju_99

Truffle-Flavored Octopus and Lobster Appetizer

트러플 풍미의 돌문어 랍스터 전채

이야기
STORY

이 메뉴는 흰눈이 소복이 내리는 겨울밤을 모티프로 삼아, 따뜻하고 포근한 계절의 감성이 오롯이 전달되기를 바라며 만든 요리입니다.

접시 위에 펼쳐진 깊은 겨울밤은 오징어먹물로 표현했고, 소복이 내리는 함박눈은 고체화한 트러플 오일로 구현해 시각적인 감성을 더했습니다. 메인 재료인 돌문어는 압력밥솥으로 부드럽게 익힌 후 숯불향을 입혀 한층 더 깊은 풍미를 더했으며, 랍스터와 함께 고급스러운 해산물의 식감을 살려 구성했습니다. 곁들임으로는 돼지감자 퓌레를 진하게 조려 부드럽고 고소한 맛을 더했고, 다채로운 색상의 작은 피클들을 플레이팅하여 산뜻한 맛의 전환과 시각적인 재미를 더했습니다.

전반적으로 부드러움, 쫄깃함, 고소함, 산미가 균형 있게 어우러지는 이 요리는 정성과 섬세함으로 완성된 겨울의 한 접시입니다. 눈 내리는 밤, 따뜻한 불빛 아래에서 즐기기에 더없이 잘 어울리는 전채 요리입니다.

With a snowy winter night as its motif, this appetizer is created to convey the gentle warmth of the season.

Squid ink captures the deep winter night, while truffle oil powder suggests soft mounds of falling snowflakes, creating a visually poetic scene on the plate.

At its heart lies tender octopus, pressure-cooked and subtly infused with smoky aroma to deepen its flavor, then paired with lobster to enrich the refined seafood texture. As accompaniments, a velvety reduced sunchoke purée offers a rich, savory note, while an array of colorful pickled vegetables adds a refreshing contrast in flavor and visual appeal.

Balancing tenderness, chewiness, savoriness, and acidity, this winter-inspired creation is gently enveloped in sincerity and finesse—a perfect indulgence for a snowy night beneath warm light.

Ingredients

8인 분량
Serves 8

돌문어*
물	1L
식초	10g
미림	20cc
소금	5g
정종	20cc
돌문어	500g
무	200g

채소 피클 3종
샴페인	375g
식초	150g
물	125g
설탕	150g
소금	10g
피클링 스파이스	5g
대추방울토마토	8개
콜라비	16조각
오렌지	16조각

고체 트러플 오일
포도씨유	30g
트러플 오일	3g
타피오카 말토 덱스트린	30g

돼지감자 퓌레
돼지감자	150g
버터	30g
생크림	100g
소금	적당량
후춧가루	적당량

돌문어와 랍스터
정제버터	50g
돌문어*	다리 8개
랍스터 집게 살	8개

가니시와 장식
(8인 기준)
오징어먹물	30g
어린싹채소	40g
사워크림	30g
크림치즈	50g
애호박 슬라이스	8개
발사믹 펄	30g
훈제소금	적당량
레몬바질 잎	8장
처빌 잎	8장

OCTOPUS*
1 L	water
10 g	vinegar
20 cc	mirin
5 g	salt
20 cc	sake
500 g	octopus
200 g	Korean radish

PICKLED VEGETABLES TRIO
375 g	Champagne
150 g	vinegar
125 g	water
150 g	sugar
10 g	salt
5 g	pickling spices
8	grape tomatoes
16	kohlrabi slices
16	orange segments

TRUFFLE OIL POWDER
30 g	grapeseed oil
3 g	truffle oil
30 g	tapioca maltodextrin

SUNCHOKE PURÉE
150 g	sunchokes
30 g	butter
100 g	fresh cream
Q.S.	salt
Q.S.	ground black pepper

OCTOPUS AND LOBSTER
50 g	clarified butter
8	octopus* legs
8	lobster claws (meat)

GARNISHES AND PLATING DECORATIONS
(serves 8)
30 g	squid ink
40 g	microgreens
30 g	sour cream
50 g	cream cheese
8	zucchini slices
30 g	balsamic pearls
Q.S.	smoked salt
8	fresh lemon basil leaves
8	fresh chervil leaves

How to make

돌문어

1. 냄비에 물, 식초, 미림, 소금, 정종을 넣고 끓어오르면 깨끗하게 세척한 돌문어를 넣고 데쳐줍니다.
- 돌문어를 삶아낸 후 남은 물은 버리지 않고 남겨둡니다.
2. 데치는 중간 돌문어를 들어올렸다 물에 담갔다를 반복해 다리 모양이 예쁘게 말리도록 합니다.
- 이 작업을 하지 않으면 다리가 예쁘게 말리지 않습니다.

OCTOPUS

1. In a pot, combine the water, vinegar, mirin, salt, and sake, then bring to a boil. Once boiling, blanch the cleaned octopus.
- Reserve the cooking liquid for later use.
2. While blanching, repeatedly dip the octopus in and out of the boiling water to help the legs curl beautifully.
- Skipping this step may result in poorly curled legs.

3. 압력밥솥에 두껍게 자른 무를 깔아줍니다.
4. 데친 문어와 문어를 삶고 남은 물(100cc)을 넣고 약 15분간 익혀줍니다.
5. 익힌 문어를 식힌 후 다리를 잘라 준비합니다.

3. Line the bottom of a pressure cooker with thick slices of Korean radish.
4. Add the blanched octopus and 100 cc of the reserved cooking liquid, then cook for about 15 minutes.
5. Remove the octopus, let it cool, then separate the legs.

채소 피클 3종

1. 냄비에 샴페인, 식초, 물, 설탕, 소금, 피클링 스파이스를 넣고 끓어오르면 불에서 내려 식혀줍니다.
2. 대추방울토마토, 껍질을 벗기고 슬라이스한 콜라비와 오렌지를 **1**이 담긴 통에 각각 넣고 2시간 이상 둔 후 사용합니다.

PICKLED VEGETABLES TRIO

1. In a pot, combine the Champagne, vinegar, water, sugar, salt, and pickling spices, and bring to a boil. Once boiling, remove from the heat and let cool.
2. Place the grape tomatoes, peeled kohlrabi slices, and orange segments in separate containers. Pour (**1**) into each container, and let them pickle for at least 2 hours before use.

고체 트러플 오일

1. 볼에 포도씨유, 트러플 오일, 타피오카 말토 덱스트린 소량을 넣고 주걱으로 가볍게 섞어줍니다.
2. 남은 타피오카 말토 덱스트린을 추가해가며 손으로 비비듯 섞어 보슬보슬한 소보로 형태로 만들어줍니다.

TRUFFLE OIL POWDER

1. In a mixing bowl, gently combine the grapeseed oil, truffle oil, and a small portion of tapioca maltodextrin, then gently mix with a spatula.
2. Gradually add the remaining tapioca maltodextrin, while gently rubbing the mixture between your hands until it resembles coarse crumbs.

돼지감자 퓌레

1. 돼지감자는 껍질을 제거하고 납작하게 채 썬 후 진공팩에 버터와 함께 넣고 스팀으로 익혀줍니다.
2. 믹서에 익힌 돼지감자와 생크림을 넣고 곱게 갈아줍니다.
3. 냄비로 옮기고 가열해 원하는 농도로 퓌레를 만들고, 소금과 후춧가루로 간을 합니다.

SUNCHOKE PURÉE

1. Slice the peeled sunchokes into coins, place them into a vacuum bag with butter, vacuum-seal, then steam.
2. Blend the steamed sunchokes with fresh cream until smooth.
3. Transfer the mixture to a pot and heat until it reaches the desired consistency. Season with salt and black pepper.

돌문어와 랍스터

1. 정제버터를 두른 팬에 익힌 문어 다리와 랍스터 집게 살을 구워줍니다.
   - 정제버터를 사용하는 이유는 버터의 고소한 풍미를 더하면서 고열에 타는 것을 방지하기 위함입니다.
2. 구운 랍스터 집게 살에 칼집을 내줍니다.

OCTOPUS AND LOBSTER

1. Heat the clarified butter in a pan, then add the cooked octopus legs and lobster claw meat.
   - The clarified butter is used to add a savory flavor and to prevent scorching over high heat.
2. Gently score the cooked lobster claw meat.

플레이팅

1. 오징어먹물을 이용해 접시에 원을 그려줍니다.
2. 오징어먹물 모양에 맞춰 고체 트러플 오일을 올려줍니다.
3. 고체 트러플 오일 안쪽에 어린싹채소와 오렌지 피클을 올려줍니다.

PLATING

1. Brush the squid ink onto a plate in a circular shape.
2. Arrange the truffle oil powder along the edge of the squid ink circle.
3. Place the microgreens and pickled orange inside the ring of truffle oil powder.

4. 오렌지 피클 위에 사워크림과 크림치즈를 섞어 만든 크림을 파이핑합니다.
5. 크림 위에 랍스터를 올린 후 칼집을 낸 공간에 콜라비 피클을 꽂아줍니다.
6. 어린싹채소 위에 돼지감자 퓌레를 파이핑합니다.

4. Pipe the mixture of sour cream and cream cheese over the pickled orange.
5. Set the lobster on top of the mixture, and insert the pickled kohlrabi into the scored cuts.
6. Pipe the sunchoke purée over the microgreens.

7. 돼지감자 퓌레 위에 돌문어를 올린 후 그 옆에 돌돌 만 애호박, 발사믹 펄, 방울토마토 피클을 올려줍니다.
- 애호박은 얇게 슬라이스해 팬에서 익힌 후 돌돌 말아 사용합니다.
8. 식용 꽃과 허브를 올려 마무리합니다.

7. Place the octopus on top of the sunchoke purée. Garnish the side with rolled zucchini, balsamic pearls, and pickled grape tomatoes.
- Pan-fry thinly sliced zucchini and roll before use.
8. Finish with edible flowers and herbs.

Abalone with Oyster Cream and Seaweed Fulvescens Aroma Oil

가정식
HOME COOKING

굴 크림과 매생이 아로마 오일을 곁들인 전복 요리

남해에서 나는 매생이는 추운 겨울, 짧은 기간에만 맛볼 수 있는 귀한 제철 식재료입니다. 특히 굴과 함께 끓인 '매생이 굴국밥'은 많은 이들이 겨울철에 즐겨 찾는 따뜻한 보양식이기도 한데요. 이 음식에서 영감을 받아 '굴 크림과 매생이 아로마 오일을 곁들인 전복 요리'를 선보이게 되었습니다.

요리의 주재료인 전복은 무를 깔고 천천히 부드럽게 익혀, 질감은 살리되 고유의 풍미는 한껏 끌어올렸습니다. 매생이는 고온에서 쉽게 풀어지고 풍미가 사라지는 특성이 있어, 이를 보완하기 위해 매생이의 향을 오일에 담아 아로마 오일로 만들었습니다. 덕분에 풍부한 매생이 향을 접시에 그대로 담을 수 있었지요.

굴 크림의 경우 진하게 우려낸 굴 육수와 밥을 함께 갈아 부드러운 크림 형태로 완성했습니다. 바다의 깊은 풍미가 느껴지는 이 크림은 전복과 완벽한 조화를 이루며, 마지막에 느껴지는 매생이 오일의 맛과 향이 전체적인 균형을 잡아주는 역할을 합니다.

한입에 전복의 부드러움, 굴 크림의 농도 깊은 감칠맛, 매생이 오일의 바다 향이 어우러지는 요리로, 겨울 바다의 정취와 따뜻함을 함께 담은 한 접시가 되기를 바라는 마음으로 준비해 보았습니다.

Often found in the South Sea, seaweed fulvescens is a rare seasonal ingredient that makes a brief appearance in the cold winter months. This dish draws inspiration from *gul-gukbap* (a warm soup of seaweed fulvescens, oysters and rice), a comforting *boyangsik* (energy-boosting dish) often enjoyed in winter.

At its center lies tender abalone, gently cooked on a bed of Korean radish to accentuate its texture and distinct flavor. As seaweed fulvescens easily loosens and loses its flavor under high heat, it is gently infused into oil to preserve its pure fragrance, faithfully bringing its richness to the plate.

The oyster cream is prepared as a smooth cream, blending deeply infused oyster stock with plain rice and other ingredients. Its profound marine flavor pairs perfectly with the abalone, while a final touch of seaweed oil completes the overall balance of the dish.

I hope this dish conveys the mood and warmth of the winter sea, harmonizing the tenderness of abalone, the rich savoriness of oyster cream, and the sea-scented notes of seaweed oil in every bite.

Ingredients

10인 분량
Serves 10

매생이 아로마 오일*

시금치	10g
포도씨유	200g
매생이	100g

전복

전복	약 100g × 10개
무	100g
물	500g
다시마	1장
미림	50g
정종	50g
간장	20g

굴 크림*

쌀	500g
전복 삶은 물	500g
굴 A	500g
다시마	1장
매생이 아로마 오일*	50g
대파	200g
마늘	50g
굴 B	500g
조개 육수 또는 물	1L
청양고추	2개
생크림	500cc

가니시와 장식 (1인 기준)

매생이 아로마 오일*	15g
전복	1개
화이트 아스파라거스	15g
굴 크림*	50g
한련화	1잎
세모가사리	1조각

SEAWEED FULVESCENS AROMA OIL*

10 g	spinach
200 g	grapeseed oil
100 g	seaweed fulvescens

ABALONE

10	abalones (about 100 g each)
100 g	Korean radish
500 g	water
1 sheet	kelp
50 g	mirin
50 g	sake
20 g	soy sauce

OYSTER CREAM*

500 g	rice
500 g	abalone cooking liquid
500 g	oysters (A)
1 sheet	kelp
50 g	seaweed fulvescens aroma oil*
200 g	green onion
50 g	garlic
500 g	oysters (B)
1 L	clam stock or water
2	cheongyang green chili peppers
500 cc	fresh cream

GARNISHES AND PLATING DECORATIONS (per serving)

15 g	seaweed fulvescens aroma oil*
1	abalone
15 g	white asparagus
50 g	oyster cream*
1	nasturtium leaf
1 piece	red algae

How to make

매생이 아로마 오일

1. 믹서에 시금치와 포도씨유를 넣고 갈아줍니다.
2. **1**이 어느 정도 갈리면 매생이를 넣고 곱게 갈아줍니다.
3. 냄비로 옮겨 가열하다가 기포가 올라오기 시작하면 불에서 내려 고운 체나 면포에 거른 후 식혀줍니다.

SEAWEED FULVESCENS AROMA OIL

1. In a blender, blend the spinach and grapeseed oil.
2. Once coarsely blended, add the seaweed fulvescens and continue blending until smooth.
3. Pour the mixture into a pot and heat until bubbles begin to form. Remove from the heat, strain through a fine sieve or muslin (cheesecloth), then let cool.

전복

1. 전복은 솔로 깨끗이 씻은 후 껍질과 내장을 제거합니다.

ABALONE

1. Brush the abalone thoroughly, and remove the shells and innards.

2. 냄비에 두껍게 자른 무를 깔아줍니다.
3. 손질한 전복과 남은 재료를 모두 넣고 2시간 정도 약불에서 가열합니다.
4. 익힌 전복을 건져냅니다. 전복을 삶은 물은 통에 담아 굴 크림을 만들 때 사용합니다.

2. Line the bottom of a pot with thick slices of Korean radish.
3. Add the abalone meat and the remaining ingredients, then simmer over low heat for about 2 hours.
4. Remove the abalone, and reserve the cooking liquid in a container for use in the oyster cream.

굴 크림

1. 쌀은 깨끗이 씻어 30분 정도 물에 불린 후 물기를 제거합니다.
2. 압력밥솥에 쌀을 담고 전복 삶은 물(전복을 익히고 남은 물)을 체에 걸러 담아줍니다.

OYSTER CREAM

1. Wash the rice thoroughly, soak in water for about 30 minutes, then drain.
2. Place the rice in a pressure cooker and add the reserved abalone cooking liquid, straining it through a sieve.

3. 깨끗이 씻은 굴A와 다시마를 올린 후 불에 올려 밥을 지어줍니다.
4. 밥이 지어지면 굴과 밥을 분리합니다.
- 밥솥 밑바닥에 눌어붙은 밥을 사용하면 추후 믹서로 가는 작업에서 색이 탁해지므로, 눌어붙은 쪽은 사용하지 않습니다.

3. Top with the kelp and cleaned oysters (A), then cook under pressure.
4. Once the rice is done, separate the rice from the oysters.
- Avoid using the scorched rice at the bottom of the pressure cooker, as it may cloud the mixture when blended.

5. 팬에 매생이 아로마 오일을 둘러줍니다.
6. 적당한 크기로 썬 대파와 다진 마늘을 넣고 볶아줍니다.
7. 대파와 마늘의 향이 우러나면 굴B를 넣고 볶다가 굴이 익으면 조개 육수와 어슷하게 썬 청양고추를 넣고 가열합니다.

5. Coat a pan with the seaweed fulvescens aroma oil.
6. Stir-fry the sliced green onion and minced garlic.
7. Once the green onion and garlic release their aromas, add oyster (B) and stir-fry. Once the oysters are cooked, add the clam stock and diagonally sliced cheongyang green chili peppers, then bring to a boil.

8. 끓어오르면 생크림을 넣고 가열합니다.
9. 굴과 매생이의 맛이 우러나면 체에 걸러줍니다.
10. 믹서에 9에서 걸러낸 국물과 4에서 분리한 밥을 넣고 갈아줍니다.

8. Once it comes to a boil, add the fresh cream.
9. When the oysters and seaweed fulvescens have infused their flavors, strain the liquid through a sieve.
10. In a blender, combine the liquid from (9) with the rice from (4), then blend until smooth.

마무리

1. 매생이 아로마 오일을 두른 팬에 손질한 전복을 넣고 노릇하게 익힌 후 먹기 좋은 크기로 잘라줍니다.
2. 먹기 좋은 크기로 자른 화이트 아스파라거스도 매생이 아로마 오일로 볶아주고 소금으로 간을 합니다.
3. 접시 중앙에 화이트 아스파라거스를 담아줍니다.

FINISH

1. Coat a pan with seaweed fulvescens aroma oil. Add the abalone, cook until golden brown, then cut into bite-sized pieces.
2. Cut the white asparagus into bite-sized pieces. Pan-fry in seaweed fulvescens aroma oil, then season with salt.
3. Arrange the asparagus in the center of a plate.

4. 화이트 아스파라거스 위에 뜨겁게 데운 굴 크림을 뿌려줍니다.
5. 전복을 올린 후 한련화로 장식합니다.
6. 불린 세모가사리를 올린 후 매생이 아로마 오일을 뿌려 마무리합니다.

4. Spoon the hot oyster cream over the asparagus.
5. Top with the abalone and garnish with a nasturtium leaf.
6. Finish with soaked red algae and a drizzle of seaweed fulvescens aroma oil.

PLATE by PLATE
플레이트 바이 플레이트

First edition printed	July 1, 2025
First edition published	July 15, 2025
Author	Kim Doyun, Song Hongyun, Kim Miryeong, Park Sungbae, Bang Kisoo, Ok Dongsik, Choi Jihyung, Shin Kyesook, Lim Taehoon, Cho Kwanghyo, Hwang Jinseon, Kim Seungmin, Lee Jingon, Sim Sungoh, Jang Hojoon, Kim Nakyoung, Kim Minseok, Kim Seakyeong, Nam Jeongseok, David Lee, Ryu Taehwan, Park Joonwoo, Park Jiyoung, Park Chanil, Sung Siwoo, Lee Daegeon, Jang Jisoo, Cho Eunju, Jo Wooram, Lee Eunhee
Translated by	Kim Yoojin, Kim Eunice
Publisher	Bak Yunseon
Published by	THETABLE Inc.
Plan & Edit	Bak Yunseon
Design	Kim Bora
Photograph	Shin Dongmin
Sales/Marketing	Kim Namkwon, Cho Yonghoon, Moon Seongbin
Management support	Kim Hyoseon, Lee Jungmin
Address	122, Jomaru-ro 385beon-gil, Bucheon-si, Gyeonggi-do, Republic of Korea
Website	www.icoxpublish.com
Instagram	@thetable_book
E-mail	thetable_book@naver.com
Phone	82-32-674-5685
Registration date	August 4, 2022
Registration number	386-2022-000050
ISBN	979-11-92855-20-2 (13590)

- THETABLE is a publishing brand that adds sensibility to daily life.
- This book is a literary property protected by copyright law, and prohibits any premise or reproduction without permission.
  In order to use all or part of the contents of this book, written consent must be obtained from the copyright holder and THETABLE, Inc.
- For inquiries about the book, please contact THETABLE by e-mail thetable_book@naver.com.
- Misprinted books can be replaced at the bookstore where it was purchased.
- Price indicated on the back cover.

❖ All of the author's royalties from the book and a portion of the publisher's proceeds will be donated to children through Save the Children Federation, Inc.